Pockets of Crime

D1500511

Pockets of Crime:

Broken Windows, Collective Efficacy, and the Criminal Point of View

PETER K. B. ST. JEAN

With a Foreword by Robert J. Sampson

The University of Chicago Press   Chicago and London

PETER K. B. ST. JEAN is assistant professor of sociology
at the University at Buffalo.

The University of Chicago Press, Chicago 60637
The University of Chicago Press, Ltd., London
© 2007 by The University of Chicago
All rights reserved. Published 2007
Printed in the United States of America

16 15 14 13 12 11 10 09 08 07   1 2 3 4 5

ISBN-13: 978-0-226-77498-5 (cloth)
ISBN-13: 978-0-226-77499-2 (paper)
ISBN-10: 0-226-77498-8 (cloth)
ISBN-10: 0-226-77499-6 (paper)

Library of Congress Cataloging-in-Publication Data

St. Jean, Peter K. B.
    Pockets of crime : broken windows, collective efficacy, and
the criminal point of view / Peter K. B. St. Jean.
        p.   cm.
    Includes bibliographical references.
    ISBN-13: 978-0-226-77498-5 (cloth : alk. paper)
    ISBN-10: 0-226-77498-8 (cloth : alk. paper)
    ISBN-13: 978-0-226-77499-2 (pbk. : alk. paper)
    ISBN-10: 0-226-77499-6 (pbk. : alk. paper)
    1. Crime.   2. Criminology.   3. Criminal behavior.
4. Neighborhood—Social aspects.   5. Neighborhood—
Psychological aspects.   6. Applied human geography.   I. Title.
HV6177.S8 2007
364.2—dc22

                                                2006036169

For improved quality of life in all the Grand Boulevard-type communities of the world, the broader Bronzeville and Wentworth communities, the wonderful City of Chicago as a whole, and the world over.

For additional inspiration within my own family tree: St. Jean (Dominica), Anthony (Dominica), Hall (Chicago), and Holloway (Chicago).

For encouragement to all those who struggle on the front lines to better understand the vexing problems of society, with the aim of finding solutions.

To the Chicago tradition of urban ethnography.

Contents

Foreword

It was usually late in the afternoon when Peter St. Jean would make his urgent visits to my office at the University of Chicago. For Peter, everything was urgent and I had little choice but to listen. (If you ever meet Peter St. Jean in person, you will understand why.) Now, it may seem odd that having someone come crashing into your office wild-eyed and flailing about could be rewarding, much less an intellectual treat, but it was all that and more. For in those early years of St. Jean's initiation into the passionate pursuit of urban sociology, I saw a budding scholar determined to break new ground. I detected a raw intellect hungry to be prodded and shaped, and ultimately to be triumphant. He was so full of energy that a typical meeting would go something like this. He would present his latest finding, we would argue and dissect it from multiple angles, and I would suggest a new angle to pursue. St. Jean would then leave more wild-eyed than upon entrance and pursue the idea for three days straight without sleep. I would receive streams of email time-stamped at ungodly hours, and days later he would urgently appear again with results a normal person would have needed months to produce. I had no choice but to answer the door, and so would begin a new round on another late afternoon in Kelly Hall 103.

What does such passion produce? In this case a gem of a study that was enthralling to mentor from initial conception to completion. The orienting idea was simple but powerful. In the mid-1990s practically all of America knew that the south side of Chicago near the Robert Taylor Homes (now defunct) was dangerous, perhaps one of the most violent places imaginable. Death and destruction were seemingly everywhere. Yet most of the time, in most of the places in this neighborhood, it was safe. As in the larger society, crime was highly concentrated in time and space. St. Jean shows us, for example, that out of sixty street blocks in the neighborhood of study, just 9 percent accounted for over half of all robberies and narcotics violations. A puzzle began to emerge, one that no one had really thought to solve before: Why does crime occur *here* and not *there* in such high-crime neighborhoods? This became St. Jean's question, one he would not let go of until he had unearthed a treasure trove of data about daily life on these otherwise mean streets.

The methodology of *Pockets of Crime* blends a concern with systematic social investigation with ethnographic discovery. (One is tempted to say that science has perhaps for the first time met urban ethnography in this book.) St. Jean began by randomly choosing a selection of blocks in the Grand Boulevard neighborhood of the south side, in the Wentworth police district. The district itself was selected based on the distribution of violent crimes in the larger city. Then St. Jean embarked on a systematic collection of empirical data using a variety of innovative methods, including intensive and often repeated interviews, videos of the streets, GIS mapping, and photographs. The interviews come from both conventional society (e.g., law-abiding residents, community leaders) and hardened offenders—approximately 150 interviews overall. Throughout the book St. Jean weaves back and forth across types of data, attempting to reconcile any discrepancies. Reliability and validity of information are always kept front and center.

Participant observation plays a key role too. For example, St. Jean attended over three hundred "beat meetings" of police and residents and personally observed over three hundred instances of participation in community organizations. Then there are the countless hours spent hanging out, observing, and speaking with people in all walks of life—prostitutes, grandmothers, store owners, ministers, street hustlers, and more than the occasional thug. In the pages to follow you will meet unforgettable characters that he met time and again in circumstances that would scare the pants off most of us. There is Icepick (a murderer and pimp very aptly named, I might add), Throat, Swift, Blunt, and Razor among others. Fortunately, I never worried about St. Jean grilling these men, demanding better answers, challenging their pat responses. His earthy qualities, physical size, dogged persistence, and just plain fearlessness of life on the streets were obvious enough early on. The interviews reveal these qualities in different ways, one of the most common being a refusal by "the researcher" (as St. Jean refers to himself) to believe initial accounts. He pushed the envelope, constantly asking why, where, and with whom? "Prove it," he seemed to demand of his informants and confidants. He even showed movies of systematic social observation (SSO) to drug and robbery offenders so they could reflect in their own words why certain crime locations were more attractive than others, or elaborate the meanings they attributed to disorder. When the perceptions of hardened offenders meet up with SSO interesting things happen. But there was another side to St. Jean as well. He knew how to listen, laugh, and show the endearing side of a man who genuinely wanted to know. I am certain that these human qualities were a key to keeping the responses flowing in at a rapid pace—so much data, so many questions.

As is well known, however, one of the fundamental challenges of ethnographic research is to make sense of all that one observes—essentially how to impose some theoretical structure on the data and yet learn anew from ongoing observations. In our afternoon meetings this issue became paramount and I have vivid memories of insisting (shouting?) "focus, focus, focus!" I feared initially that St. Jean was in danger of drowning in data without a theoretical frame of interpretation. This tension pervades urban ethnography, but *Pockets of Crime* provides a commendable example of the struggle to negotiate difficult boundaries. As will be evident upon inspection, St. Jean went into the field with a clear goal that was primed by immersion in a set of sharp theoretical questions and thus expectations of what to look for, what to ask about.

He specifically wanted to collect data that would allow him to interrogate two theoretical perspectives on crime—"broken windows" and "collective efficacy." The former theory focuses on the physical and social cues that urban disorder is hypothesized to send to potential offenders. Collective efficacy theory is at bottom about social action—how shared expectations and social interactions among city residents shape the likelihood that existing criminal motivations will successfully eventuate in acts of crime. Testing and extending these theories provided the motivating questions and structure to shape a research design for collecting the data. Yet true to ethnographic form, St. Jean learned from the incoming messages the data were sending and he began to challenge and revise certain aspects of each theory. He had questions he wanted answered, to be sure, but this was no rote search. Rather, St. Jean operated as a detective might in trying to solve a crime—he had necessary priors and goals but discovery was essential.

The insights gained are more than worth the price of the book's admission. It is not my job to spoil the show, so I will only hint at what is to come with respect to substantive findings. Suffice it to say the reader will gain new knowledge of what makes offenders tick, in particular what aspects of urban space count the most in the decision to commit a crime. Both collective efficacy and broken windows theories find support, but both are also challenged by what St. Jean refers to as "ecological advantage." What he means by this is that the ecological position a block occupies in the larger structure of the community plays a direct role in determining its criminal advantage, regardless of the actions of residents or what appears to a middle-class eye to be disorder. More generally, offenders know how to use space in very specific ways that betray a sophisticated knowledge of street ecology. In the words of one offender, they know how to "build up a spot." If a block offers expropriative advantages, say because of a mixture of liquor stores, bars, and other establishments that provide cash-laden passersby or a demand for drugs, they will exploit it regardless of other conditions. As the drug dealer Quick puts it when queried about cues of disorder thought by "broken windows" theory to motivate crime: "You pay no attention to what the place be looking like, the condition of the lawns and buildings, if people be throwing trash and such." What matters is criminal opportunity, and for drug dealers and robbers that means vulnerable people with cash or contraband. St. Jean discovers why disorder is associated with crime—the bars, liquor stores, and other land-use types that generate available targets simultaneously generate disorder (often by offenders themselves), producing a spurious association.

Collective efficacy theory comes in for critical inquiry as well. St. Jean finds that collective action on the part of a block's residents has a fighting chance even in areas of high violence overall, but the odds of success are highly conditioned by local ecology. Interestingly, blocks with *low* collective efficacy (and usually high disorder) are virtually ignored by offenders if they do not offer the mixture of criminogenic commodities they seek. He also finds that the notion of a general trust in neighbors is misleading because it fails to distinguish between trust about personal information and trust regarding the guardianship of property, with the result that trust must be contextualized to understand the viability of collective efficacy. Another contribution will be found in the book's analysis of the variable demand for collective efficacy by residents and in its form of execution. Intervening on behalf of others exacts a cost, and how these costs are perceived and evaluated becomes important for understanding how collective efficacy is created.

In the end St. Jean offers us a revised theoretical conception of the ecological and social interactional conditions under which crime thrives, and those in which it is extinguished—all within the confines of a seg-regated black ghetto. It should go without saying, of course, that the canonical explanations offered by structuralist sociological theories of crime—poverty and segregation especially—fail at the very posing of St. Jean's question. Virtually everyone in *Pockets of Crime* is poor and black. These factors do not, and cannot, explain the fundamental variations of interest. Thus St. Jean's effort may be seen as part of new wave of urban research that is seeking to make sense of the proximate social mecha-nisms, interactions, and ecological structures that help explain crime. As he notes, the book is about social actions that are not determined by structural position. All of this is not to say that economic disadvantage is irrelevant. Quite the opposite—disadvantage looms everywhere as a sort of brutal machine that continuously produces a motivated pool of of-fenders. *How* the underlying motivations get translated into actual crimi-nal events is the puzzle that is solved, connecting St. Jean's work to the now classic "routine activities" conception of how to think about crime.

Another insight gleaned from St. Jean's data turns on how crime is conceptualized in ghetto settings. We find that crime is "managed." As just noted, there is no getting around crime's existence given the struc-tural conditions of the ghetto. What matters is avoiding becoming a "random victim." This is an intriguing idea, one that goes against much common wisdom about victimization risk. The residents take for granted that most crime is predictable and occurs among participants (offenders and victims alike) in the underbelly of illicit action. Even within a single block there are "normal" crimes and there are "random" crimes. Most of the residents St. Jean interviewed are conventional Americans but they know that in their world, the task is to avoid the latter and manage the rest. People organize to "push certain crimes into strategic locations," such that collective efficacy is often about displacement, but with the hope that with increased "pushing" away of crime the overall rate of commission will decline. Based on what we know about the short-term impulses and opportunistic nature governing the commission of most crimes, this logic is rational, if quite different from the more middle-class way of thinking, which is to "prevent" crime. The everyday reality of crime in the ghetto sets up a dynamic that demands savvy (or what has recently been called "street efficacy") on the part of residents if they are to survive. It also means a constant negotiation between law-abiding and law-violating neighbors to manage "normal" crimes, especially when both parties come from the same block and sometimes even family.

There are many other insights, but it is time for me to exit and for the reader to engage. I am confident the pages to follow will be rewarding and spark your imagination. They certainly did mine, and I am delighted to see St. Jean's innovative work on Chicago's hard-bitten streets make it into the pages of the University of Chicago Press. There could hardly be a more natural outlet, not to mention research setting, for the latest installment of the transcendent Chicago School of urban studies.

Robert J. Sampson
Harvard University

Acknowledgments

Without the assistance of a long list of devoted people and organizations that I owe a great debt of gratitude, the completion of this book would not have been possible. I first thank the many residents of Chicago, particularly those of Wentworth, and more specifically of Grand Boulevard, for being so giving of their time to allow me access to the most vulnerable aspects of their lives.

Thanks to the many active and reformed offenders who so freely and patiently schooled me on how to discipline my vision and thinking to understand how they viewed and negotiated their worlds. Drug dealers and robbers unlocked the secrets of "success" in their dreaded professions and allowed me as much access as I wished, within the boundaries of my ethics. They allowed me into an underworld that is invisible to many, even when in plain view. They accommodated my probing questions about why and how they did what they did, and my explanations of the relevance of academic theories that seemed both interesting and laughable to them. They tolerated my boldness in identifying inconsistencies in their statements, and took the time to clarify or sometimes honestly admit the shameful truth whenever I "busted" them with rebuttal evidence. I particularly thank Icepick, Throat, and Razor, who were the most patient, sometimes affectionately calling me "Brother" or "Black Man." They did so especially while taking extra time to teach me not only how to recognize how they selected a "good" person to rob but also how to protect myself from being robbed or otherwise becoming injured as I negotiated some of the most dangerous and frightening neighborhood corners. Their lessons from the streets of Chicago have proven to be invaluable as I now negotiate similarly dangerous streets in my ongoing research in Buffalo, New York. Although I perhaps did this enough in person, I here again apologize to the robbers and drug dealers for my clumsiness, which afforded them much laughter at my expense, but intermittently frustrated them with concern for my safety as well as their own. As I flattened the learning curve associated with knowing the life of the streets, I relied on comments of those experienced offenders to gauge my progress. I express condolences to the families of two of those men who lost their lives through violence in Chicago before I left the city in 2002. During interviews, those men wished that by allowing their points of view to be told, they could pay a debt back to society to repair some of the social damage caused by their criminal behavior. They asked me to discourage others from living the criminal lifestyles that consumed them. I hereby convey this message, and hope that the work will speak for itself.

I thank the Wentworth residents who frequently enjoy the self-imposed label of "law-abiding citizens" for their cooperation. They were particularly helpful with explanations about the formation, causes, and consequences of neighborhood disorder and collective action. They were open about their dense networks with offenders and their visions for an improved community. I am particularly grateful to the many residents who actively participated in the hundreds of CAPS meetings and community events that I attended. You know yourselves—thank you for allowing me special access into your homes, churches, meetings, and family events. Thanks too, for the encouragement and advice that you provided, as well as the pride that you displayed when you learned that my research was in part my dissertation project at the Department of Sociology, University of Chicago. Although you sometimes questioned whether my strange Caribbean (Dominica) accent disqualified me from being African American, I felt comfort in your acceptance of me as a black man, and your frankness that despite some reservations, you were confident that I was not a traitor of your community. I hope that the contents of this book, as true as they are, do not betray that trust. I must also express my discomfort about the fact that the first book that I published about your neighborhood focuses on its pockets of crime rather than its pockets of safety. I hope to balance this picture in the coming years.

I thank the many police officers of Wentworth, particularly the beat officers, their supervisors, and the detectives who knew me for keeping a watchful eye on me while I researched those dangerous streets, sometimes perhaps at inappropriate hours. Thanks for reminding me, although often months or years afterward, of instances when I could have been vulnerable in the field if not for your marked or unmarked cars in fixed or changing locations keeping surveillance for my protection. I knew that good research skills and good luck were not enough for safety, and drew comfort in my knowledge of your sometimes invisible presence.

I thank the officers of Beat 213 for participating in my interviews, taking extra time to respond to questions that could not be addressed during public meetings, and for providing me with insights into their own flaws and those of their department. Your trust was very reassuring. Former Wentworth police commander Perry, I thank you for encouraging your officers to support my research from multiple angles.

Support from the faculty, staff, and my fellow doctoral students at the University of Chicago allowed me to complete the research with good speed and sanity. Robert J. Sampson, Richard Taub, Andrew Abbott, and Wesley Skogan (of Northwestern), thanks for the guidance you provided throughout the time you served on my dissertation committee, but particularly during my defense when you grilled me beyond imagination. Rob, thanks for encouraging me to focus, focus, focus and take some time to think carefully about the sort of book that should emerge from the study instead of rushing to publish at the first opportunity. Rob, as the chair of my dissertation committee, thanks again for being so unselfish with your time and knowledge. Thanks too for your continued mentorship and friendship after our formal relationship ended in Chicago. Edward Laumann, Omar McRoberts, Saskia Sassen, Donald Levine, Patrick Heuveline, William Parish, Terry Clark, James Davis, Andreas Glaeser, and Charles Bidwell, thank you all for the special encouragement that you provided during my most troubled times. Special thanks to some of my former Chicago classmates for their constant encouragement: Fabio, Mito, Harris, Yildirim, Marc, Anne, Arthur, and Rachelle. Linnea, Alta, and Ray, thanks for your help with navigating administrative hurdles.

Since I moved from Chicago to Buffalo in 2002, I have received tremendous support from the Buffalo community, especially among those with whom I volunteer as a participant-observer in my ongoing Buffalo Area Neighborhood Study (BANS). Buffalo has afforded me an opportunity to scrutinize in tight focus some of the factors I began to explore in the Wentworth Area Neighborhood Study (WANS), upon which this book is based. Members of the Buffalo Local Action Committee (BLAC), Stop the Violence Coalition, Parents Encouraging Accountability and Closure to Everyone (PEACE), Buffalo Block Clubs, and the Buffalo Police Department, thanks for your constant encouragement to get this Chicago-based book completed so that I can complete one based on my ongoing research in your wonderful city. I hope that meanwhile *Pockets of Crime* finds relevance among you.

Colleagues at the University at Buffalo, thank you for comments on drafts and your encouragement: Robert Wagmiller, Mike Farrell, Brenda Moore, and Debra Street. I also thank some of my former University at Buffalo graduate students for their comments on drafts: Clarke Gocker, Daisy Henderson, Cassi Meyerhoffer, Autumn Foster, Timothy Sentman, Daniel Nickolai, Gabrielle Alfieri, Kristin Prusinski, Yi-Ping Shih, Li Lu, and Shannon Azzarelli. My friends, Liz Adrien, Corinne Francis, and Juliette Matthews, thanks too for your comments on drafts. Sharon Martin, thank you for your assistance and encouragement during the early stages of the research. Thanks to the anonymous reviewers whose comments strengthened the manuscript as it progressed.

Last but certainly not least, I thank my immediate family members for their love, support, encouragement, and reading of drafts: my wonderful wife and partner, Zahrain, a native of Chicago; our children, Sergio P. K. B., P. K. Breanna, and Patrice K. B.; my mother, Isaline; siblings, Agnes (Marilyn), Jacqueline (Cecilia), and Anthony (Newton); niece, Chanda; and nephews, Wayne and Wilbur. To my Chicago relatives in the Holloway and Hall families, especially Michelle, Brenda, Carolyn, Mary Ellen, Konrad, Vita, Sharon, Gloria, and Gladys, thanks for your frequent inspiration, outpouring of love, and interest. Your holistic support has been fuel to my everyday fire.

ONE

Introduction and Overview

Introduction

Why is it that, even within the same general high-crime area, crimes such as robbery, drug dealing, and assaults occur much more frequently on some neighborhood blocks than others? Is it because, compared to the low-crime blocks, high-crime blocks have more unpleasant appearances created by abandoned buildings, broken windows, boarded-up windows, overgrown lawns, vacant lots, littering, loitering, and panhandling (neighborhood disorder)?[1] Or might it be that, compared to the low-crime blocks, high-crime blocks exhibit a diminished sense of community—less trust among neighbors, less solidarity among them, and less willingness on their part to intervene to create a safer neighborhood (collective efficacy)?[2] These claims constitute the core of two popular and competing theories proposed to explain causes and consequences of neighborhood crime: the first widely known as *broken windows,* and the second as *collective efficacy.*[3] These two theories have been widely assessed by researchers who examine them from the point of view of law-abiding citizens. However, to date no research effort has been made to take these claims into neighborhoods; to place them under ethnographic scrutiny, especially within the world of hardened offenders; or to evaluate how closely the theories correspond to the realities of everyday community life. This is one objective of the ongoing

1. Wilson and Kelling 1982.
2. Sampson, Raudenbush, and Earls 1997; Sampson and Raudenbush 1999.
3. Both theories are further explained in chapter 2.

Wentworth Area Neighborhood Study (WANS),[4] the source of data for this book.

I have chosen to focus on broken windows and collective efficacy theories because they have recently received considerable attention for their competing explanations of why crimes are more likely to occur in some neighborhoods than in others. Each theory is further explained in chapter 2, so it will suffice to offer only a brief introduction here. Broken windows theory posits that a high level of neighborhood disorder indirectly influences high crime through a chain of events that begins with neighborhood disorder and then advances to dynamics such as fear of crime and weakened social control—which serve as a breeding ground for more serious crime. There are two components of neighborhood disorder: physical disorder and social disorder. Physical disorder refers to conditions that suggest lack of care for the physical environment of a neighborhood. These conditions include abandoned buildings, broken and/or boarded-up windows, graffiti, overgrown lawns, and untidy vacant lots. Social disorder refers to unpleasant and potentially intimidating patterns of social interaction such as panhandling, loitering, and public drinking. Broken windows theorists argue that such neighborhood disorderly conditions also signal to offenders that no one cares about the neighborhood, and that therefore there are few costs to committing crime there (Wilson and Kelling 1982). If left unchecked, neighborhood disorder will continue to increase, petty crimes will increase, and residents will perceive that more serious crimes are also on the increase. Fearful of crime, law-abiding citizens will then refrain from using public spaces, become less attached to the neighborhood, and eventually move out of the area only to be replaced by less attached people. Serious crimes will then follow (Wilson and Kelling 1982). Proponents of broken windows theory therefore argue that to reduce the potentials for serious crimes to occur, petty and disorderly crimes such as panhandling, loitering, and public drinking must be aggressively suppressed (Kelling and Coles 1996; Skogan 1990; Wilson and Kelling 1982). However, the aspect of broken windows theory that is of greatest concern to this book is the reference to offenders' interpretation of neighborhood disorder as an invitation to commit crimes with impunity, and their

4. The Wentworth Area Neighborhood Study (WANS) is an ongoing research effort aimed at understanding factors associated with neighborhood quality of life in Wentworth, a section of Chicago's South Side. The project began in 1997 as my dissertation research while I was a student at the Department of Sociology, University of Chicago. After completing the dissertation in 2002, I have continued my research in Wentworth from my new location at SUNY-Buffalo. The ongoing research has primarily focused on factors relevant to gentrification and various aspects of quality of life in the area.

subsequent actions aligned with this interpretation of disorder. Never before have offenders such as drug dealers, robbers, murderers, and others been given the opportunity to make their contribution to the broken windows debate. This book has allowed them to explain their decision making process and actions in colorful and sometimes shocking terms that punctuate the complexities of their everyday realities.

Collective efficacy theorists, on the other hand, argue that high crime flourishes not because of high neighborhood disorder, but rather, as a result of low collective efficacy—a low sense of community for the public good—or low capacities for collective action for the public good. Collective efficacy is defined as a combined measure of trust, solidarity, and the willingness of residents to intervene on behalf of the public good. One example of the public good is the desire to cultivate a safer neighborhood for everyone (Sampson et al. 1997). Collective efficacy theorists contend that high capacities for collective action for the public good (or high collective efficacy) is best realized when the relationships among persons acting on the behalf of a neighborhood are characterized by mutual trust, solidarity, and similar expectations about what is acceptable behavior and what they can accomplish together (shared expectations for action). Therefore, in order to reduce potentials for serious crimes, stronger communities—that is, communities in which precisely the relationships just described are prevalent— must be developed and maintained.

Pockets of Crime evaluates the claims and assumptions of broken windows and collective efficacy theories through five years of intensive neighborhood research within Wentworth, a police district on the south side of Chicago, Illinois, that has historically been among the highest violent and predatory crime areas of the city. Among the important features of this book are candid interviews and neighborhood tours with hardened offenders whose criminal histories include crimes such as murder, robbery, drug dealing, burglary and battery. These offenders explain in detail how various crimes are committed and describe their perceptions of how the claims of broken windows and collective efficacy theories relate to the process of their criminal activities. Data for the book also come from field notes I made as a participant observer in the community;[5] from analyses of police crime statistics cross-validated against a neighborhood survey of residents' knowledge of crime hotspots; from videos that show both sides of neighborhood blocks;[6] from maps; and from interviews with police officers, local business persons, and law-abiding residents.

5. Participant observation.
6. Systematic Social Observation.

The main finding from the research is that while the level of physical disorder[7] (one of the key variables of broken windows theory) is not significantly associated with higher levels of street drug dealing, robbery, or battery, both social disorder[8] and collective efficacy[9] were found to be significantly associated with all three types of crime. However, the relationships are not as straightforward as either broken windows theory or collective efficacy theory assumes. I found that among the blocks that ranked high on social disorder, about an equal proportion experienced high and low levels of crime (see appendix A). This suggests that while low social disorder may help to condition low crime, high social disorder alone is insufficient to produce high crime. The relationships between the level of collective efficacy and the level of these three crimes were also somewhat complicated. While lower crime was found on blocks whose residents exhibited high levels of collective efficacy, residents of blocks with lower levels of collective efficacy experienced high and low levels of crime in approximately equal proportions. This suggests that while high collective efficacy may condition low crime, low collective efficacy may not be sufficient to produce high crime. The question remains, why? These complications found in the statistical data were supported by field observations and the nonstatistical information for this study, including interviews with offenders to explore why such is the case.

This research contextualizes previous work on crime in neighborhoods, both lending support to and contradicting broken windows and collective efficacy theories. Using the concept of *ecological disadvantage,* I offer extensions of both broken windows and collective efficacy theories. *Ecological disadvantage* posits that (a) urban space is unevenly developed,

7. Physical disorder was measured in terms of the condition of buildings, the properties around them, and vacant lots. The measures of physical disorder were derived using a technique I refer to as handcoding. In the year 2000, equipped with a large folded structural base map outlining each parcel of Beat 213, I walked through all of the 58 neighborhood blocks and visually evaluated the physical condition of all 649 structures (530 residential, 96 commercial, and 23 mixed) and 545 vacant lots in the neighborhood. The standards for measurement were adopted from the Project on Human Development on Chicago's Neighborhoods (PHDCN) and from Taub, Taylor, and Dunham 1984.

8. Loitering, panhandling, and public drinking. Measures of social disorder were obtained from the survey of neighborhood experts and cross-validated with my own field observations. For each block, respondents were asked to indicate how many days of the week, and for how many hours per day, persons would be "hanging out" (loitering), panhandling, and drinking alcohol in public spaces on the block (loitering). Mean and standard deviation measures were derived to determine high, midrange, and low levels of social disorder. It turned out that high social disorder blocks were those where such activities occurred more than 4 days a week, and more than 6 consecutive hours per day.

9. Measures for levels of collective efficacy were derived from the survey of neighborhood experts. I used the same questions utilized in the PNDCN. See Sampson, Raudenbush, and Earls 1997.

and (b) different crimes are habitually committed in particular locations that offer offenders specific advantages. Therefore, (c) the influence that factors such as neighborhood disorder and collective efficacy may have on the formation of crime hotspots[10] cannot be adequately understood without first considering how the spatial positioning of the location independently places it at a disadvantage for certain criminal opportunities.

For instance, as subsequent chapters demonstrate, for various reasons, both street drug dealers and robbers in the research site are primarily attracted to locations with businesses such as liquor stores, grocery stores, check-cashing outlets, and fast-food restaurants.[11] Such businesses are most typically found at or near major and busy street intersections. Most drug dealers and robbers commonly find little interest in street locations that are remote and exclusively residential.[12] Therefore, even given the same levels of neighborhood disorder and collective efficacy, neighborhood blocks with the businesses mentioned above are, because of this ecological disadvantage, more likely to emerge as drug dealing and robbery hotspots. Researchers, therefore, must situate explanations in the influence of broader spaces within which a crime hotspot is located. Spatial positioning has profound impacts on the interpretations[13] of neighborhood disorder, as well as on the *demands*,[14] and *returns*[15] for collective action against crime (collective efficacy).

Several studies[16] have been conducted on the general topic of crime

10. Crime hotspots are locations where, compared to others, crimes occur most frequently.

11. With the exception of some drug dealers who prefer to operate out of large public housing buildings.

12. Except in some instances where drugs are sold out of homes on quiet streets, and relatives or acquaintances rob each other within their own domiciles or recreational spaces.

13. As will be demonstrated, interpretations of neighborhood disorder are affected by preexisting assumptions about race, class, age, and gender that are used as cues to determine what section of the city one is in and what is expected to occur there.

14. In collective efficacy, "demands" refers to (a) whether or not collective neighborhood action against crime will become a *necessity* and (b) the *form* such action takes–whether it is as simple as requesting that a powerful neighborhood resident, business owner, or associate make a phone call to solve the problem; having a small meeting among concerned persons to plan a response; or (n the extreme case) having a large group of concerned residents arise in uproar.

15. "Returns" refers to expected results for collective action against crime in terms of: (a) *benefits:* whether there will be widespread notice of the actions, whether there will be widespread confidence among neighbors about the results of collective action against crime; and (b) *costs:* how much, and what form of resistance offenders will express against such collective actions, and the real and perceived losses to participants in collective actions against crime.

16. Lersch 2004; Brantingham and Brantingham 1991, 1998, 1999; Jeffery 1971; Block and Block 1995; Bursik 1999, 1986; Burgess 1967 [1925]; Byrne and Sampson 1986; Eck, Gersh, and Taylor. 2000; Eck 2001; Felson 1986; Langworthy and Jefferis 2000; Miethe and McCorle 2001; Sampson 1985, 1986, Sampson and Groves 1989; Sherman 1995, Shaw and McKay 1942; Taylor and Harrell 1996; Wilson and Kelling 1982, Sampson, Raudenbush, and Earls , Sampson and Raudenbush 1999.

hotspots,[17] but mainly through analyses of official crime data and information derived from presumed law-abiding citizens. Despite the important contribution of such studies, more effort needs to be made to understand, mainly from the point of view of offenders themselves, how various crime locales are selected, sustained, and abandoned, and how accurately those processes are reflected in current theories. *Pockets of Crime* responds to this gap in knowledge by using the approach of extended case methods[18] (Burawoy et al. 1991) to provide up-close field research analyses of the reasons offenders give for committing certain crimes, how they commit them (especially the critical space-related factors associated with their decision making process), and how accurately those thoughts and actions are reflected in the two theoretical frameworks.

Both broken windows and collective efficacy theories are intuitively appealing, and researchers have found moderate to strong empirical support for their core assumptions. Still, there is a need to "take them to the field" and scrutinize them ethnographically to further determine whether and how the theories resonate with the various ways offenders commit crimes. To the extent that contradictory findings arise that do not mesh well with the assumptions of these theories, such findings can be used to build the theories[19] by incorporating nuance or specifying scope conditions in the face of new evidence. For instance, what is the relevance of these theories to the actions of drug dealers in their quests to find and maintain lucrative locations in which to conduct sales; and for robbers, in their search for prey? How do these theories relate to the processes involved in high instances of interpersonal crimes such as battery? I have chosen to focus on the crimes of narcotics violations, robberies, and batteries because, as discussed later in this chapter, they are based on different structures of opportunity and motivation and therefore provide a richer context for understanding the strengths and

---

17. Locations with a disproportionately higher incidence of crime than others.

18. Extended case method focuses on theory building through participant observation. It advocates that "methodology provides the link between technique and theory . . . the reciprocal relationship between data and theory" (Burawoy et al. 1991, 271). Extended case method "is realized not through induction of new theory from the ground up but through the failure of and then *reconstruction of existing theory*. . . . We search for theory that highlight some aspect of the situation under study as being anomalous and then proceed to build (rather than reject) that theory by reference to the wider forces at work, be they the state, the economy, or even the world system. . . . [W]e seek to place ourselves in a wider community of social scientists by taking the flaws of existing theory as points of departure. . . . The dialogue between participant and observer extends itself naturally to a dialogue among social scientists—a dialogue that is emergent rather than conclusive, critical rather than cosmetic, involving reconstruction rather than deconstruction" (Burawoy et al. 1991, 6–7, emphasis in original).

19. Again, in harmony with the methodological and theoretical protocols of extended case methods (Burawoy et al. 1991).

weaknesses of the two theoretical frameworks as they relate to the various ways crimes are actually committed.

Chicago's History of Crime, and Recent Efforts to Combat It

Chicago is the *known* city; perhaps more is known about it, how it is run, how it kills, how it loves, steals, helps, gives, cheats, and crushes than any other city in the world. Chicago is a new city; it grew to be bigger in one hundred years than did Paris in two hundred. There are men now living in Chicago whose fathers saw it in its infancy and helped it grow. Because Chicago is so young, it is possible to know it in a way that many other cities cannot be known. The stages of its complex growth are living memories. (Wright 1945, xviii)

Much of Richard Wright's analyses of Chicago are as true today as they were in 1945. Much has changed in Chicago since its early days of development, but certain themes have remained the same: its high racial and ethnic segregation, the caring hearts of many residents, the somewhat flamboyant leadership, its prominence as a hub for commerce, its wonderful parks, and complex criminal situations that demand innovative responses from law enforcement agents and the citizenry.

From its inception, Chicago has been an American city of great interest to locals and visitors alike. For instance, during the 2005 American Society of Criminology Meeting held in Toronto, and at the 2006 Eastern Society of Sociology Meeting held in Boston, several scholars who conducted research there introduced Chicago as the most studied city in America. Yet, much is still to be known about Chicago: the complex aspects of life that unfold within it, and the manner in which it inspires the intellectual and literary interests entrenched in its daily routines. "Chicago, it seems, has a way of leaving its imprint upon those who live in it" (Wright 1945, xviii).

The mass of land that is currently known as Chicago did not became widely known to persons other than the Potawatomi Indians until 1673, when the French Canadian explorers Jacques Marquette and Louis Jolliet passed through the area on their way to Quebec (Cromie 1984). In the Potawatomi language, "Checagou" (Chick-Ah-Goo-Ah) or "Checaguar" means "wild onion" or "skunk"—a reference to the smell that filled the air of that swampy area. In 1779, Jean Baptiste Point du Sable, a Haitian of African descent, became the first non–Native American settler in Chicago (Andreas 1975). With a population of 350, Chicago became incorporated in 1833, and by 1840 its population had increased to more than 4,000; its population continued to increase dramatically in subsequent decades, to more than 90,000 by 1857 and to some 300,000 by 1871. One of the earliest recorded disasters in Chicago was the 1871 Great Chicago Fire, which killed approximately 300 people, left more than 100,000 residents homeless, and destroyed nearly 18,000 buildings (Cromie 1984).

Some other notable aspects of Chicago's history include the following: the world's first skyscraper in 1885; the founding of the University of Chicago in 1890; the elevated train (the el), which began operation in 1891; the 1893 World's Fair; the Pullman Strike in 1894; a race riot in 1919; the Valentine's Day Massacre in 1929; the assassination of Mayor Cermak, who was killed while riding with President-Elect Theodore Roosevelt; the stormy 1968 Democratic National Convention; the 1973 opening of the Sears Tower, which was the world's tallest building for thirty years; election of the city's first woman mayor (Jane M. Byrne) in 1979, and its first African American Mayor (Harold Washington) in 1983; the 1992 Chicago flood; the 1995 Chicago Heat Wave; the closing of Meigs Field in 2003; and the 2004 opening of Millennium Park (Wikipedia 2006).

One of the most publicized aspects of Chicago's history has been its struggles with criminal lifestyles, including the innovative strategies adopted by criminal justice agents and residents to create safer communities. Gangsters such as Johnny Torrio, his protégé Al Capone, and many others may readily come to mind. Chicago's infestation with gangs attracted the attention of some of the earliest American sociologists such as Thrasher (1927) and Shaw and McKay (1942), who examined a variety of neighborhood and socioeconomic factors associated with juvenile delinquency and gang involvement in the city. Such scholars found that for many young persons, gangs served as a social network to compensate for lack of bonds in their lives, and especially as a buffer against the ills of poverty, violence, intimidation, and discrimination.

Chicago's police department faced serious crime problems throughout most of the twentieth century, and by the summer of 1991 the city's homicide rate was the fourth highest in the nation. Built on the foundation of a turbulent criminal past, Chicago in the summer of 1991 was marked by a conspicuous change in criminality that provided the impetus for a change in strategy against crime in the city. Wes Skogan and his research colleagues provide a good picture of Chicago at that time:

Pay telephones were no longer a neighborhood amenity; instead, residents reported they attracted street drug traffickers. The term "drive-by-shooting" entered residents' lexicon. Beginning with the early 1990s, the percentage of homicides attributed to gangs grew higher. Assaults became increasingly lethal as the proportion of murder weapons that were automatic or semi-automatic jumped sharply. The courts prosecuted larger numbers of gun-toters so young that special measures had to be taken to try them as adults. Children also died violently in record numbers. Gang wars erupted over the control of lucrative drug-selling sites. Some of the city's most notorious public housing projects echoed with gunfire almost nightly. Crime appeared to be the number one local issue, and the public wanted something done about it. The question was, what would the city do about the crime rate? (Skogan et al. 1994, 2)

The Chicago Community Alternative Policing Strategy (CAPS) became the answer in Chicago. CAPS was timely since the city was facing increasing crime problems, population withdrawal in response to crime concerns, racial conflicts, a shortage of public funds as a result of the profound economic depression of the time, and a mayor who was seeking re-election (Skogan and Hartnett 1997). To be sure, 1991 was an unusual year not only for homicides but also for other crimes in Chicago. Robberies had increased by 7,000 over the previous year; assaults increased by 1,000 (up by almost 5,000 compared to 1989); serious crimes on the trains and buses had also reached a record high of 2,400 in 1991. The use of guns in violent crimes had also increased, accounting for about 66 percent of all homicides in Chicago. Between 1988 to 1994, murders with automatic and semiautomatic machine guns had increased by a whopping 650 percent (Skogan and Hartnett 1997). Between 1985 and 1991, Chicago's children were dying in record numbers as a result of violent crimes. Meanwhile, juvenile arrests for murder had increased by 230 percent during that period (Skogan and Hartnett 1997).

Chicago has long been one of America's most segregated cities, and its pattern of crime is also disproportionately distributed among its population, with the poorest and least represented racial and ethnic citizens (particularly Hispanics and African Americans) suffering the most as victims and perpetrators of violent crimes. In 1993, houses in predominantly African American neighborhoods were twice as likely as those in predominantly white neighborhoods to be burglarized. African Americans in Chicago were more than four times more likely to be raped or robbed than whites, and two times more likely than Hispanics. In African American neighborhoods, crimes involving guns were seven times more frequent than in white neighborhoods, and four times more frequent than in Hispanic neighborhoods. Compared to white neighborhoods, drug offenses were four times higher in Hispanic neighborhoods, and 11.5 times higher in African American neighborhoods (Skogan and Hartnett 1997).

In response to rising crime problems and to the increased public pressure to *do something about it,* community policing was formally implemented in Chicago on April 29, 1993. The idea was to restructure the city's police department by decentralization and to forge a new relationship with residents and the business community collectively to identify, prioritize, and resolve community problems that directly and indirectly related to crime. The vision, structure, and protocols for the Community Alternative Policing Strategy (CAPS) was formulated and launched as a pilot project in five police districts that were quite varied in terms of income, racial composition, and existing crime rates. These districts were Englewood (District 7), Marquette (District 10), Austin (District 15), Morgan Park (District 22), and Rogers Park (District 24) (Skogan et al. 1994).

A core of the CAPS program is monthly community meetings in each police district. At these "beat meetings,"[20] residents, police, representatives from the business community, and others gather in a designated location (usually a church or community center) to discuss strategies to combat crime problems, to prioritize those problems, and to decide the various roles different actors will play; participants leave the meetings committed to action. They then return to the next meeting to update each other on the progress of their efforts. As crime problems are resolved, they are removed from the priority problem list and replaced by other pressing problems. CAPS provides a template for running beat meetings, but local actors may slightly modify that guideline to suit the idiosyncratic problems at hand. On some occasions, specific problem-solving meetings are held by small groups of residents who are actively working on prioritized problems. During such meetings, the idea is to focus on the specific problems at hand. Alternatively, in general beat meetings, beat facilitators (the chief representative for residents) and police team leaders guide discussions where new complaints are submitted and strategies to address them are formulated.

By May 1995, almost all uniformed Chicago police officers had completed two days of problem-solving training that included procedures on how to use the main service delivery process. Chicago's police department was on its way to transforming police work into yet another vital city service aimed at satisfying the needs of its customers—the general public in need of safety and protection. This was done through collaboration with residents, businesses, and faith-based communities.

---

20. There are 25 police districts and 279 beats in Chicago. A beat is a subsection of a district – usually several street blocks. Elaborations are elsewhere in this book.

The year-two evaluation of CAPS indicated that "An analysis of reported crimes figures and survey reports of victimization and neighborhood problems found there were significant decreases in perceived crime problems in all five prototype areas" (Chicago Community Policing Evaluation Consortium 1995; all data reported in this paragraph are from this report). Most notable were significant decreases in gang violence, drug dealing, building abandonment, and littering on the streets and sidewalks. In four of the five pilot areas, citizens' confidence in the police had increased. However, police leadership at beat meetings had also increased, gradually morphing community/police partnership into police domination.

In 1996, the Chicago Police Department boasted that "For the fifth year in a row reports of major crime declined in Chicago. The 3.3 percent decrease in 1996 followed a 4.4 percent decrease in 1995. These decreases followed declines of 1.2 percent in 1994, 3.9 percent in 1993, and 7.5 percent in 1992. The 263,166 index crimes reported in 1996 were the lowest total in more than a decade" (Chicago Police Department 1997, 14).

Eight years later, the Chicago Police Department continued to enjoy substantial decreases in serious crimes in the city. "Reported index crime declined consistently in the ten years from 1995 through 2004. The overall decline was 32.9 percent or 3.36 percent per year on a compound annual basis. Between 2003 and 2004 the decrease was 3.7 percent" (Chicago Police Department 2005, 4). Most notably, in 2004 there were 448 murders in Chicago, representing a 25.2 percent decrease from the 599 murders of 2003. This 2004 murder figure was Chicago's lowest in thirty-eight years. Robberies declined by 8.2 percent, and assaults by 5.4 percent.

One of the strengths of the CAPS program has been its ability to actively involve residents and the business community in keeping neighborhoods safe. Annual evaluations of CAPS have indicated that the program is often most active where it is most needed: in the high crime sections of the city. However, there are noticeable variations across beats in the extent to which residents and their police are functioning partners. In some beats police dominate the meetings, while in others the partnership is more conspicuous through their actions. Ultimately, CAPS provides a more or less effective framework for addressing disorderly neighborhood conditions and serious crimes. In the process, individuals are afforded the opportunity to build collective efficacy: to increase trust in relationships, solidarity, and agreement on shared expectations for action, all of which influences their willingness to intervene on behalf of the common good. Of course, this willingness to intervene does not function in a vacuum. Individuals and groups who are willing to act on behalf of improved quality of life in their community must also have the opportunities and resources to act. In Chicago, CAPS provides them with such a framework. Only time will tell how successful this approach will be in the future, and what key factors will ultimately make the difference. Meanwhile, we are left with the task of determining what neighborhood disorder means to active offenders, and how (and to what extent) collective efficacy may influence neighborhood crime.

The Research Site

I chose to study the city of Chicago, Illinois, where other scholars recently conducted intensive research testing both broken windows and collective efficacy theories.[21] A subsection of Chicago was selected for intensive ethnographic and other field research conducted over five years (1997–2002). Several studies have identified the variables of race and income as important factors in determining high and low crime neighborhoods. Therefore, in an effort to focus on a neighborhood within a high-crime area and control for income and race on the broad neighborhood level,[22] I selected from among Chicago's twenty-five police districts (Table 1.1 and Figures 1.1–1.3) one that best exemplified the following categories: (1) highest serious (index) crime rate, (2) lowest income, and (3) highest concentration of African Americans. Table 1.1 provides the following data for all twenty-five Chicago police districts: 2000 median household income, percent Black (2000 census), index crime[23] rates for each year from 1998 to 2002, and the yearly ranking of each of the twenty-five districts in terms of index crime rate. Figures 1.1–1.3 outline the police districts of Chicago in terms of the variables of concern: high percentage of African American residents, income, and average index crime rate (1998–2002).

District 2 (Wentworth) is highlighted in Table 1.1 because it was selected as the one that best fits the criteria. Note that among the three police districts with the highest percentage of African Americans (2, 6, and 7), Wentworth had the lowest median household income in 2000

21. I refer here to the Project on Human Development in Chicago Neighborhoods (PHDCN), from which several papers have been published by Robert J. Sampson and his colleagues.

22. I have also elected to closely study a neighborhood within an area where race and class are controlled to scrutinize the claim of collective efficacy theorists that collective efficacy is significantly and negatively associated with crimes even when neighborhood disadvantage is controlled (Sampson, Raudenbush, and Earls 1997).

23. Homicide, criminal sexual assaults, aggravated battery, burglary, theft, motor vehicle theft, arson.

Table 1.1. Income, Race, and Index Crime Rates (per 1,000) for Chicago's Twenty-five Police Districts (1998–2002).

District	Size	Medinc00	Perblk	98rt	99rt	00rt	01rt	02rt
1	3.94	62050	29%	448	421	395	340	324
2	**3.77**	**16591**	**98%**	**196**	**174**	**142**	**124**	**115**
3	6.04	25569	94%	121	107	102	104	92
4	27.27	36649	62%	80	74	68	67	68
5	12.8	35888	95%	99	86	87	79	79
6	8.1	33519	99%	119	108	109	103	100
7	6.56	23454	98%	134	123	112	111	106
8	23.12	44037	24%	63	58	57	57	57
9	13.09	32785	15%	69	62	64	59	58
10	7.87	28109	35%	64	57	56	56	52
11	6.11	24434	92%	130	111	103	102	105
12	5.47	32775	25%	117	99	96	79	77
13	4.21	37249	21%	111	94	91	87	94
14	6	38438	7%	101	81	86	83	80
15	3.82	29135	96%	111	86	80	74	72
16	30.95	50431	1%	41	37	38	33	32
17	9.62	43234	3%	54	49	47	43	42
18	4.69	66610	15%	149	128	117	105	102
19	5.57	59004	4%	79	70	66	58	61
20	4.37	36985	12%	51	47	44	37	35
21	4.92	33718	58%	113	104	88	80	67
22	13.46	53755	62%	63	55	53	52	54
23	3.01	43002	13%	64	54	50	45	43
24	5.43	40276	20%	54	49	47	40	41
25	10.91	40878	19%	75	64	61	58	56

Size = square miles.
Medinc00 = median household income, 2000.
Perblk = percent population Black or African American.
Example, 98rt = Index crime rate (per 1000 residents) for 1998.

($16,591) and the highest index crime rate for all the years from 1998 to 2002. Between 1998 and 2002, index crime rates in Wentworth ranked second highest among the twenty-five police districts in Chicago. There are approximately 1,300 street blocks in Wentworth.

The geographic boundaries of Wentworth are 35th Street at the north, Cottage Grove Avenue at the east, 61st Street at the south, and the Dan Ryan Expressway at the west. The community areas of Wentworth are Grand Boulevard, Washington Park, and a section of Douglas. This section of Chicago is commonly referred to as Bronzeville. Wentworth is

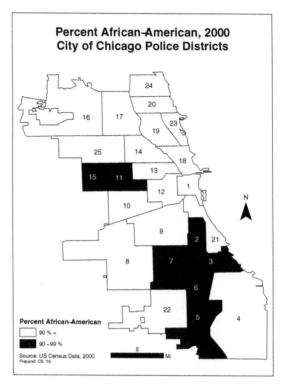

Figure 1.1. Chicago police districts with African American populations greater than or equal to 90 percent (2000).

home to some of Chicago's most notorious housing projects, including Stateway Gardens, which was identified as the poorest area in the United States in 1980 and 1990; Robert Taylor Homes; Madden Park; and Ida B. Wells. In their book *Black Metropolis*,[24] St. Clair Drake and Horace Clayton described Bronzeville as the heart of the African American community in Chicago. They identified the northern boundary of Bronzeville as slightly further north than 35th Street, and the southern boundary as about the same as that of Wentworth. In the 1940s to the late 1950s, Bronzeville was known as the Black Metropolis. Drake and Clayton described it as very vibrant, with an active businesses section especially along 47th Street and its environs. Richard Wright also wrote about life in Bronzeville, especially in *Black Boy*.[25] Like Drake and Clayton, he too

24. Drake and Clayton 1970.
25. Wright 1964.

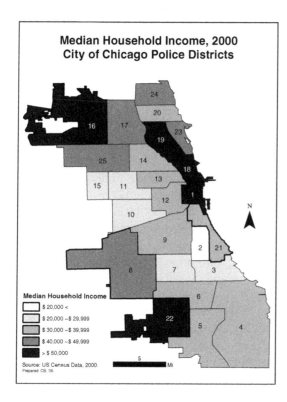

Figure 1.2. Median house-
hold income, by Chicago
police district (2000).

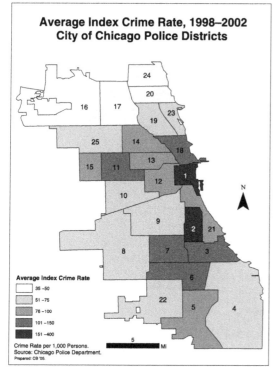

Figure 1.3. Index crime
rates by Chicago police
district (1998–2000).

described this area as a segregated but commercially thriving section of Chicago in the 1940s and 1950s. Between the late 1950s and the late 1990s, however, poverty, joblessness, crime, and other social problems devastated the area. In 1999 and 2000, 47th Street was still the busiest shopping area within Bronzeville, but many of the businesses that operated there in the past had either been liquidated or relocated.

William J. Wilson's *When Work Disappears* and *The Truly Disadvantaged* document many of the socioeconomic changes that have occurred in Bronzeville's neighborhood processes. Bronzeville is undergoing yet another period of change, particularly since the period of my study ended. Since development in the northern sections of Chicago has reached its limits, the city is being forced to expand gentrification southward. Therefore, Bronzeville is rapidly undergoing gentrification, marked by the demolition of many public housing units, especially down the State Street corridor where Stateway Gardens and the Robert Taylor Homes high-rise buildings that housed many of the poorest Americans were located.

The southeastern section of Wentworth borders on Hyde Park, one of the wealthiest communities in Chicago and home of the University of Chicago. The shocking socioeconomic contrasts between Hyde Park and Wentworth can easily be seen as one travels across any of the arteries, such as 47th Street, 51st Street, 55th Street, or 61st Street, that run east to west. One could travel east on any of these streets, across the Dan Ryan Expressway, through Wentworth, and end in Hyde Park, which borders on Lake Shore Drive and the shores of Lake Michigan.

While I was interested in closely observing crime-related processes on the street block level, it was impractical to study all 1,300 blocks within Wentworth District. Therefore, a smaller section was selected at random. In this study, a street block is defined as an address block: both sides of a street with addresses within the same hundred-number range. For example, 501 through 599 E. Pershing Road is identified as the 500 block of East Pershing Road.

Selecting a Neighborhood within Wentworth

Chicago's twenty-five police districts are further divided into beats. Each district has nine to fifteen beats. This forms a total of 281 beats in the entire city.[26] Each beat ranges from about 50 to 125 street blocks. The beat is one of the most important units for neighborhood action because it is on that level that police officers, city agents, and residents most

26. See www.cityofchicago.org/police.

Table 1.2. Wentworth Index Crime Rates by Beat (1999–2002).

Beat	Pop00	Medinc00	Rate99	Rank99	Rate00	Rank00	Rate01	Rank01	Rate02	Rank02
211	5425	161143	117	7	97	10	126	5	128	5
212	6441	9840	68	11	73	11	75	11	65	12
213	3386	15018	93	9	126	7	130	4	111	6
214	4108	15555	94	8	195	3	102	8	81	11
221	5038	10239	119	5	158	4	114	6	87	10
222	4946	26926	92	10	39	12	92	10	101	8
223	5968	18030	52	12	103	9	94	9	101	9
224	3028	16273	118	6	155	6	145	3	158	3
231	1532	5500	258	2	385	1	260	1	254	2
232	2093	17430	517	1	291	2	260	1	282	1
233	5183	20658	206	4	111	8	102	7	108	7
234	3820	22803	216	3	156	5	161	2	143	4

commonly assemble to mobilize themselves around issues of common concern. The size of each police beat has been determined by administrative decisions that take the volume of crime problems experienced in that space as a top priority. Higher crime areas tend to be divided into smaller police beats. However, many beats are similar in geographic size and population (see Table 1.2 and Figure 1.4).

There are twelve police beats within Wentworth. Although the beats vary somewhat in size, they possess similar residential spaces, because sections of the larger beats are occupied by train tracks, commercial spaces, parks, and other public spaces. Table 1.2 indicates that although some of the beats in Wentworth are similar in population and income, their index crime rates varied considerably between 1999 and 2002.

Beat 213 Selected as the Research Site

A random selection procedure was used in Statistical Package for Social Sciences (SPSS) to select one of the twelve police beats in Wentworth for a close analysis of each of its blocks. Beat 213, Grand Boulevard, emerged as the selection. There are fifty-nine blocks[27] within Beat 213. The boundaries are Pershing (39th Street) to the north, Cottage Grove Avenue to the west, 43rd Street to the south, and Calumet Avenue to the east (Figures 1.5 and 1.6).

27. Be reminded that a block refers to an address block.

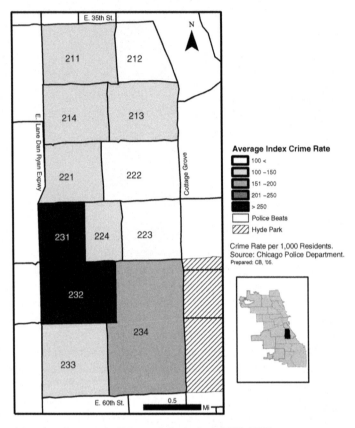

Figure 1.4. Index crime rates by Wentworth district beat (1998–2000).

In 2000, the total population of Beat 213 was 3,386 residents, 98.3 percent of whom were African American. Systematic Social Observation (SSO) data indicated that in 2000 there were 530 residential structures, 96 commercial structures, 23 mixed-use structures, and 545 empty lots in Beat 213. As can be seen in Table 1.2, the population and median household income of Beat 213 are about midrange when compared to the other eleven beats in Wentworth. Furthermore, although Wentworth has been the Chicago police district with the second highest index crime rate from 1999 to 2002, among the twelve beats in that district, the index crime rate in Beat 213 has been midrange over those

Chicago Police Beat 213: Grand Boulevard

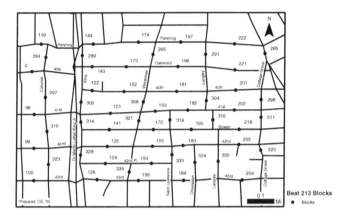

Figure 1.5. Beat 213: Grand Boulevard.

Spatial Distribution of Targeted Locations by Orthophoto, 1999–2000

Figure 1.6. Aerial photograph of Beat 213.

years, ranking ninth, seventh, fourth, and sixth, respectively (Table 1.2). These observations further establish Beat 213 as an appropriate slice of Wentworth to be further analyzed for an understanding of the processes in question. Grand Boulevard is, therefore, an average crime beat within a very high-crime district.

19

Focusing on Three Crimes: Narcotic
Violations, Robberies, and Batteries

Although the data presented so far have focused on the broad category of index crimes on the city and district levels, this book really focuses on the violations of street narcotic dealing, robbery, and battery aggregated to the address block level.[28] I have chosen to focus on these crimes because they are examples of three different categories of crime that function based on various structures of motivation and opportunity. Street narcotics violation is an example of an entrepreneurial crime, robbery an example of violent and predatory crime, and battery an example of violent interpersonal crime. Focusing on these crimes provides a diverse and rich array of circumstances that allows us to understand the complexities associated with the emergence, persistence, or decline of various crime hotspots, especially as this relates to the assumptions of broken windows and collective efficacy theories.

Entrepreneurial crimes such as drug dealing and prostitution flourish based on market opportunities. They depend on opportunities for easy and predictable transactions between seller and client, easy escape from the police, and deniability—the ability to deny that one is present in the area solely to participate in the exchange of drugs or sex for money.

Predatory crimes such as robbery flourish on opportunities for access to suitable targets. High-opportunity places for predatory crime are often in close proximity to banks, check-cashing outlets, liquor stores, grocery stores, hair salons, and certain other commercial properties. Close proximity to the offender's residence often contributes to opportunities for predatory crime. Each crime chapter provides details about how these opportunities are realized and capitalized upon and the relevance of broken windows and collective efficacy variables in the process.

Grievance crimes such as battery flourish based on opportunities for intensified conflicts and spontaneous access to targets when unresolved conflicts escalate. Battery hotspots are often disruptive residential spaces, dense public areas, bars, grocery stores, fast food locations, and other business spaces where conflicts emerge as a result of perceived poor customer service. Unresolved and intensified conflicts are also common among idle groups of adults and teenagers and with disruptive family members and their associates. Table 1.3 outlines the structures of opportunity for these three categories of crime.

28. An address block is both sides of a street with addresses within the same hundred-number range. For instance, crimes that occurred on 510, 518, and 599 39th Street are referred to as crimes on the 500 block of 39th Street. The address block is the unit of analysis in this study.

Table 1.3. Structures of Opportunity for Various Categories of Crime.

Crime Category	Examples of Crimes in Category	Opportunity Structure Needed to Flourish
Nonviolent entrepreneurial	Narcotics, prostitution	Market opportunities.
Predatory	Strong-arm and aggravated robberies, sexual assault, theft, motor vehicle theft, burglary, criminal trespass to property, criminal damage to property	Easy and spontaneous access to suitable targets.
Grievance	Homicide, simple and aggravated batteries, simple and aggravated assaults	Unresolved and intensified conflicts with easy access to target.

Focus is placed on the single crime of battery instead of all crimes in the broad category of assault, which often includes verbal assaults, sexual assaults, and physical assaults (batteries), for several reasons. First, verbal assaults are believed to be the most unreported crimes in the research site. This is based on the researcher's direct observations and statements from various neighborhood experts. On most field visits, approximately two to ten unreported verbal assaults were observed within two hours. Most of these verbal assaults were statements such as "am a kick your ass," "am a fuck you up," "am a beat you up," "am a ice you," and "am a burn down this mo'rfucking place." Verbal assaults are seldom reported to the police except for instances in which they are made directly to owners or employees at fast food restaurants, grocery stores, liquor stores, and other business establishments. Domestic verbal assaults are quite frequent and very seldom reported to the police, except for instances in which restraining orders are being violated or the victim wants to officially record the history of abuse to strengthen a legal case in the courts.

Second, neighborhood experts found it difficult to identify the blocks on which a higher number of verbal assaults occurred. When asked to identify blocks they perceived to be considerably higher on verbal assaults, their most common response was that verbal assaults are everywhere, and it is very difficult to tell which blocks are higher. In a pilot test of the neighborhood experts' survey, some neighborhood experts refused to answer this question because they thought verbal assaults were too commonplace. On this basis I surmised that police statistical accounts of verbal assaults would not provide a credible account of where most of these crimes actually occurred. Moreover, since neighborhood experts were not sure where the verbal assault hotspots were, it would be very difficult to ascertain whether or not the police statistics portrayed a reasonably accurate spatial distribution of those crimes.

Sexual assaults were omitted from the analysis because although they often involve physical assault (battery), this is not always the case. There was no way to sort out in the data set used for this study which instances of sexual assault included battery and which instances did not. Furthermore, there are often different logics to the ways that sexual assaults and nonsexual assaults function in place. Therefore, this study has omitted discussions of sexual assaults and placed emphasis only on the spatial distribution of batteries, to provide more focus in the discussion about mechanisms associated with crime and place. The discussion about crime and place would have been less accurate and less focused if it combined verbal and sexual assaults with batteries.

Nor is much emphasis placed on the motivations to engage in crimes such as drug dealing, robbery, and battery. In this area of concentrated disadvantage, because of structural constraints, perceptions of limited opportunities, high levels of drug dependency, unresolved social conflicts, and other social problems, the motivation to offend is rampant among a segment of the population. More focus is placed on the opportunities to act on that criminal motivation, and the relevance of broken windows and collective efficacy variables to the perceptions and behaviors of offenders. Such opportunities are differentially presented in spaces by virtue of their ecological (dis)advantages, the reputation spaces have gained for having commonly hosted particular crime-related actions over time, and how neighborhood actors are organized around particular salient issues of concern.

Pockets of Crime

Data presented in later sections of this book show that even though a poor, urban African-American district may have the highest violent and predatory crime rate in a city, an overwhelming majority of blocks within that district may still have a low incidence of such crimes. This suggests that while reference to race and class[29] may be useful to identify broad sections of a city as crime hotspots, other factors must be relied upon to explain how, within subsections of those areas, crime hotspots

29. Such as a poor African-American section of a city.

become strategically clustered, persist, or change over time. Multiple sources of data that include street interviews with active and former offenders, the police, and other neighborhood actors help to explain these factors in reference to broken windows and collective efficacy theories.

This large, predominantly poor African-American section of Chicago reflects high incidence of selected crimes mainly because of patterns of activities among groups of residents and acquaintances who are responding to daily realities that are rooted in the economic, social, and political difficulties occurring in their vicinity. William Julius Wilson's books *When Work Disappears* and *The Truly Disadvantaged* provide compelling explanations of how these forces have combined to produce conditions of high crime in the Wentworth area. Therefore, instead of rehashing these processes, I focus on how and why, within this high-crime area, selected crimes become more densely clustered on some blocks and not others. The findings show that smaller neighborhoods, such as blocks within a certain area, are not equally dangerous or equally likely to attract and host criminal elements. Instead of a broad crime hotspot, what I have observed by looking more closely into this area are "pockets of crime": most crimes occur on particular blocks while other blocks remain practically untouched.

The conditions of diminishing employment and out-migration of the black middle class described by Wilson, as well as other conditions, have resulted in the concentration of a ready supply of motivated offenders actively seeking—and sometimes stumbling upon—opportunities to commit certain crimes in that area. This is not to suggest that most of the residents are agents of crime. Indeed, many of the criminal agents in this area do not reside in Wentworth, but travel there to commit particular crimes. However, since crimes function based on different structures of opportunity, and neighborhood blocks do not evenly or randomly supply those opportunities, crimes are differentially clustered across street blocks. This book explains the different kinds of opportunities associated with street entrepreneurial crimes such as drug dealing, violent predatory crimes such as robbery, and crimes of interpersonal conflict such as battery.

Street interviews with active offenders, police officers, neighborhood reformers, and victims of crime show that while it is possible for the crimes in question to occur on many blocks, there are certain ecological disadvantages that make some blocks particularly attractive to certain motivated offenders. Those ecological disadvantages also make it more difficult for police officers and neighborhood reformers to infiltrate and otherwise control that space. Moreover, there are enablers—people who directly or indirectly profit from the financial or other gains of such crimes; and there are also noncompliants—people who do not directly or indirectly profit but who are too afraid, closely tied, or otherwise unwilling to cooperate against active offenders. These anomalies challenge both broken windows and collective efficacy theories that do not account for the ecological disadvantage of high-crime locales, and the regulatory limitations of dense networks of dependency and fear among neighbors.

Ecological disadvantages, the limitations of dense networks of dependency, and fear among neighbors help create opportunities for offenders such as robbers and street drug dealers who are actively seeking paths of least resistance. They capitalize on those ecological and social disadvantages of neighborhoods to conduct crimes. As a result, hotspots will persist until some conspicuous shocks are introduced to those spaces or active offenders are displaced, killed, incarcerated, or reformed, or otherwise change their behaviors without being replaced by a new or rotating stock of their kind. An understanding of how these complex processes function requires multiple sources of data.

Multiple Methods Used to Gather the Data

Data used in this study were obtained from many sources, including official crime statistics, mapping, a neighborhood survey, in-depth interviews, and Systematic Social Observation (SSO). Although ethnographic data were gathered through the entire duration of the study (1997–2002),[30] the analysis of official crime statistics on the block level reflects only crimes that occurred during 1999 and 2000. This is because changes to the Chicago Police Department crime database limited available block-level data to only 1999. After the 2000 data had been collected by the department, changes in department policies and procedures denied me access to block-level data for subsequent years. The department's refusal to provide updated data has been explained by shortages in staff and existing agreements with other researchers.

In an attempt to account for unreported crimes, a survey was conducted with neighborhood experts,[31] and those data were cross-referenced with the official police crime statistics. Neighborhood experts were not asked to identify each instance of crime that they knew.

30. The Wentworth Area Neighborhood Study (WANS) upon which this book is based is ongoing, although the used here are restricted to those gathered between 1997 and 2002.
31. Persons very familiar with the happenings of the neighborhood.

Instead, they were asked to identify blocks in the neighborhood they recognized as hotspots. Hotspots were defined to them as places where most incidents of that particular crime appear to occur, in public and private. The survey asked neighborhood experts to rank each block as low, midrange, or high in to the incidence of various crimes, including narcotics violations, robbery, and battery. These accounts were compared to the hotspots identified through analysis of the official police statistics of reported incidents of crime. A block was designated as a hotspot for a particular crime if the total number of that crime was a standard deviation above the mean of that crime reported for the entire beat. There was a very strong correlation between the blocks that neighborhood experts identified as various crime hotspots and those identified through the use of the official Chicago police crime statistics. More specifically, all of the blocks that were tabulated from the police data as crime hotspots in 1999 and 2000 were reported as hotspots by all of the neighborhood experts. This high level of agreement provided confidence that the incidence of street narcotic violations, robberies, and batteries reflected in the police statistics did not deviate appreciably from residents' understandings of where most of those crimes occurred in their neighborhoods.

As a participant observer, I served as a member of local block clubs and a volunteer with the community policing program. The field data included 223 interviews with 45 former and current offenders who had committed crimes such as narcotic violations, robbery, battery, burglary, rape, weapons possession, and car theft; 153 interviews with 62 community leaders, police officers, local business owners and employees, and other residents; field notes from attending 327 community policing beat meetings and from 305 instances of participating in formal and informal neighborhood events such as block club meetings, festive and sporting events, and self-help projects; and notes and observations gleaned while "hanging out" to observe and participate in various aspects of neighborhood life as they unfolded.

A rich vault of ethnographic data was accumulated over an array of diverse and intense first-hand neighborhood interactions that included conducting observations on all of the blocks with former drug dealers, robbers, veteran police officers, neighborhood reformers,[32] and other neighborhood actors, each of whom brought a particular viewpoint and area of expertise. These informants explained their understandings of

32. Persons constantly involved in bringing about what they consider positive neighborhood changes.

how each block served as a microcosm of the broader neighborhood, especially in terms of attracting, hosting, and suppressing crime-related activities. Several street-level interviews were conducted with motivated offenders such as Icepick, Throat, Nightlife, Swift, Razor, and others who explained in detail the logic they used for crime-related operations such as setting up a lucrative street drug-dealing business and staging robberies.

Snowball sampling was used to obtain leads for interviews with offenders. I was introduced to the offenders mainly through referrals from relatives, customers, friends, and acquaintances who, after several months (sometimes years), trusted me as someone whose only motive was to understand life in their neighborhood. For instance, the first three drug dealers I interviewed were introduced by their close relatives. Toward the end of each interview, I asked for leads to other subjects, with the first three interviews resulting in eleven additional leads. Occasionally, street drug dealers and robbers indicated that the interview was allowing them to reflect on themselves, their lives, and their work in ways that they had never done before, and they wanted their "boys" (colleagues) to have a similar experience. Therefore, they eagerly provided additional leads and asked that they be identified as the person who provided the referral. On several occasions, I was approached by offenders who knew I was conducting interviews of persons like themselves and who were willing to be interviewed themselves.

Most interviews with offenders and other neighborhood experts were conducted in public spaces such as street corners, vacant lots, public library rooms, and park benches. Some interviews were conducted in private spaces such as the inside of my car while parked in a safe location along a major street. Others were conducted at the subjects' residences. Many individuals consented to tape-recorded interviews with the understanding that the tapes would be transcribed and then destroyed.

Systemic Social Observation (SSO) was also used in this study. My method was a partial replication of the techniques described by Sampson et al. (1995).[33] SSO is a data gathering method that uses video data from cameras mounted in each side of a vehicle while it is slowly driven through neighborhood streets so that physical and social appearances can be captured for in-depth analyses. Such analyses include quantitative coding of the conditions of buildings, properties, and vacant lots, and the prevalence of behaviors like loitering, public drinking, and panhandling. Qualitative analyses of the video data were also used as

33. See also Sampson and Raudenbush 1999.

a cross-reference to obtain a visual sense of the features of street blocks that make them attractive to offenders such as drug dealers.

While conducting field interviews in 1999, I found that it was difficult to visualize clearly certain features that made locations attractive to drug dealing and other crimes without being on the location or having a picture of it. Therefore, to make this process less time-consuming and more understandable, I devised a particular form of video ethnography: SSO data simultaneously depicting both sides of each street in Grand Boulevard were compressed and converted into a QuickTime movie and transferred to the hard drive of a laptop computer that was brought to the field and used during interviews. The SSO movie allowed subjects to give me a tour of the neighborhood while pointing to particular features that explain how spaces function in terms of various crimes. For instance, drug dealers and robbers were able to use the SSO movie to explain in detail how and why certain locations are more attractive than others. It also allowed offenders to identify the specific features of neighborhoods that they considered distasteful, and to explain associated meanings, especially as such meanings pertain to the crimes they commit. Viewing the SSO movie of the neighborhood during the interviews refreshed the subjects' memories of relevant events that they often claimed they would have forgotten to mention otherwise. An audio tape recorder was used to capture the descriptions so that they could be transcribed. I refer to this technique as SSO video ethnography.

Finally, Geographic Information Systems (GIS) was used to produce maps of the various crime hotspots to observe how they are clustered or scattered throughout the research site. The narratives from interviews were used to understand why those places, as opposed to others, hosted more crime. The narratives, SSO, and video ethnography are also combined to better understand why street blocks with similar levels of neighborhood disorder and of collective efficacy exhibit different levels of crime and different levels of attractiveness to various offenders. Such analyses provide a rich context to understand the various meanings associated with neighborhood disorder and the relevance and effectiveness of collective efficacy.

Findings and Strategies

Appendix A shows that most of the blocks in Grand Boulevard had no narcotic violations, robberies, or batteries reported in 1999 and 2000, while a few of the blocks accounted for most of the crimes in question.

For example, in 2000, out of the fifty-nine blocks in the beat, five (9 percent) contributed 60 percent of the narcotic violations, 53 percent of the robberies, and 44 percent of the batteries. This seems to indicate that the crimes are not randomly distributed over all blocks. Chapter 2 pursues a more rigorous approach to the question of randomness. In addition to the observation that most of the crimes are generated from a small number of blocks, a review of arrest reports indicates that most of those crimes are being committed by repeat offenders.[34] Based on arrest data obtained from the Chicago police for 1999 and 2000, approximately 70 percent of the narcotic violations, 65 percent of the robberies, and 70 percent of the batteries were committed by an offender pool of forty-three offenders, thirty-six (84 percent) of whom are repeat offenders.

Among the forty-three offenders arrested for narcotic violations, robberies, and batteries that occurred in Grand Boulevard in 1999 and 2000, thirty-three (77 percent) provided home addresses indicating that they reside in Beat 213; an additional six (14 percent) provided addresses for elsewhere in Wentworth. Four (9 percent) provided home addresses that were outside the district. These figures indicate that most of those neighborhood crimes are being committed on a relatively small number of blocks and by a very small segment of the residential population. Thus, the challenges are to identify the differences between the blocks observed as hotspots and coldspots and how the offenders select their targets and locations. Then enumerate the similar features among hotspots that explain their existence and persistence, especially as this relates to the assumptions of broken windows and collective efficacy theories.

While many residents and city agents in this concentrated disadvantaged African-American area of Chicago understand that the neighborhoods are stripped of many of the resources necessary to regulate themselves according to pro-social principles and values, they understand that they are not completely helpless. They perceive that the biggest threat of neighborhood crime is to become a random victim. Therefore, they attempt to control certain crimes by influencing where they occur—organizing themselves to cluster or push certain crimes into strategic locations. In this way, they attempt to "de-randomize" crime, hoping that it will be reduced in the process. Meanwhile, motivated offenders, especially crime entrepreneurs, go about selecting places based on the ecological and social advantages that they offer. Therefore, when crimes become clustered, motivated offenders capitalize on

---

34. Arrest records were identified for all of the narcotic violations, 77 percent of the robberies, and 86 percent of the batteries recorded in 1999 and 2000.

the perceived advantages offered by that space and keep their activities there until they are encouraged or forced to move elsewhere, or until they retire from such criminal activities altogether. These block-level actions are repeated on intermediate neighborhood levels of organization such as police beats, and are further observed as macro neighborhood crime rates on the district level.

Structure of the Study

Chapter 2 provides an overview of broken windows and collective efficacy theories as they relate to neighborhood crime. It discusses the major arguments of the theories, identifies their strengths and limitations, and points to the various ways in which the current study uses the concept of *ecological disadvantage* to extend each theory. This concept posits that urban neighborhoods are unevenly developed as a result of urban planning, zoning, and patterns of neighborhood development (or the lack thereof). This reality functions together with offenders' tendency to seek certain advantages out of preferred locations in choosing where to attempt different crimes. Since spaces do not equally offer those advantages to offenders, they are not equally attractive to them. Therefore, if neighborhood disorder at the macro level, across a whole neighborhood, means anything to robbers and drug dealers, such meanings will be secondary because those offenders are already disinterested in certain locales that offer them little or no ecological advantage. Similarly, since habitual offenders are only interested in committing certain crimes in particular locales because of perceived ecological advantages, this will pose different problems for collective efficacy. In other words, *ecological disadvantage* precedes both conditions of neighborhood disorder and capacities of collective efficacy.

Chapter 3 introduces the research site by presenting the new method of SSO Video Ethnography used to provide a meticulous description of each block on the outer boundaries of Grand Boulevard where all of the crime hotspots are situated. The video ethnography coincides with a movie that can be accessed through www.peterkbstjean.com.

Chapter 4 outlines perceived sources of neighborhood disorder from the different perspectives of offenders and law-abiding residents in the research site. Pictures are used to contextualize the quotations from interviews conducted in the field. This chapter lays the foundation for the three ethnographic chapters that follow it, in which offenders reveal intimate details associated with committing crimes such as drug dealing, robbery, and battery, the rationale being that understanding the perceived sources of neighborhood disorder is an important precursor to understanding how offenders interpret neighborhood disorder in reference to undertaking their criminal activities.

Chapter 5 explains how drug dealers interpret neighborhood disorder and understand the effects of collective efficacy on their business decisions. The chapter highlights the various ways that the information both supports and contradicts the claims of broken windows and collective efficacy theories, and how ecological disadvantage extends each theory. Implications of the findings are presented in subsequent chapters. The reader will be introduced to offenders such as Icepick, Throat, Swift, and Razor, who were very generous in their explanations of how street drug dealing functions. The same procedure is followed in chapter 6, which focuses on robbers' interpretations of neighborhood disorder and reactions to collective efficacy.

The battery chapter (chapter 7) indicates that it is sometimes quite appropriate to think of "people as hotspots," because the presence of disruptive families has a major influence on which blocks experience the highest number of batteries. Regardless of where they reside and congregate, members of disruptive families frequently assault each other, their friends, and their acquaintances. Alcohol abuse, drug abuse, and a tremendous amount of idle time are common factors in this process. The effects of those factors are explained in the ethnographies. The concept of ecological advantage is used to explain why disruptive families are more likely to be situated on some blocks than on others.

Chapter 8, the final chapter, summarizes the major findings of the research and outlines the implications for theory, methods, and policy. It shows that there is considerable potential for both broken windows theory and collective efficacy theory. However, these theories and their policy implications will be better understood when they account for the independent factors associated with ecological disadvantage.

Appendix A, the Methodological Appendix, outlines the crime hotspots as they were tabulated from the 1999–2000 crime statistics obtained from the Chicago Police Department and cross-checked against a neighborhood survey. The spatial distributions of neighborhood disorder and collective efficacy are also outlined and discussed. The appendix is mainly statistical and presents many of the puzzles that are explained in the qualitative chapters where offenders who commit crimes like drug dealing, robbery, and battery explain in detail how those crimes are committed, and the relevance of neighborhood disorder and collective efficacy in the process.

Explaining Crime Hotspots

Overview and Extensions of Broken Windows
and Collective Efficacy Theories

Introduction

Over the last seven years, broken windows theory and collective efficacy theory have received increased attention
from researchers and policymakers who seek to understand
and address crime problems in society. The purpose of this
chapter is not to provide a comprehensive review of such
research. Appendix B and Appendix C offer a summary of
recent trends in literature on broken windows and collective efficacy, respectively. In this chapter, I discuss the fundamental logics of these two theories as they relate to the
subject at hand: namely, why crimes occur more frequently
in certain neighborhood locations as opposed to others. I
explain the various ways that data from the Wentworth
Area Neighborhood Study (WANS) support, explain, and
challenge the fundamental claims of each theory. I also
propose the concept of *ecological disadvantage* to extend
each theory by resolving problems posed by their limitations and oversights.

One of the major findings of this research is that physical disorder—one core component of broken windows
theory—does not matter (statistically or substantively) for
any of the three crimes analyzed (narcotic violations, robberies, or batteries). However, while social disorder (a second component of broken windows theory) and collective

efficacy both have statistical and substantive significance in reference to those crimes, they were both observed as necessary but insufficient conditions. More specifically, statistical analyses (see Appendix A) indicate that when social disorder was low, all selected crimes were also generally low. However, when social disorder was high, all crimes were almost equally likely to be high or low. Similarly, when collective efficacy was high, all crimes were generally low, but when collective efficacy was low, crimes were almost equally likely to be high or low. In subsequent chapters I present interview, ethnographic, and mapping data to show that those quantitative findings are further supported by the qualitative data, which are then used to explain the puzzles found during analysis of the statistical data. The qualitative data show that the ecological positioning of a particular street block, in terms of what is within and around it, has a profound influence on the logic motivated offenders use to select perceived advantageous spaces for their crime-related activities. These factors require much more theoretical consideration than is offered in broken windows and collective efficacy theories.

Both broken windows theory and collective efficacy theory focus on the *reactive* rather than the *proactive* aspects associated with offending. They portray offenders as reacting to neighborhood conditions—whether such conditions are signs of neighborhood disorder in the physical and social environment, or of levels of collective efficacy, capacities for collective action among the opposing law-abiding population. This study shows that the proactive aspects of offending, such as assessment of the ecologically advantageous factors offenders actively seek in their efforts at committing crimes, require greater attention.

The tendency of research has also been to portray offenders as relatively strange and unintelligent people who act on their wicked impulses and who succeed because of something that law-abiding people fail to do. Whether these failures are not fixing broken windows or not developing adequate trust and cohesion in order to create public goods such as safer neighborhoods, the presence of crime is attributed by conventional theories to the failure of others, not to the successful strategies of offenders.

The data in this book show that most offenders, especially crime entrepreneurs such as drug dealers and robbers, are quite proactive in their crime-related ambitions. They capitalize on various advantages locations offer by virtue of the sort of broader space within which they are embedded, notwithstanding levels of neighborhood disorder or collective efficacy. I refer to these space-specific (dis)advantages to criminal opportunity as *ecological (dis)advantage*[1] and use this concept to extend both broken windows and collective efficacy theories.

The Logic of Broken Windows Theory

Broken windows theory operates on the commonsensical logic that *a stitch in time saves nine*. The general idea is that if small problems are left unresolved, bigger problems will inevitably follow, especially in neighborhoods near the tipping point, "where a window is likely to be broken at any time and must quickly be fixed if all are not to be shattered" (Wilson 1985, 88). The theory posits that, from the law-abiding residents' perspective, disorder is *indirectly* linked to serious crime through the process of weakened social control that is fueled by citizens' fear of crime. These realities create "the conditions in which crime can flourish" (Bratton and Kelling 2006, 2).

However, from the offenders' point of view, the link between disorder and crime is more *direct*. Offenders interpret disorder as a signal that no one cares about the neighborhood, and that therefore they can commit crimes there with relative impunity. This assumption of broken windows theory has not been directly tested by empirical research focused on offenders' interpretations and reaction to neighborhood disorder. That gap in research is the focus of this book.

To date, scholarly responses to broken windows theory have mainly focused on two factors: (1) the association between neighborhood disorder and various crimes[2]—which is the focus here; and (2) broken windows policing, which is an attempt to reduce serious crimes through aggressive police enforcement of minor misdemeanors and offenses of disorderly conduct.[3] This is the focus that has received the most attention and stimulated the most controversy, especially based on research conducted by Robert J. Sampson and his colleagues, who have published numerous major journal articles that challenge broken windows hypotheses as well as broken windows policing. By publishing his research

---

1. I admit that the term "ecological disadvantage" may appear relatively biased, favoring conditions that create safer neighborhoods rather than those that enable offenders to do better in their criminal pursuits. In other words, those ecological conditions are advantageous to offenders, but disadvantageous for the pursuit of crime reduction.

2. Harcourt 2001; Sampson and Raudenbush 1999; Skogan 1987, 1990; Taylor 2001.

3. Corman and Mocan 2002; Decker and Kohfeld 1985; Funk and Kugler 2003; Giacopassi and Forde 2000; Golub et al. 2003; Harcourt 1998, 2001; Herbert 2001; Jacob and Rich 1981; Kelling and Coles 1996; Kelling and Bratton 1998; Roberts 1999; Sampson and Cohen 1988; Wilson 1968, 1975, 1981; Wilson and Boland 1978; Whittaker et. al. 1985.

in journal articles and in a recent book, *Illusions of Disorder,* Bernard Harcourt has registered his own attacks on broken windows policing (see Appendix B). However, two advocates of broken windows theory, William Bratton[4] and Geoge Kelling,[5] have not responded kindly to those scholarly criticisms. They protest that "Ideological academics are trying to undermine a perfectly good idea" (Bratton and Kelling 2006, 1). Academics, they argue, many of whom have not spent much time conducting field research, continue to misrepresent broken windows theory as assuming a direct link between disorder and serious crime. Bratton and Kelling further lament that some academics who attempt to debunk broken windows theory have been very selective in their interpretation of data and have omitted from their accounts research that has found support for broken windows theory (Bratton and Kelling 2006).

My intention in setting out on this research was neither to support nor to refute broken windows theory. Instead, I have mainly sought to understand and explain the relevance of the theory to offenders in their everyday deliberations with crime and neighborhood life. It is important to disclose here that I was the last student to receive his Ph.D. under the chief supervision of Robert J. Sampson before Sampson left the University of Chicago's Department of Sociology in 2002. (Sampson is currently the chair of the Sociology Department at Harvard University.) At no time have I felt influenced by Sampson's work to initiate my own attacks on broken windows theory, or to be more sympathetic toward collective efficacy theory. Instead, I have taken on both theories in plain view to assess their relevance to street crimes, especially from the perspective of offenders—a viewpoint that is currently missing in the debate between these two theoretical perspectives. At the end, the chips will fall where they may.

The third main focus of research on broken windows theory has been on the effects of neighborhood disorder on individual psychological dimensions such as stress, powerlessness,[6] and neighborhood attachment.[7]

It is important to reiterate that this book does not focus on verifying the idea that "when police pay attention to minor offenses—such as prostitution, graffiti, aggressive panhandling—they can reduce fear, strengthen communities, and prevent serious crime" (Bratton and Kel-

---

4. The current chief of the Los Angeles Police Department.
5. A professor of criminal justice at Rutgers University.
6. Geis and Ross 1998), fear of crime (Perkins and Taylor 1996; Skogan 1990; Taylor, Gottfredson, and Brower 1985; Taylor and Shumaker 1990).
7. Taylor 1996; Taylor, Shumaker, and Gottfredson 1985

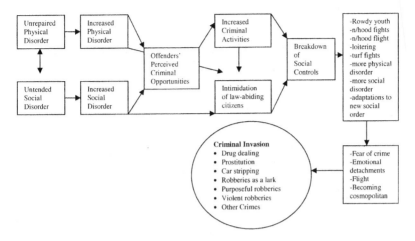

Figure 2.1. Broken windows model.

ling 2006, 1). The ethnographic investigation of this claim is one focus of my ongoing work within the Buffalo Area Neighborhood Study (BANS). BANS builds on some of the findings from the Wentworth Area Neighborhood Study (WANS) upon which this book is based. The task here is to explain, mainly from the perspective of offenders, the social meanings of neighborhood disorder and how these meanings influence offenders' criminal decisions and actions.

The foundational assumption of broken windows theory that is most relevant to this book is that offenders interpret neighborhood disorder as a sign that nobody cares about the neighborhood, and that, therefore, their chances of apprehension are significantly reduced in disorderly neighborhoods.[8] Based on this interpretation, offenders will commit crimes in disorderly neighborhoods because they anticipate little or no cost for their actions. A chain of events then ensues in affected neighborhoods: First, disorder will continue to accumulate. Second, law-abiding citizens will perceive that violent crime is on the increase and will then become more fearful of crime. Third, as a result of that fear, they will refrain from intervening in the neighborhood and will avoid the use of public spaces. Fourth, they will then move out of the neighborhood, only to be replaced by less attached citizens. Finally, and almost inevitably, serious crime will follow (Skogan 1990; Wilson 1975; Wilson and Kelling 1982; Wilson 1985).

8. Wilson and Kelling 1982.

There are two types of neighborhood disorder invoked by broken windows theory: physical and social. Physical disorder refers to the dilapidated or unkempt conditions of the physical neighborhood environment. This includes the condition of buildings, of properties around buildings, and of vacant lots that have become eyesores. Social disorder refers to patterns of social activities and interactions that are visible to the public eye and are viewed to be deviant or distasteful to most citizens.

Physical Disorder

At the community level, disorder and crime are usually inextricably linked, in a kind of developmental sequence. Social psychologists and police officers tend to agree that if a window in a building is broken and is left unrepaired, all the rest of the windows will soon be broken. This is as true in nice neighborhoods as in rundown ones. Window-breaking does not necessarily occur on a large scale because some areas are inhabited by determined window-breakers whereas others are populated by window-lovers; rather, one unrepaired broken window is a signal that no one cares, and so breaking more windows costs nothing. (It has always been fun.) (Wilson and Kelling 1982, 31)

Physical disorder is assumed to be a cue to wayward people, both petty and serious offenders, that they can get away with doing whatever they please in that space; it is further assumed that law-abiding citizens will become afraid of perceived crime, retreat behind their curtains, avoid intervening, and then eventually move out of the neighborhood (Wilson and Kelling 1982, 30–32; Kahan 1997, 370–71). Social disorder is assumed to have a similar effect.

Social Disorder

Signs of social disorder include the presence of "not violent people, nor, necessarily, criminal, but disreputable or obstreperous or unpredictable people: panhandlers, drunks, addicts, rowdy teenagers, prostitutes, loiterers, the mentally disturbed" (Wilson and Kelling 1982, 30). However, among all these categories of people, the panhandler holds a special place:

The unchecked panhandler is in effect the first broken window. Muggers and robbers, whether opportunistic or professional, believe they reduce their chances of being caught or ever identified if they operate on streets where potential victims are already intimidated by prevailing conditions. If a neighborhood cannot keep bothersome panhandlers from annoying passersby, the thief may reason, it is even less likely to call the police to identify a potential mugger or to interfere if the mugging actually takes place. (Ibid., 34)

Wilson and Kelling speculate about the process that most likely leads to the entry of panhandlers and more serious law breakers. They believe that just as physical neglect of a neighborhood is an invitation to wrongdoing, ignoring certain forms of social interaction leads to more problematic behavior and crime:

We suggest that "untended" behavior also leads to the breakdown of community controls. A stable neighborhood of families who care for their homes, mind each other's children, and confidently frown on unwanted intruders can change, in a few years or even a few months, to an inhospitable and frightening jungle. A piece of property is abandoned, weeds grow up, a window is smashed. Adults stop scolding rowdy children; the children, emboldened, become more rowdy. Families move out, unattached adults move in. Teenagers gather in front of the corner store. The merchant asks them to move; they refuse. Fights occur. Litter accumulates. People start drinking in front of the grocery; in time, an inebriate slumps to the sidewalk and is allowed to sleep it off. Pedestrians are approached by panhandlers. (Ibid., 31–32)

The presence of this first panhandler and the developments that follow are presumed to trigger an important turning point in the neighborhood: increased fear of crime.

At this point it is not inevitable that serious crime will flourish or violent attacks on strangers will occur. But many residents will think that crime, especially violent crime, is on the rise, and they will modify their behavior accordingly. They will use the streets less often, and when on the streets will stay apart from their fellows, moving with averted eyes, silent lips, and hurried steps. "Don't get involved." For some residents, this growing atomization will matter little, because the neighborhood is not their "home" but "the place where they live." Their interests are elsewhere; they are cosmopolitans. But it will matter greatly to other people, whose lives derive meaning and satisfaction from local attachments rather than worldly involvement; for them, the neighborhood will cease to exist except for a few reliable friends whom they arrange to meet.

This new fear of crime and emotional detachment from the neighborhood will lead to a breakdown in social control, which will eventually lead to actual increases in crime:

Such an area is vulnerable to criminal invasion. Though it is not inevitable, it is more likely that here, rather than in places where people are confident they can regulate public behavior by informal controls, drugs will change hands, prostitutes will solicit, and cars will be stripped. That the drunks will be robbed by boys who do it as a lark, and the prostitutes' customers will be robbed by men who do it purposefully and perhaps violently. That muggings will occur. (Ibid., 32)

Referencing broken windows theory, researchers and policy makers have suggested that neighborhood disorder must be aggressively suppressed to prevent serious criminal invasions. For instance, broken windows theorists have been credited for providing the conceptual framework used in New York in the 1990s by Mayor Rudolph Giuliani and Police Commissioner William Bratton to reduce crime.[9] The assumption that unpleasant neighborhood appearances lead offenders to commit crimes with expectations of little to no costs continues to be the main impetus of community policing programs in the United States and elsewhere—despite the fact that little effort has been made to examine empirically some of the key assumptions of this theory, which begins with offenders' interpretations of neighborhood disorder.

However, as Harcourt (2001, 109–21) observes, much is still unknown about the social meaning of disorder, which is the fundamental assumption upon which broken windows theory is based. Harcourt (2001, 120) identifies the need for more "in-depth interviews of informants, participatory observation, and other investigatory or experimental techniques that probe the structure of meaning." He argues that such research is important because disorder may mean different things to different people, and this reality needs further exploration (2001, 15–17). This book is a response to that call.

Extending Broken Windows Theory

While the claims of broken windows theory appear intuitive, and indeed some research has found empirical support for its predictions,[10] some obvious limitations require attention. Let us first examine the overall logic of the theory. Few reasonable people disagree with the notion that if small problems are left unchecked, they will develop into larger, more serious ones. Since this appears to be true with issues such as the timely stitching of an open wound, the timely sewing of torn pants, the timely

9. Barnes 1998; Bernstein 1998; Conklin 2003; Harcourt 2001; Jones 1997; Kelling and Bratton 1998; Kelling and Coles 1996; Nifong 1997; Rosen 2000; Witkin 1998.
10. Kelling and Coles 1996; Corman and Mocan 2002; Funk and Kugler 2003, Golub et al. 2003; Skogan 1990.

changing of motor oil in an automobile, and the swift correction of children, it seems quite logical that timely response to petty crimes and disorderly conduct can deter more serious crimes. But is that really the case, and if so, how exactly is that deterrence achieved? What are the exact processes through which heavy enforcement of disorderly conduct and petty crimes such as panhandling, loitering, and public drinking prevent murders, rapes, and robberies?

It seems logical that if an open wound on one leg is stitched promptly, such action will likely save that leg, not the other one, from amputation; timely sewing of a torn shirt will save that same shirt from ruin; timely oil changes on an automotive engine will save that same engine from seizing; and swift correction of a child will help deter that same child from getting into further trouble.[11] But how can the arrest of the loiterer, panhandler, or public drinker prevent murders, rapes, and robberies?[12] One way might be if the same petty offenders were about to become perpetrators, accessories, or victims of the more serious crimes in question. However, in the many instances when participants in disorderly conduct are not perpetrators, accessories, or victims of more serious crimes, how will their arrests deter other, more serious offenders from committing mayhem on society? For instance, how will the arrest of the elderly and middle-aged panhandlers or public drinkers I introduce in chapter 4 deter young men such as those under the age of twenty-five years from killing each other over drug deals or from robbing and assaulting their peers? How will the arrests of those senior residents deter habitual offenders such as those interviewed in this book, who are often below the age of thirty, from robbing strangers, friends, and family members alike? Moreover, how will such arrests deter assaults and homicides that occur behind closed doors among romantic partners?

The fundamental question is, however, if a heavy enforcement effort directed at minor offenses deters more serious crimes, how exactly does that work in everyday life? The broken windows response to this question is that offenders perceive small signs of disorder to mean that no one cares about the neighborhood and that there is no significant cost to committing crimes there. Therefore, in this study, I have focused on this claim by attempting to find answers through direct interactions with the offenders themselves and with other participants in neighbor-

11. Additionally, any other benefits are side effects of effectively confronting the direct cause.

12. I fully acknowledge that "fixing" social problems is much more complex than simply stitching wounds, sewing pants, and changing engine oil—in response to objects that are not engaged in social interaction.

hood life. The findings reveal the complexities associated with localized interpretations of such measures of neighborhood disorder.

First, the presence of trash, graffiti, panhandlers, and other publicly visible signs of neighborhood disorder receive different interpretations on different blocks; some of these interpretations are unrelated to the costs of committing crime. Although the data do not completely support this claim, let us assume that offenders are really more likely to commit crimes in locations where they believe no one cares. Do they really interpret neighborhood disorder as the primary cue that no one cares? As the discussions will show, offenders such as drug dealers and robbers will frequently continue to operate in places where they constantly face opposition from neighborhood reformers, even their own relatives who they know care greatly about the neighborhood. Why? Because, regardless of the level of resistance they face, offenders remain interested in particular locations that offer them certain advantages, and they are not willing to easily abandon those locations. These ecological advantages are explained in upcoming sections.

Regarding the interpretation of neighborhood disorder, broken windows theory assumes a universal meaning. It does not acknowledge, for example, that insiders and outsiders to a particular neighborhood may have different interpretations of the conditions of the physical and social environment. If indeed cues of disorder are important signposts for motivated offenders to select locations for crime, and if it is also true (as ethnographic data suggest) that insiders and outsiders to a neighborhood have different interpretations of disorder, it follows that offenders who are insiders and outsiders to a neighborhood will not have the same interpretations of disorder. Therefore the broken windows thesis has erred in assuming a fixed set of responses to the physical and social conditions of neighborhoods.

Second, the broken windows thesis views disorder through the bias of a middle-class lens. To that perspective, the *absence* of trash, graffiti, panhandlers, abandoned buildings, boarded-up buildings, and the like suggests that everyone cares about the neighborhood. Therefore, the presence of any of those conditions suggests not that people cannot afford to conduct repairs, or that they are under severe social distress, but that no one cares. Many persons who reside under conditions of concentrated disadvantage have different interpretations of neighborhood disorder. To them, it does not suggest that no one cares, but rather that the city's government does not care about the neighborhood. To many Wentworth residents, the presence of trash on the street often means the absence of sufficient trash cans in an area, or the sporadic services provided by the city's streets and sanitation department. Graffiti often signals the marking of gang turf, or the lack of availability of organized programs where youths can vent frustrations through display of their artistic talents. Finally, the presence of panhandlers often means the representation of the unemployable underclass, or yet another informal economy in the city. Therefore, it is important to provide ethnographic representations of the multiple meanings of neighborhood disorder. Such representations are offered in this study in the various chapters that discuss drug dealing, robberies, and batteries.

Third, broken windows theory wrongly assumes that neighborhood disorder is the most salient condition offenders consider in their quests to commit crimes. The ethnographic data suggest otherwise. When seeking cues for a place conducive to their questionable activities, most motivated offenders such as drug dealers, robbers, car thieves, and burglars do not pay much (if any) attention to certain signs of neighborhood disorder. When selecting places where they can easily "get away" with their questionable activities,[13] most motivated offenders select places based on conditions of (1) *ecological advantage*[14] and (2) their knowledge of the capacities for action within local social networks. In other words, to many motivated offenders, the direct indication of where they can get away with committing crimes is more related to *something* about where the place itself is located[15] and to concrete knowledge about the capacities for intervention within social networks in and around that place.

Chapter 5 shows that although drug dealers are not completely oblivious to neighborhood disorder, they report that the relationship between neighborhood disorder and street drug dealing is not as simple, straightforward, and linear as broken windows theory suggests. The findings

13. Keeping in mind that many times, and depending on the nature of the crime or disorderly act in question, motivated offenders perform crime-related activities simply in the areas where they live, spaces "given" to them (for example, spaces allocated by drug bosses to subordinate dealers), or in other spaces that they stumble upon after a previous space becomes unavailable.

14. This relates to the extent to which a location makes concealment of activities or escape from the police or capable guardians easy to accomplish. For example, many drug dealers indicate that it is easier to deal in intersections where they can "spot" the police approaching from any angle or where it is easy to locate "look-out men" around strategic corners or within buildings, and where it is easy to conceal drugs in the home or car of a sympathetic relative or friend. Thieves reveal that it is easier to snatch purses close to the train station, or at a check-cashing outlet located near an intersection rather than in the middle of the block. Furthermore, some places for theft, robbery, and drug dealing are selected simply because they have had a reputation for producing "good hits."

15. Recall that as the concept of *ecological challenge* suggests, since urban space is unevenly developed, and different offenders seek different *ecological advantages* out of preferred locations, some spaces are by default more attractive to offenders than others, regardless of the levels of broken windows or collective efficacy.

show that drug dealers interpret widespread neighborhood disorder in a large section of the city as denoting that the area is depressed, that there is high demand for illegal drugs, and that there is a willing and available army of young men desperately seeking employment opportunities, for whom drug dealing would be an attractive alternative to legitimate employment. Yet, when selecting a micro neighborhood location such as a street corner on which to conduct sales, drug dealers pay little attention to neighborhood disorder, especially physical disorder. Street-corner congregations are sometimes used by drug dealers as an opportunity to blend into the crowd to avoid detection. However, these congregations are not all instances of social disorder, since they also include instances when law-abiding people are standing at bus stops awaiting transportation and traveling back and forth to local businesses. Chapter 5 also illustrates that in many instances, depending on who is involved in instances of loitering and public drinking, drug dealing is deterred rather than encouraged.

Fourth, the broken windows theory erroneously assumes an almost inevitable sequence of events that begins with offenders' interpretation of neighborhood disorder as an invitation to commit crimes, then leads to neighborhood decline, increased fear of crime, the flight of law-abiding citizens, criminal invasion, and maximized dangerousness. It does not acknowledge that in many instances signs of neighborhood disorder are precursors to reestablishment of neighborhood vitality. Neighborhood disorder is often perceived by committed residents as a call to action rather than an alarm indicating that they should flee the neighborhood before "things get worse." Thus, broken windows theory does not sufficiently acknowledge the various ways disorder is interpreted by different categories of residents. It ignores the interpretations of some who are already invested and active in the local milieu.

Fifth, broken windows theory does not acknowledge that interpretations of neighborhood disorder are considerably conditioned by acknowledgment of the sort of broader space within which the particular location being observed is situated. In American society, interpretations of social phenomena are considerably affected by presumptions about race, class, and gender. An abandoned or boarded-up building will be interpreted in one way in the poor black or Hispanic side of town, and in quite another on the white side of town.

Within the black metropolis itself, broken windows of buildings situated on the corner of a busy intersection are interpreted differently from those in a remote corner. Interpretations also vary if the properties are owned privately or by the city; if they are within a predominantly commercial, residential, or mixed zone; or are public or private housing. Properties that are city-owned are often interpreted to mean that, for the moment, the city does not care so much about that section of Chicago. Furthermore, high neighborhood disorder is a reminder that one has arrived in the "hood"—the most disadvantaged section of the city. When buildings are privately owned, their dilapidated conditions are often associated with redlining, absentee landlords, or the inability of owners to make repairs because of financial constraints that may result from unemployment, underemployment, or insufficient retirement income. Street congregations of young men are subject to different types of scrutiny than those by young boys. Young girls are viewed as needing help and protection, while boys are often perceived as needing discipline and punishment.

Finally, broken windows theory pays no attention to what motivates people to commit various crimes in the first place. It assumes that serious crimes result when minor offenses do not receive aggressive response. However, without acknowledgment of the conditions that cause both petty and serious crimes to occur, in its current form broken windows theory is not prepared to offer long-term solutions to neighborhood crime problems.

It is important to reinforce, however, that according to broken windows theory, this downward neighborhood spiral begins with offenders' interpretations of neighborhood disorder. Therefore, I contend that one good way of testing this theory is to seek concrete evidence that offenders do in fact interpret neighborhood disorder in this manner, and that residents mainly react in accordance with the predictions of that theory. The need for such data has been identified as a crucial step to further determine the utility of broken windows theory.[16]

The Logic of Collective Efficacy Theory

Collective efficacy theory is an offshoot of social disorganization theory that relates the prevalence of social problems to the capacity of groups to realize common values and maintain effective social control (Sampson 2004a). Collective efficacy is defined as a "link of cohesion and trust with shared expectations for intervening in support of neighborhood social control" (Sampson and Raudenbush 2001, 2). Social control is the

16. For an extensive review of findings relevant to broken windows theory see Harcourt 2001.

capacity of a group to regulate itself according to desired principles and values (Sampson and Raudenbush 1999; Janowitz 1975).

Since 1997, collective efficacy researchers have produced several publications outlining research findings that contradict broken windows theory. They agree that understanding neighborhood disorder in public spaces is fundamental to understanding urban neighborhoods; however, they reject the notion that neighborhood disorder causes crime. Indeed, they argue, disorder may play an important role by affecting the perceptions of insiders and outsiders about neighborhood life. Overwhelmed by neighborhood disorder, employed, law-abiding, and tenured residents who can afford it may eventually flee the neighborhood. Potential employed residents and homeowners may be turned away by neighborhood disorder and not replace those of their kind who have fled. Those left behind will mainly be concentrated in disadvantage. In some instances, activities such as graffiti painting, loitering, and soliciting prostitution, which are considered neighborhood disorder, are indeed crimes, or ordinance violations, not precursors to more serious crimes (Sampson and Raudenbush 2001).

However, Sampson and his colleagues have found no convincing evidence leading to the conclusion that neighborhood disorder is a direct cause of crime. Instead, they argue, "Disorder and crime have similar roots: The forces that generate disorder also generate crime. It is structural characteristics of neighborhoods, as well as neighborhood cohesion and informal social control—not levels of disorder—that most affect crime" (Sampson and Raudenbush 2001, 4). They argue further that "These two forces—structural characteristics of neighborhoods and human intervention—are interrelated, working jointly and reciprocally to affect crime and disorder" (2001, 2). See Figure 2.2.

In their 1995 study[17] examining the relationships among neighborhood disorder, collective efficacy, and crime, Sampson and his colleague used Systematic Social Observation (SSO) to measure neighborhood disorder directly and independently instead of deriving such measures from public perceptions. The rationale for their study was as follows:

If broken windows thesis is correct, and disorder directly causes crime, then disorder should mediate the effects of neighborhood characteristics and collective efficacy on crime. By contrast, if disorder is a manifestation of the same forces that produce

17. The Project of Human Development in Chicago's Neighborhoods (PHDCN), conducted in 1995.

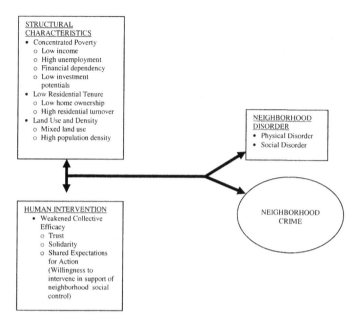

Figure 2.2. Collective efficacy model: rebuttal of broken windows model.

crime, then collective efficacy and structural characteristics should account for the relationship between disorder and crime. (Sampson and Raudenbush 2001)

Their study concluded that, except for robbery,

Overall, the findings did not support the thesis that disorder directly causes crime. First, although it is true that where survey-reported violence was high, levels of disorder detected by SSO tended to be high, the relationship was not strong. Second—and more importantly—is the finding . . . that the level of disorder varied strongly with neighborhood structural characteristics, poverty among them. Once these characteristics and collective efficacy were taken into account, the connection between disorder and crime vanished in most instances. (Sampson and Raudenbush 2001, 4)

Sampson and Raudenbush indicate further that "Concentrated disadvantage and residential instability undermine collective efficacy, in turn fostering increased crime and, by implication, public disorder" (2001, 2). This statement suggests that disorder is not so much a cause of crime as an indication of concentrated disadvantage and weakened collective efficacy. Therefore, policies that seek to reduce crime and eliminate disorder simply by applying aggressive law enforcement tactics, as broken windows theorists recommend, are misguided (ibid.). If policy makers attempt to reduce crime by focusing exclusively on eliminating disorder, the common causes of crime and disorder, especially of the former, are left relatively unexamined. Sampson and his colleagues suggest an alternative approach:

> Perhaps more effective would be an approach that focuses on how residents' efforts to stem disorder may reap unanticipated benefits in greater collective efficacy, which in turn would lower crime in the long run. Informally mobilizing a neighborhood cleanup, for example, would reduce physical disorder while building collective efficacy by creating and strengthening social ties and increasing awareness of the residents' commitment to their neighborhood. Such a mobilization might also demonstrate to participants and observers alike that neighborhood residents can be relied upon to maintain public order. By contrast, a police-led crackdown on disorder would probably produce a very different response by residents. (Sampson and Raudenbush 2001, 5)

Such different responses by residents often include feelings of alienation and resentment of police tactics. This leads to further alienation of the disadvantaged and subsequent escalations of neighborhood disruption and crime (Sampson 2004b).

These findings of collective efficacy research beg for further empirical verification of the mechanisms that link neighborhood disorder, collective efficacy, and crime. Broken windows theory posits that disorder is a direct cause of crime through offenders' interpretations of disorder as an indication that residents lack control over their environment. In rebuttal, collective efficacy theory argues that neighborhood disorder, like crime, is due to the breakdown of collective efficacy, which is reciprocally linked to the structural characteristics of neighborhood disadvantage (Figure 2.2).

Further verifications of these claims are certainly necessary. To be sure, several other studies have been conducted to further test the claims of each theory (see Appendices A and B), yet none have undertaken the task at hand in this book: utilizing intensive field research and extensive interviews with offenders and others to understand how abstract measures of neighborhood disorder and collective efficacy influence their crime-related actions in everyday life.

Extending Collective Efficacy Theory

Although research by collective efficacy theorists has challenged the broken windows approach by demonstrating that collective efficacy and not neighborhood disorder is the active ingredient for neighborhood crime, there are some limitations to collective efficacy theory that require further attention. First, let's return to an early definition of collective efficacy: "Social cohesion among neighbors combined with their willingness to intervene on behalf of the common good" (Sampson, Raudenbush, and Earls 1997, 918), and later, "This link of cohesion and trust with shared expectations for intervening in support of neighborhood social control" (Sampson and Raudenbush 2001, 2).

The logic of these definitions seems to be that crime will be reduced if residents organize themselves for collective action aimed at social control—that is to say, if they organize collectively to regulate themselves according to the desired principles and values associated with reducing crime in their neighborhood. Furthermore, Sampson and Raudenbush argue that this capacity for action is best fostered under conditions of cohesion and trust: "Where there is cohesion and mutual trust among neighbors, the likelihood is greater that they will share a willingness to intervene for the common good" (2001, 2). It appears clear that *collective action* against crime can very likely lead to reductions in crime. But how does the willingness to intervene, or shared expectations for action, translate to real action or action with results? The research by Sampson and his colleagues did not measure the extent to which people have intervened in the past, but rather their expressed willingness to do so in the future. Where is the guarantee?

As chapters 5 to 7 show, there are many conditions in which neighborhood people intervene *reluctantly*, while others who express a great willingness to intervene remain silent out of conflicts of interest with the issues at hand[18] or fear of retaliation. Collective efficacy theorists have not acknowledged the fact that, in many neighborhoods, especially those characterized by concentrated disadvantage, people are often forced to act against their will—including taking actions against those they want to protect.[19] To their credit, as time has progressed, Sampson (2004) has refined the definition of collective efficacy to be

---

18. Mainly because of close blood or other connections with the offender.

19. Especially considering the fact that taking action against crimes committed by residents often involves prosecution and potential incarceration in a criminal justice system they do not trust.

more task-specific and to reflect a reliance on *action* instead of *capacities for action* that, as I have argued, is no guarantee for action itself: "Collective efficacy is a task-specific construct that draws attention to shared expectations and *mutual engagement by residents* in local social control" (Sampson 2004a, 161; emphasis added). This focus on action has been emphasized more succinctly as "collective action for problem-solving" (2004a, 165).

Moreover, if intervention against neighborhood crime depends on conditions of mutual trust and cohesion among neighbors, does this mean that such must be cultivated before collective action against crime can be mobilized? In other words, is it true that people will not be able to organize themselves effectively for collective action against crime unless there is mutual trust and cohesion among them? Sampson and Raudenbush argue that "Where the rules of comportment are unclear and people mistrust one another, they are unlikely to take action against disorder and crime" (2001, 2). It appears clear that people will not intervene collectively if they are not sure about what they should intervene against, and when.[20] However, it is not clear what trust means, and why it is so important for collective action against crime that such action may not occur without it. Residents of Grand Boulevard think of trust and distrust in terms of the level of confidence one has in the integrity, ability, and judgments of others.

Data presented in the following chapters indicate that under conditions of concentrated disadvantage in Wentworth, many residents remain actively organized for collective action against crime because they *distrust* the police to do an effective job, and also distrust residents who are part of their working community policing group. They often remain active in collective action against crime through community policing with the belief that if they do not participate, the efforts will stop or take a form that does not meet with their approval. They often trust their neighbors with issues such as watching their children and returning borrowed money, but not necessarily with keeping promises to participate actively in the organized efforts necessary to reduce neighborhood crime. These efforts include being present at future meetings and completing tasks assigned to them during prior meetings. Many residents would prefer not to be active in collective neighborhood efforts but

20. This is why community policing beat meetings are so important. They provide residents, business owners, the police, politicians, and other neighborhood actors a setting through which they can comprehend what others believe is reasonable and unreasonable to do in the neighborhood.

remain active out of distrust in the integrity, work ethics, and abilities of others tasked to keep efforts sustained.

Therefore, particularly in desperate situations, distrust can be a major motivating factor for involvement in collective action. It is important to note, however, that the point here is not that distrust should be cultivated for collective action to be activated. Instead, I argue that trust is a complex issue that requires further clarification especially as it relates to collective action against crime. Also, in many situations, mistrust serves as a precursor to such actions. Therefore, trust should be viewed as a conditional rather than a global phenomenon.

Although under certain conditions mistrust serves as a catalyst for participation, I have observed that in situations where residents and others are organized under a prevailing atmosphere of mistrust, their efforts are much more stressful, sporadic, and confrontational. Meetings intended for strategic planning against crime often become group therapy sessions where participating groups and individuals who mistrust each other constantly argue over issues that appear to be petty, but require attention before real progress can be made. Meetings often revert to retelling of certain episodes of the past where people did not perform according to expectations. Examples include instances when people volunteer to assist with a neighborhood event but never show up; when they promise to make phone calls that are never completed; or, worst of all, when they misuse organizational funds or resources. Mistrust is also embedded in social networks in which residents are called upon to organize against criminal activities where the perpetrators are family members or close friends of the organizers. Group members often remain involved in collective action because they distrust the capacity of other members of the group or of the community, people who are supposed to be impartial, to act in the best interests of the neighborhood. Therefore, they "hang around" to serve as watchdogs, but otherwise remain active in the process.

Perhaps more importantly, people residing or working in this area of concentrated disadvantage have often learned, through life experiences, to trust no one—or to always remain skeptical. Their surrounding area is often used by insiders and outsiders to obtain funding that produces few deliverables. They are constantly made promises with little follow-through, and most people who make promises eventually end up being more "shady"[21] than they seemed in the beginning. People are

21. Pretentious.

almost always suspected of having ulterior motives. This is also because they have often had long histories of competing for scarce resources and of engaging in family feuds and other conflicts that have created divisions and deep distrust among them. However, they realize that on some level they are all affected by crime problems that require their collective attention, and they believe that it can occur notwithstanding the personal conflicts among them.

Considering these realities, it would perhaps be fruitless to focus directly on developing trust among certain neighborhood people as a precursor to collective action. Instead, trust is often earned over time as people learn more about each other through the process of collective action for problem-solving. As their bad experiences become outnumbered by more pleasant ones through the process of collaborating to achieve the common goal of a safer neighborhood, trust develops (although they remain cautiously skeptical). Working relationships based on trust have several advantages over those based on distrust.

When neighborhood collective action is undertaken based on mutual trust and admiration, it is often more emotionally rewarding, less confrontational, less convoluted, and more consistent over time. Those who have confidence in the integrity, work ethics, judgments, and abilities of others are more willing to work closely together to achieve collective goals. This is demonstrated by the fact that certain groups and individuals will only work with others whom they trust to produce results. Trust reduces many of the latent costs associated with collective action. When people already trust each other they do not have to spend time searching out enemies among them that could be better spent organizing against opposing forces. In Grand Boulevard, some of the churches and individuals also enjoy long histories of strong and healthy working relationships characterized by mutual trust and admiration. Others continue to work together and achieve results under clear conditions of distrust. It is important, therefore, to question meanings of trust as they relate to localized capacities for action. As data in subsequent chapters show, trust is manifested in different ways and has varied implications for collective action.

In the quest to critique and extend collective efficacy theory, I present statistical relationships between collective efficacy and neighborhood crime hotspots. I also question the social meanings of trust, solidarity, the willingness of residents to intervene, and the notion of neighborhood safety as a public good. These social meanings have yet to receive adequate attention from collective efficacy theorists, and this is one of the ways my research extends that theory.

For instance, this study has identified a distinction between objective[22] and subjective[23] solidarities. It argues that subjective solidarity refers to subjective social distance, which is important for the formation of trust. On the other hand, objective solidarity refers to the level of familiarity citizens have with their neighborhood, its citizens, and its history. Objective and subjective solidarity are sometimes at odds with each other.

As ethnographic data show, sometimes the longer people live in a neighborhood and the more they get to know their neighbors, the more they realize that they cannot or should not trust them—the more they realize that they cannot "do things" together. In Grand Boulevard, these divisions are most clearly reflected along religious lines and in neighborhood organizations competing for the same resources. In other instances, citizens may not know each other well, but may use certain social indicators to construct notions of trust among themselves. The clearest example is of residents who reside on blocks with well-manicured homes and who have little or no interaction with their newly-arrived busy professional neighbors. During interviews, however, these residents express deep belief that their new neighbors are trustworthy people because they

22. Objective solidarity refers to the level of familiarity neighborhood citizens have with each other. Residential tenure is one of those indicators. Other indicators are the frequency and depth with which citizens "do things" together, perceive themselves as "close-knit," or feel, for one reason or another, that this is a neighborhood they would miss greatly if they were to stop their current residential or other affiliations with it. In my ethnographic measurements, it is an estimation of how well residents know each other, especially in terms of knowing what sorts of lifestyles others lead, what their social networks are, and how they are expected to act or react under certain circumstances, especially those that relate to placing neighborhood safety under challenge.

23. Subjective solidarity is trust: a sort of positive affective disposition citizens have toward each other—the disposition that others will look after their well-being. Ethnographic data in this research have indicated that for most citizens, trust refers to the level of confidence that, in their absence or presence, another person (or persons) will look after their best interests. I have found that citizens often make statements such as, "I do not trust the people who live in the brick two-flat across the street." When they are questioned deeply about what they really mean, they often communicate the idea that they are not confident that, in their presence or absence, the people who live in that house will not try to do something to harm them if the opportunity presents itself. Hence, they try to interact with those persons in ways that do not present them with opportunities to harm them. Avoiding interaction altogether, or as much as possible, is one way to reduce the opportunities for harm. This is often why, under conditions of low trust, concerned and able persons prefer to engage in individual as opposed to group forms of intervention. They never know when and how the persons they do not trust may find an opportunity to do something hurtful to them. It is also very apparent that while persons who trust others in one way are likely to trust them in other ways, this is not always the case. In some instances, persons may trust others to watch their children, borrow money, or even watch their house or apartment while they are out of town. However, they may not trust the same persons to withhold information from offenders—information about their active participation in interventions against the questionable activities of those offenders. This is often the case when citizens make statements such as, "I can trust them with anything except to keep their damn mouths shut."

are quiet and take good care of their property. Without even knowing their neighbors well, they assume that they will be able to count on them to help intervene against crime on the block, because, after all, the new neighbors will want to protect their investment. These more seasoned residents have been very surprised when the trusted newcomers and some neighborhood veterans respond with indifference about intervention against crime, indicating that this is why they pay taxes—for the police, not themselves, to assume the responsibility of crime prevention. In most instances, however, a small body of residents repeatedly joins their neighbors in collective action against crime.

Often, the realization that the police are not very reliable creates a demand for collective efficacy, forcing residents to know their neighbors and to be more active in locally initiated collective action against crime. Indeed, distrust among offending and law-abiding neighbors is another strong catalyst that calls residents to action. Their involvement in collective action against crime is not driven by trust among them per se, but rather by a desire to protect themselves and the neighborhood from the wrongful actions of their own neighbors. Sometimes there is considerable tension among those involved in the collective action, but they are forced to put these differences aside to work together against the crime problems that affect them all. Newcomers to the neighborhood often join neighborhood groups such as block clubs that are organized against crime because they view this setting as an opportunity to know each other better and to participate in activities that can help protect their existing or planned investments in real estate.

This reality, the potential inconsistencies between objective solidarity and trust (or subjective solidarity) in reference to collective action against crime, requires more clarification and theoretical attention. Such attention is provided in subsequent chapters, which also include discussions about different types of trust, such as trust with information and trust with property. Thus, this study concludes that although the data offer qualified support for collective efficacy theory, there is a great need for more clarification as to how its key components actually work together in everyday life. In the concluding chapter I suggest ways this can be achieved.

The research also shows that several conditions challenge the expectation that high collective efficacy causes low crime and high crime is a result of low collective efficacy. This study indicates that neighborhoods have certain ecological features and reputations that make them differentially useful or attractive to offenders, especially crime entrepreneurs such as drug dealers, prostitutes, thieves, and burglars.

Therefore, although law-abiding citizens[24] may seek to reside in neighborhoods perceived to be of high collective efficacy, offenders do not explicitly seek out crime locales because they are low on collective efficacy.

However, once offenders are established in an area, the level of collective efficacy can have considerable influence on their decisions to exit the neighborhood or to stay and fight back. For instance, depending on the location occupied, street drug dealers will engage in different levels of resistance against neighborhood intervention. They are more likely to resist intervention in areas that have proven to be financially profitable to them. Urban spaces become of interest to different actors at the same time. The question is, what really makes a place of interest to certain offenders, and why? The answer goes far beyond the presence or absence of certain forms of collective action against them.

Offenders are often more proactive than reactive in developing their interest in a particular space. Such interest relates to how *ecologically advantageous* the space in question is to them—such as how close a block is to their residence, the highway, the bus stop, the elevated train, or the boundary of another beat or jurisdiction. Other ecological features may also offer advantages: for instance, the presence of liquor stores, grocery stores, fast-food locations, and check cashing outlets that cause people to congregate in specific locations and otherwise give offenders a legitimate reason for being there. A particular location's reputation as a congenial venue for crime-related activities is another part of the ecological advantage it offers to offenders; at the same time, it poses *ecological challenges* to other neighborhood actors. This ecological challenge has major implications for collective efficacy as it determines the *demand* for collective *efficacy,*[25] and the *format,*[26] *impact,*[27] and *costs* of collective efficacy.[28]

Residents of different locations do not receive the same level of benefit for similar levels of collective action against crime. These returns are conditioned not only by the actions of the people within the location in question, but also by those around them. Furthermore, such returns are also conditioned by ecological challenge: the sort of space within which the location in question is embedded, and what is going on around it.

24. And even certain offenders such as successful drug dealers.
25. The extent to which neighbors will be called upon to intervene against crime.
26. What type of efforts they will be required to undertake against crime.
27. How effective collective action will be against crime.
28. The level and form of resistance that will be encountered from offenders, and the type of personal sacrifices, even threats to life, they will be forced to endure as a result of their participation in collective efficacy.

Although collective efficacy theorists are leaders in demonstrating the impact of "spatial (dis)advantage" and "spatial dependency" (Sampson and Morenoff 2004) on homicide rates in Chicago, they have not applied these concepts to collective efficacy. I do this here by invoking the notion of ecological challenge.

The concept of social dependence indicates that, contrary to what is proposed by the urban village model, neighborhoods are not intact social systems that function as islands unto themselves. Instead, they are affected by the wider sociodynamics of the city. For example, interpersonal crimes such as homicide are based on social interaction and are affected by factors such as concentrated disadvantage and acts of retaliation in surrounding neighborhoods. Homicides are also shown to be affected by levels of collective efficacy not only within the location in question, but also in locations around it (Sampson and Morenoff 2004).

The WANS data indicate that conditions of collective efficacy are also affected by ecological factors. The demand for collective efficacy and its form, benefits, and returns are all affected by what is within and around a neighborhood location, even one as small as a street block. Neighborhood blocks in or adjacent to commercial or mixed land use blocks face a greater ecological challenge than those situated within strictly residential areas. Similarly, owners of private homes on blocks that are closest to public housing complexes are under greater challenge to organize against crime than those embedded among other privately owned homes. The presence of adjoining grocery stores, liquor stores, check cashing outlets, busy street intersections, and bus or nearby train stops also place more challenge on neighborhood blocks, and in turn affect the demand, form, benefits, and costs of collective efficacy.

Since urban and other areas are developed unequally, and since offenders prefer certain neighborhood features over others, locations are differentially *at risk* for criminal invasion, notwithstanding their levels of collective efficacy and neighborhood disorder. These levels of risk determine the demand, format, potential impact, and costs of collective efficacy. These risk factors vary on different neighborhood levels; it is more likely that blocks near liquor stores, grocery stores, check-cashing services, and busy intersections in Grand Boulevard will be at greater risk of hosting drug dealing and robbery than those in Hyde Park. However, in Grand Boulevard itself, certain blocks, by virtue of what is next to and around them, are at greater risk for those crimes. Blocks that are at greater risk for drug dealing and robbery stimulate a higher demand for collective action against crime. On such blocks, residents are constantly challenged to organize against those crimes, and they continue to face repeated infractions even while their efforts are in progress. Consequently, because they are situated in lucrative drug dealing and robbery locations, they encounter more resistance from offenders and suffer higher costs, such as retaliation, for their participation in collective action against those crimes. Therefore, residents on such blocks, although more organized, sometimes express more reluctance to intervene, although they have reluctantly intervened on several occasions in the past and may do so again in the future.

By contrast, residents on blocks with less ecological disadvantage—that are less attractive to drug dealers and robbers—because such blocks are "out of the way," will be presented with less challenge for collective action against crime. Whenever residents on those blocks are faced with crime challenges, they can often displace offenders with relatively little effort, because the offenders already do not consider such blocks lucrative enough to be worth their trouble. Such residents will enjoy high returns on small efforts against crime. They will also encounter lower costs for intervention. However, this is not because of higher levels of trust, cohesion, and willingness to intervene against crime. Instead, it is because they are fortunate to reside in locations robbers and drug dealers consider ecologically inconvenient for business. These blocks are, consequently, under less criminal challenge.

Residents of blocks that are under less criminal challenge often express greater willingness to intervene against crime. Since they are called upon to do so less frequently, the interventions are often brief; they encounter little resistance, and therefore, experience low costs. Their willingness to intervene, therefore, is not based on mutual trust and cohesion among them, but rather on the low level of challenge they face on their block by virtue of its positioning—in reference to the ecological advantages that some offenders are actively seeking. Based on the location of their block, they will have enjoyed tranquility and experienced little cost in maintaining it in the past, and will anticipate the same for the future.

By contrast, residents of more ecologically disadvantaged blocks, having experienced greater costs associated with intervention in the past, are more likely to express reluctance to intervene—notwithstanding levels of trust and cohesion among them. In fact, trust and cohesion are less likely to develop among residents on blocks with greater ecological disadvantage because, unlike those on the low-challenge blocks, they are frequently called upon to intervene against their own neighbors. This complicates the issue by imposing greater conflict of interests and less willingness to intervene against relatives or close friends. This is especially the case when residents already distrust the criminal justice system to return such persons to the neighborhoods as better individuals than when they left. This also shows that reluctance to intervene is not always associated with anticipated retaliation from offenders. It is also often related to the anticipated loss of friends and close associates who may be prosecuted as a result of localized actions against crime. These factors require considerable attention if the potentials for collective efficacy are to be fully realized. The narratives in chapters 5 to 7 provide up-close accounts of how these processes occur on the ground and serve as extensions to collective efficacy theory.

THREE

Here's the Neighborhood

A Video Ethnographic Tour
of Grand Boulevard, 2000

This chapter provides a video ethnographic description of Beat 213, which includes all of Grand Boulevard[1] and the east side of Calumet Avenue between 39th and 43rd Streets. The words Grand Boulevard and Beat 213 are used interchangeably to describe the same area. Video ethnography is a component of Systematic Social Observation (SSO), a research method used to document aspects of neighborhood life as they occur and in a manner that can be replayed or reexamined. In this instance, SSO data were gathered using a slow-moving vehicle with cameras mounted on each side of the interior, to simultaneously produce video images of both sides of each neighborhood street.

Video ethnography is the procedure through which video images are carefully reviewed and described in print to help explain social phenomena of concern. The SSO data also include recordings of the verbal descriptions of what the crew observed while driving through the streets. This includes descriptions of images and patterns of interaction that were not visible to the cameras. Video ethnography can also include written headnotes if, as was true in this case, the researcher preparing the notes was also a member

1. The official boundaries of Grand Boulevard are 39th Street and King Drive at the northwest corner, 39th Street and Cottage Grove at the northeast, Cottage Grove and 43rd Street at the southeast, and 43rd Street and King Drive at the southwest.

of the crew that recorded the images. Headnotes are written comments based the researcher's memory of previously observed events.[2] Still photos will also be used to provide yet another image of particular sections of the neighborhood. We begin this spring 2000 tour of Beat 213 at the northeast corner of the intersection of Cottage Grove Avenue and Pershing Road (39th Street).

That intersection can be seen at time-code[3] 00:40 in the Quicktime movie made from the spring 2000 SSO footage and can be viewed at www. peterkbstjean.com. We will travel westbound along Pershing Road, south on Calumet Avenue, east on 43rd Street, then north on Cottage Grove Avenue to return to the intersection where the tour began. This will cover the entire rectangular boundary of Beat 213. This trip is 2.2 miles long and it takes about fifteen minutes of driving at about 3–5 miles per hour to video record the entire route.

The aerial photograph of Beat 213 (see Figure 1.6) shows that the land at the southwest corner of the Cottage and Pershing intersection was still an empty lot in 1998 when that picture was taken. That area was later developed into Mandrake Park, which officially opened in the summer of 2001. The 2000 SSO movie shows Mandrake Park in its early stages of development. There were still security rails around the park to prevent pedestrians from entering the property while it was under construction. In 1999 and 2000, the development of Mandrake Park was a signal to many Grand Boulevard residents of the changes that had begun and that would continue in the area. Residents had already noticed many new buildings being raised in previously vacant lots. They had also seen presentations by many developers with plans for future development in the area. During community meetings, residents commonly expressed belief that the new park was a signal that more young working families were about to settle in the area, or at least that they were being invited to do so. Residents viewed this as a welcome change, stressing the need to have parks used by families rather than by gang members who often engage in illegal drug sales and violent activities in Ellis Park, located three blocks north on Cottage Grove, but in another neighborhood (Beat 212).

Mandrake Park occupies most of the 700 block of Pershing Road and stretches southward onto Oakwood Avenue, which has historically been known as a neutral gang territory. Residents were hopeful that since

2. I distinguish headnotes from fieldnotes, which were written while observations were still in progress.

3. The changing numbers in the lower corner of the movie screen, which display the time elapsed between the beginning of the movie and the scene being viewed.

Mandrake Park is located in a neutral gang territory, gang members engaged in questionable activities based in Ellis Park would be discouraged from bringing their activities into this new park. To add to this disincentive, local residents organized a schedule of events for the park that left very little time unaccounted for. Various days of the week were to be allocated for teen games, adult games, basketball, baseball, and softball. Gang members could use the park, but they would have to share it with other residents' scheduled activities instead of appropriating it for their own activities. The residents were concerned that if gang activities flourished in the new park, the general public would be intimidated and would avoid using the park.

Residents of Grand Boulevard had also begun to notice the many newcomers who began settling in the area, most of whom were young, middle-income African Americans. The new residents quickly began using the running track across the street from Mandrake Park, in the North Kenwood community. The track was paved and completed shortly before groundbreaking began in Mandrake Park.

In the beginning, using the park was an odd event to many longtime residents of the area, in part because they were not accustomed to seeing recreational activities in this area. It was also odd because the park was positioned directly across Pershing Road from Madden Park Homes, which itself was across the street from Ida B. Wells Homes. Many users of the track, especially newcomers to the area, had expressed discomfort about using the track because it was directly across the street from the huge vacant lots and abandoned buildings that were visible in Madden Park. It was not uncommon for residents of Ida B. Wells to walk through the running track on their way to other destinations. I obtained a few interview contacts by beginning conversations with such persons.

I also habitually used that track while conducting fieldwork in the area. My running and walking companions frequently commented on how ironic it was to be exercising across the street from the Madden Park homes, which by that time had been almost completely evacuated. The brownstone three-story buildings, which can be seen on the right screen of the SSO movie, were once home to many lower-income residents, some of whom were notorious for their involvement in criminal activities. But many decent people also lived there. One of them was my walking mate in the summer of 2000. He was one of the positive leaders in Madden Park, and he recounted several instances less than five years ago when violence erupted, causing people to seek cover in the lot where the running track is now located. As mentioned earlier, the area of the new park is also neutral gang territory. Like several other residents of the area, my

Figure 3.1. Center for Inner City Studies.

running partner from Madden Park homes could not have imagined five years ago that this space would be used as a running track. He perceived this as a sign that the future would bring improvements in the neighborhood environment, but he remained skeptical about how much progress could be made, particularly because several factors such as departing businesses had not changed along Pershing Road and its surrounding area, leaving the area vulnerable to the negative impacts of poverty.

As we continue westbound on Pershing Road we observe an Abraham Lincoln Center that has been serving the community since 1905. It is a center for youth and elderly recreation, after-school services, and individual development. The exterior of the building is in fair condition, its interior is well maintained, and a security guard is on duty during operating hours.

The left camera shows the largest building visible from this section of Pershing. This is the Center for Inner City Studies, located at 700 East Oakwood Boulevard (Figure 3.1). It is a satellite campus of Northeastern Illinois University, whose main campus is on the north side of Chicago. Several community meetings are held in this building. The cafeteria in the basement is where Beat 213 community policing meetings are usually held, at 7:00 P.M. on the third Wednesday of each month. On weeknights, and on any given Saturday, college classes and Afrocentric cultural events are held at the Center for Inner City Studies. This building is one of the key institutions of Grand Boulevard. The main entrance to the building is located on Oakwood Boulevard, but the parking lot is located at the rear of the building along Langley Street, which runs north-south through the entire length of Beat 213.

Langley also marks the end of the 600 block of Pershing Road. At the southwest corner of Langley and Pershing is a large one-story abandoned building that was once a lumber yard. The building is frequently discussed at community policing meetings because it is a temporary home for a few homeless men in the area. A police officer once recommended at a beat meeting that residents simply place a lock on the gates at the entrance of the property because the owner resides elsewhere and is seldom in the area. Residents questioned whether that was legal only to receive the following response from the officer: "That would take care of the problem, now won't it?" Following the officer's advice, residents placed a lock on the gate and there were no more complaints of squatting in that location for about one year.

Next to the abandoned lumber yard is another large empty lot that is securely fenced. However, immediately west of that fenced vacant lot is a large unfenced lot of about nine-tenths of an acre. According to neighborhood elders, the lot has been the location of several businesses, including a McDonalds Restaurant and a pharmacy. The lot has been vacant for more than fifteen years. The SSO video shows an ongoing picnic in that vacant lot (left camera, 1:24). Four vehicles, including a minivan and a car with an open trunk, can be seen parked on the roadside; barbeque smoke is visible and the smell of chicken fills the air. Classic soul music can be heard coming from the white car with the open trunk. Immediately across the street, at the Ida B. Wells Homes (Figure 3.2), adults can also be seen preparing barbeques, teenagers are playing on the sidewalks, and children are playing Double Dutch with a jump rope. This is not a crowded area. So far in the video, there have been about twelve persons in sight.

Next to the vacant lot where the barbeque is being held is a brown one-story building used as a family health center. The building does not look as if it is being used, mainly because it is badly in need of external repairs and fresh painting. The empty lots on the east and west sides of the building allow the walls to be plainly visible to the camera. There are no windows visible on the east, north, or west sides of that health center. I have accompanied residents to this center for dental and medical

Figure 3.2. Ida B. Wells Homes.

visits. Just inside the entrance to the building are the waiting room and the pharmacy, straight ahead. A tall glass window separates the patients from the front desk attendants, who are dwarfed by shelves of patients' charts visible behind them. The health center staff was quite courteous to the patients, most of whom had walked from their residence at Ida B. Wells. The elderly African American who entered the door with me the last time I visited that health center was there to have his dentures adjusted. Since he was only walking to the clinic from his Ida B. Wells apartment immediately across the street, he did not bother to wrap the dentures in a handkerchief or a napkin, as I had seen others do in the past. He told me that he had waited until he saw the dentist walking to work and then left his apartment timed to arrive about five minutes after her. This was to allow her time to settle in. He had been a regular patient at this health center for several years. He spoke highly of the health services he had received at the center. As soon as the dentist saw him, she called him by name and urged him to walk to the head of the line. She then quickly adjusted his dentures, returning them to him in about four minutes. He said, "This is why I keep coming here. It is right cross the street and I get taken care of right away." Other patients I spoke to at this family health center also expressed a liking for the place because of the convenience and the much-needed service they received there. Others, however, were not so satisfied.

The dental attendant at that time was an elderly Asian woman who frequently used public transportation to get to work. She had worked there for several years. To get to work she rode a bus to the corner of Cottage and Pershing, and walked the two blocks from there to the center. I once asked her how it felt to walk the streets of this neighborhood, especially since it was quite apparent that she did not live in the immediate area. She expressed no concerns for her safety, stressing that many of the residents are her patients, and would not allow anyone to harm her. I came to realize that although the exterior of the building was in poor condition, the services within it were invaluable to the residents, especially the poor who reside within walking distance. Staff at the building felt reassured that their patients would help ensure their safety even in this location marked by high deterioration.

Continuing west along Pershing Road, Vincennes Street is at the next intersection (Figure 3.3). Like Langley, Vincennes runs north-south through the entire Beat 213. It is also the boundary of the two census tracts that comprise Grand Boulevard, and a political boundary between two different aldermanic wards. The other buildings located between

Figure 3.3. Vincennes and Pershing.

the clinic and Vincennes Street are also in poor condition. The three-story building immediately west of the health center was at one time or another home to several small businesses. The building west of that one is a storefront Baptist church. Next to that building is a yellow one-story structure with several boarded-up windows; it is clearly not serviceable at this time. The open space near the corner of Vincennes and Pershing Rd. ranks high on social disorder mainly because it is a "hang-out spot" mainly for middle-aged men who sometimes engage in public drinking, but mostly sit and socialize (Figure 3.3).

On the other side of the street, the lawns in front of the two-story Ida B. Wells buildings look as if they have recently been cut. However, several pieces of trash can be seen on most of them. Children appear to be happily playing on the grass as well. There is a huge barbeque pit made out of an oil drum mounted at the front of one of the Ida B. Wells houses. This is frequently the site for outdoor barbecue parties, but not today. There is hardly any grass on the vacant lots on the northeast side of Pershing and Vincennes. The lot is sometimes used as a parking lot when persons wish to avoid parking on the streets. Pershing separates Beat 213 from Beat 212. Although the north side of Pershing is outside of Beat 213, it is important to observe the social events that occur on that side of the street since they often have spillover effects on the south side of the street, in Beat 213.

One of the spillover effects is due to the fact that all of the local businesses on Pershing Road between Cottage Grove and King Drive are located on the south side of the street, within the jurisdiction of Beat 213. In addition to the health clinic, there are three grocery and liquor stores, one gas station, one motel, one laundromat, and one take-out restaurant. Many customers of the local businesses on Pershing come from the north side of the street, from Ida B. Wells. On any given day, traffic heading in either direction on Pershing must yield to children, youths, adults, and elders who are crossing the street to obtain goods.

Maps in Appendix A show that the intersection of Pershing and King is one of the stable hotspots of street drug dealing, robbery, and battery. Much of this is explained by the fact that this is one of the more vibrant locations in the beat (Figure 3.4).

In interviews presented in chapters 5 and 6, drug dealers and robbers explain the ecological advantages that locations such as this offers to offenders. In the late 1980s and early 1990s, this section of Pershing Road was a hotbed for different types of heroin trafficking. The area saw several turf fights during that time. Currently, these turf fights occur less frequently because local drug dealers are cooperating more with each other

Figure 3.4. Pershing and Martin Luther King Drive.

and are less in direct competition with the products being sold. Some specialize in the sale of various forms of crack cocaine, heroin, and cocaine. In the past, local drug dealers were more involved in general sales. Therefore, there was more competition for turf because they sold the same products. Since the business has become more specialized, the issue of turf fighting is less important, and street drug dealers are more focused on keeping customers and avoiding agents of the law. The fights that now occur among them are more associated with envy and jealousy than with claiming and holding turf. Some drug dealers are much more successful than others. This earns them enemies among their peers. Those enemies sometimes rob the more successful drug dealers at gunpoint, or by other forceful methods. However, these events are not very common on this particular block because it is within a secondary street-drug-dealing area. The more lucrative areas are located about seven blocks west on Pershing, along the State Street corridor where the high-rise Stateway Gardens and Robert Taylor Homes housing project buildings once dominated the skies but are steadily being demolished at this time.

The 300–400 block of Pershing Road near King Drive is also a robbery hotspot, mainly because it is an area where people can be found with money in their possession and distracted while patronizing local

Figure 3.5. Pershing and Martin Luther King Drive.

establishments. It is also a battery hotspot because many idlers, drug addicts, and public drinkers who congregate in the area frequently engage in verbal and other conflicts with each other. These conflicts often escalate into physical confrontations. On other occasions, the fights begin elsewhere among couples or friends, and then unfold on that section of the street while people are drinking, socializing with friends, or awaiting public transportation (see time code 2:25–2:44 on SSO movie to get a sense of this block). Dr. Martin Luther King Drive is the next major street that crosses Pershing Road (Figure 3.5).King Drive is the largest street in this area. On a clear day, the top section of Sears Towers can be seen from the intersection of King and Pershing. From 6:00 A.M. to 8:00 P.M. on weekdays, various public buses travel through this intersection at five- to ten-minute intervals. This is clearly the busiest intersection in Beat 213.

As we ride westward along Pershing and cross King, a tire repair shop can be seen on the left screen. It is the first business in a small adjoined brick business complex that stretches along the entire south side of the block to the alleyway before Calumet Avenue. A barber shop, a beauty shop, a bar, and a barbeque house are the other businesses in that complex. The north side of that block begins with a large vacant lot next to Vegas Food and Liquor Store and Dollar Plus, which are located at the alleyway. Across the alleyway on the north side of Pershing is a three-story brick apartment building in fair condition. This side of Pershing is also a hotspot for drug dealing, robbery, and battery, for the same reasons explained earlier in reference to the east side of King. Direct quotes from offenders interviewed in this study will highlight how such places are capitalized upon for entrepreneurial crimes such as street drug dealing and robbery.

We turn left from Pershing southward on Calumet toward 40th Street. On the right screen we see that the entire 3900 block of Calumet Avenue is a vacant lot overgrown with weeds and small trees. Residents who live in the adjoining area can frequently be seen walking diagonally across that lot as a short cut. Two well-worn footpaths have resulted from this frequent traffic. The eastern side of Calumet also has three vacant lots, as well as two three-story brick buildings that are in fair condition. Next to these buildings is a taller senior citizens' home that is in excellent condition. The fence surrounding that building appears to be freshly painted, the lawn is freshly cut, the hedge is well manicured, and no pieces of trash are visible on the lawn (Figure 3.6).

An out-of-service elevated railroad track runs to the northwest from Cottage Grove and Bowen Avenue, forming an underpass at the intersection of 40th and Calumet. The rusty metal overpass is supported by two solid concrete foundations, portions of which are painted in white to erase the graffiti that was once there. This railroad foundation can also be seen on the 4100 block of King, near the Ritz Hotel, which is located on the corner of King and Oakwood. In that location, as at the Cottage

Figure 3.6. Senior citizens' home, 3900 block of Calumet.

Figure 3.7. Mural, Cottage Grove between Bowen and 41st.

Grove site, the railroad track foundation is used as a background on which Afrocentric murals are painted (Figure 3.7).

Continuing south on Calumet past 40th Street, we observe barbeque pits on both sides of the street, and children, teenagers, and adults are congregating. On the west side of the street, teenage African American males can be seen sitting on the curb in front of the doorway of a four-story brick apartment building. On the eastern side of the street an African American man and woman are standing between two vehicles, facing each other and laughing in what appears to be a friendly conversation.

Two buildings to the south on the same side of the street, two African American girls about five years old can be seen playing in the patch of grass between the curb and the sidewalk. They are at the front of a three-story brownstone building with boarded-up doors and windows. A wire fence more than six feet tall at the front of the building gives a clear indication that it is not serviceable and that trespassing is prohibited. Across the street from the children are two young African American males standing with their feet about shoulder-width apart and hands in their pockets. One is standing against the fence in front of a building. There are several vacant lots and abandoned brownstone buildings on the 4000 block of Calumet Avenue. Such types of buildings have been renovated and converted into condominiums in several locations along King Drive. The same is expected to happen to the buildings here on Calumet as gentrification penetrates more deeply into the neighborhood.

The 4100 block of Calumet looks more appealing than the previous block. Although there are some vacant lots, they are well maintained. Two new houses were also recently built on the block, and two more were newly renovated. There is also a very well maintained senior citizens' home located on this block. Similar to the one on the 3900 block of Calumet, this building is in immaculate condition on the outside—the lawn and trees are well manicured, and the fence appears to be new or freshly painted. Huge vacant lots can be seen along the remainder of the 4100 block of Calumet. The grass is freshly cut in some empty lots, but overgrown in others.

The two buildings on both sides of the intersection of 42nd and Calumet are in good condition. The building on the left is newly built and a couple of its windows are boarded up, suggesting that it is still undergoing finishing touches. The two-story gray-stone on the right was recently renovated and is now known as a local mansion. Chicago police statistics, narratives from beat meetings, and a survey of neighborhood experts have all identified this block (4200 Calumet) as one of the prostitution hotspots. The location lives up to its reputation during this SSO run; a street prostitute can be seen waving at the vehicle (right camera time code 05:13–05:17), then following the vehicle as I drive away (off camera). Several vacant lots and poorly maintained properties can be seen along the 4200 block of Calumet, which ends on 43rd Street. A few other buildings on that block are also in fair condition.

Like most of the other numbered streets in Chicago, 43rd Street runs in an east-west direction. Like 39th Street, 43rd Street is another struggling commercial street in Grand Boulevard. The north side of 43rd Street forms the southern border of Beat 213. Our journey down Calumet from 43rd begins with a large vacant lot on the east side; on the west side is a two-story brick commercial building that has large boarded-up windows on the upper floor and a corner grocery store on the ground level. A large painted mural that occupies the entire eastern side of the first floor of the building depicts African American women wearing various hairstyles. This is an advertisement for a hair salon that was once located on the first floor of that building.

The Calumet/43rd Street intersection is also one of the busiest sections of this area because of its close proximity to both a stop on the elevated train (el) and a nearby popular liquor and grocery store. As early as 7:30 A.M. on any warm or hot day, several middle-aged men and women can be seen congregating under the el after obtaining products from the corner store. Figure 3.8, taken from SSO footage (video photography), shows local residents crossing the 43rd and Calumet intersection from different directions after completing nearby shopping.

Further east along 43rd Street, large one-story abandoned commercial buildings occupy both sides of the street. The building on the right had been home to bars and night clubs for several years. A bar is still open in the building on the north side of 43rd close to King. Both buildings on the south side of the street clearly look abandoned, since their windows are all boarded up and the wire security gates on the doors are very rusty.

We arrive at the intersection of 43rd Street and King Drive. Although King is a large two-way street, there are one-way streets running with the flow of traffic on each side of the street. Those north- and southbound one-way streets are separated from the larger four-lane two-way section of King by a median about twelve feet wide with concrete curbs on each side and well-manicured grass between the curbs. These one-way streets allow persons who reside along King Dr. to park their vehicles away from

Figure 3.8. 43rd and Calumet.

Figure 3.9. Northwest corner, 43rd and King (2000).

the busy section of the street. They also allow for slow-moving vehicles to travel along King Drive without impeding the flow of faster traffic.

If one stood on the northwest corner of King and 43rd (Figure 3.9) and began walking north along the southbound one-way section of King Drive, one would first pass a liquor store, then a laundromat, both of which are still open for service.

Continuing northward, one would then pass a three-story rooming house where transients[4] often live. Next to the rooming house is a vacant lot; north of the vacant lot is a four-story gray stone building that was once a house of refuge, mainly for African Americans who migrated from the south seeking employment in the area. According to local accounts, that building had suffered several fires as a result of residents smoking while still in bed. If renovated, this building could easily be one of the most beautiful structures in that section of the neighborhood.

Immediately north of the former refuge house is a large vacant lot where middle-age male and female alcoholics congregate for at least 15 hours every day of the week during warm weather. The wine of choice is often Wild Irish Rose, which is relatively inexpensive. The interactions in this vacant lot on the 4200 block of King have become a subject at many Beat 213 community policing meetings. According to police accounts, that vacant lot belongs to the city of Chicago. The more affluent residents often complain that the men and women who socialize and drink in public in that lot are an eyesore to the area. They express concern about property values potentially declining as a result of the

4. Transients are people who live in locations temporarily because they are frequently in transition from one job or residence to another.

presence of those public drinkers, among whom minor fights occasionally break out. These public drinkers and their associates are predominantly middle-aged and elderly men, and a few women. However, residents have mainly expressed discontent about the littering, loitering, public urination, loud laughter, and quarrels that result from such street-corner congregating. They are often sympathetic to the plight of the middle-aged and elderly idlers, whom many have known to be peaceful people. During beat meetings, residents have suggested that an "old man's park" or "idlers' park" should be built for such persons so that they can have their own space and not resort to occupying whatever empty lot seems to be available. Police officers have responded to residents' complaints by making occasional searches, some of which have led to arrests or citations for matters such as disorderly conduct, drinking in the public way, and outstanding warrants. However, the police have usually instructed the public drinkers to clean up after themselves, to stop congregating on the section of the lot that is most visible from King Drive, and to keep their voices low. I spent several hours on different days socializing with those men and women to understand how they make sense of their world. Some of the data will be presented in the chapters on drug dealing, robbery, and battery later in this book.

In 2001, when renovation began in a nearby building, the middle-aged men and women who congregated in the empty lot on the 4200 block of King Drive moved about 300 feet southward along the alleyway neat 43rd St. and King Drive. The demolition of a few buildings on that block had created an open space, and the men and women told me that the owner of the space had told them they were allowed to congregate there as long as they cleaned up after themselves. As of 2005, the space was still being used for the same purposes (Figure 3.10).

Our video tour has now returned to the intersection of King and 43rd. One resident recalled twenty years ago, when all the bars on that corner were open for business, seeing many bloody fights at this corner in the early morning hours. Residents also recall that in the 1950s, 1960s, and 1970s this was a thriving, major intersection. A doctor's office was said to have been located in the white two-story commercial building that appears on the right screen (time code 6:20) as we cross King. That building now has a sign on the northwest corner that reads "43rd News Stand." However, the windows are boarded up, indicating that the business has folded.

Beyond that building is a vacant lot, then a church called God's House for All Nations. This is one of the locations I visited to observe services. As at many of the other churches in this area, Sunday teachings

Figure 3.10. Northwest corner, 43rd and King (2005).

at God's House are tailored to respond to the hurt and suffering many residents of this area express about daily life. These feelings are often associated with the lost of loved ones to violence; with the hardships of poverty, unemployment, and underemployment; with frustration about the school system, the social welfare system, and the criminal justice system; with frustrations about insufficient safe play areas for children and teenagers and lack of opportunity for organized recreation; with involvement in abusive relationships; with police brutality; and with more general struggles with the realities of low human capital, various forms of discrimination, and scarce resources. This church and others in the area provide members with, among other things, an opportunity to praise their God and to attempt to live on despite their pains and sufferings.

Beyond the church is a vacant lot, then the building where the Checkerboard Lounge is located.[5] For many decades, the Checkerboard has been the home for great blues music, as is evidenced by the blue sign that reads "Home of the Blues." Muddy Waters and several famous blues musicians have performed here. The building is in poor condition and

---

5. The lounge has since relocated to the Hyde Park neighborhood.

residents have expressed a belief that the neighborhood will eventually lose this landmark as a result of gentrification, or continued failing businesses. On Thursday nights the Checkerboard Lounge becomes a popular socializing place for many University of Chicago graduate students, most of whom are white and who love the blues. They usually travel in carpools and are escorted by Checkerboard employees from and to their parked cars, which remain under the watchful eyes of security officers while they are at the Lounge. At this time, Vance Kelly is the musician most commonly featured at the Checkerboard Lounge.

Across the street from the Checkerboard is a Women Infants and Children (WIC) building where pregnant women and mothers go for services, which include obtaining nourishment for themselves and their babies. Next to the WIC building is a vacant lot, overgrown with weeds, in which an abandoned vehicle sits. An alleyway separates this vacant lot from three adjoining one-story brick buildings.

The first building is a storefront church and homeless shelter. The pastor has been asked to find another location for her church because the building has been cited for several code violations and is considered unsuitable for human use. She is expected to relocate in less than one year. The building next door, once a bar, is now closed. Next to that building is an antique furniture store. The worker at this store frequently laments that he could have owned several pieces of property in this area for what he called "dirt cheap." He once said that a gray stone building located one block south was purchased by one of his friends for $45,000; two years later, having invested less than $25,000 in repairs, he sold the building to a young couple for $215,000. The owner of the furniture store was also given notice by his landlord to vacate the premises because the building is in need of major repairs. The furniture store is expected to relocate within one year. Next to the furniture store is another empty lot, on the corner of Vincennes and 43rd. The northeast corner of that intersection is also a large vacant lot overgrown with grass. Large vacant lots can also be seen on the south side of 43rd Street, which is in the jurisdiction of Beat 222.

There are very few people in evidence on this street. Three are standing at the bus stop. One man, dressed in a long Afrocentric gown, is on one of his usual long walks around the neighborhood, which he uses as a form of exercise and socializing. He lives about six blocks away, in the same building that houses his church. He will most likely walk all the way to Hyde Park, as he has done several times in the past.

The entire section of 43rd Street between Vincennes and St. Lawrence is a large vacant lot, with only one abandoned building. New buildings are being constructed all along the north side of 43rd Street between St. Lawrence and Champlain. Piles of building materials for these structures are placed on the ground in the vacant lots. No construction workers can be seen on the property at this time.

Further east on 43rd, the section between Champlain and Langley begins with a fenced vacant lot that resembles a junkyard, with many vehicles, some clearly unserviceable. The two white Cape Cod houses next to that lot are followed by a single-story brick commercial building that houses a hair salon. Next to the hair salon, on both sides of 43rd Street, are two newly built three-story apartment buildings, both in such excellent condition that they actually look out of place on that block. Residents believe that in less than five years, these buildings will no longer be the exception, but the norm. Plans are in place to construct buildings like these all along the 400–600 block of 43rd Street. Many residents are happy about that. In 1998, I interviewed four seasonal workers who had gained temporary employment clearing away the bricks and debris from the building that had been demolished to make way for these new apartment buildings. Those laborers were thankful for the work, but lamented that they would not be able to afford to live in the apartments that would be built there.

The 700 block of 43rd Street is one of the drug dealing, robbery, and battery hotspots in Beat 213. It begins on the east side of Langley and ends on the west side of Cottage Grove. We first drive pass a corner store, a church, and an abandoned storefront before getting to the largest building on 43rd Street. It is the fourteen-story Judge Slater Apartments, originally designed as a residence for seniors (Figure 3.11).

Some of the residents who live in this building are active in the community and attend beat meetings occasionally, especially when a serious crime is committed on or near the property. At the time of the study, the building was also home to some disabled middle-aged men and women, some of whom were recovering alcoholics and drug addicts.[6] The more seasoned residents are quick to express discontent about the younger group of residents who are still involved in lifestyles the older ones condemn. This has caused some of the seniors to relocate, but others have remained there, believing they have no better options. Some of the seniors who live there take pride in their apartments and keep them clean, even though the building itself is often neglected. Several apartments in the building are unserviceable, as is evidenced by the boarded-up win-

---

6. Since the end of the study, the building has been designated as a residence exclusively for senior citizens.

Figure 3.11. Judge Slater Apartments.

dows. A tour through the building clearly indicates the need for better maintenance and updates in the common areas.

Several senior citizens who reside in this building are proactive in reporting crime to the police. They frequently spend time sitting at their windows observing life as it unfolds on the streets. Some residents on the east side of the building have a view of Lake Michigan, more than a mile away. These residents also have a clear view of the intersection of 43rd and Cottage Grove, where most of the commercial activities in that area occur.

Tenants residing on the north side of the building can view many of the larger buildings such as the Sears Tower located in downtown Chicago, which is 8.6 miles away. They and residents of the other high-rise building on the complex occasionally witness sexual acts that occur in vehicles parked on the 700 block of 42nd Street. That quiet block is known as one of the areas to which prostitutes accompany johns in their vehicles to engage in sexual activities. Some seniors who reside on the north side of the buildings are so vigilant that they called the police to report my car as a suspicious vehicle when I was filming the SSO footage used in this book. I was driving slowly on the 700 block of 42nd Street, then I stopped to replace one of my cameras because of a technical problem. Within five minutes, a police car with flashing lights raced toward me in response to the call. The officer, who knew me from several beat meetings we attended, laughed at the episode and told me that I had just received a firsthand account of how some residents in this area do not tolerate suspicious behavior.

An alleyway separates the senior building on 740 E. 43rd Street from four storefront properties with boarded-up windows and other indications of disrepair (time code 8:35–8:38). A barbershop and beauty salon still functions out of one of those storefronts. Next is a three-story commercial building on the northwest corner of 43rd and Cottage Grove (Figure 3.12). A Western Union check-cashing outlet, a grocery and liquor store, and a take-out outlet called "Tasty Beef" are located on the first floor of the building. The entrances to all of these businesses are on the east side of the building located on Cottage Grove. The bus stop is also located in front of this building. At any given moment between 7:00 A.M. and 9:00 P.M., anywhere from five to ten people can be seen standing in front of this building, awaiting the bus, going to or leaving from one of the businesses, panhandling, drinking in public, or simply socializing. Many of the customers who use these businesses reside in the two senior citizen homes, just described, that are around the corner. In subsequent chapters, drug dealers and robbers explain how the social life of this street corner relates to their criminal entrepreneurial activities.

Turning left from 43rd Street, we head north on Cottage Grove. A middle-aged African American man who was engaging in conversation with the driver of a slow-moving car has to quickly run out of the center of the intersection when the light changes. We observe a large sign

Figure 3.12. Northwest corner, 43rd and Cottage Grove (1999).

that reads "Jamaica Food and Liquor Inc." painted in red on the yellow background of the entire front of the building (time code 9:10–9:27). The two upper floors of this building cannot be seen on camera, but all of their windows are boarded up because they were broken several years ago. According to the Arab tenants who own the grocery store inside this building, within one year the owners of the building will begin a complete renovation. The store owners are concerned that their rent will increase after that is done.

African American men can be seen standing on the corner and sitting on the bench at the bus stop. The wall of the building is decorated with a large red Chicago Bulls logo and a black White Sox sign. Three African American men can be seen together just north of the White Sox logo. One swings his arms while talking. In the empty lot immediately north of Tasty Beef, three individuals can be seen drinking in public while two others look on.

Immediately north of that empty lot is a three-story mixed-use brick building. Located at 4248 Cottage Grove, it has been home to New Age Chicago Furniture for more than seventy years. A hair salon is also located on the first floor of the building. Like the building just south of it, this building is structurally in good condition but is in need of considerable repair, as is evident by the rusty metal, cracked paint, and outdated signs.

The drive further north on Cottage Grove is dominated by the view of open space and vacant lots. The brown building on the left screen (time code 9:38) is one of the two Judge Slater apartment buildings to which reference was made earlier. The large fenced yard of that building stretches to the curb of Cottage Grove. The two churches and their large parking lots take up the entire west side of the 4100 block of Cottage Grove. Heading further north, the entire western block face[8] between Bowen and 41st Street is occupied by an abandoned railroad foundation on which a mural has been painted, and a condemned three-story multipurpose building. Another building in the same condition is located along the 4000 block of Cottage Grove. One block further north is yet another abandoned building which is only single-story and was once occupied by a hair salon and a grocery store.

The tour of the outer boundaries of Beat 213 ends on the 3900 block of Cottage Grove. Holy Angels Catholic Church can be seen in the background. A large wire fence encloses the parking lot where the children assemble during school hours, and buses are parked there at night. A large vacant lot occupies the south corner of the intersection of Oakwood Boulevard and Cottage Grove. An abandoned fast food outlet stands alone in the background. Mandrake Park is located directly across the street from the vacant lot and abandoned commercial building. As was indicated at the beginning of this video ethnographic tour, Mandrake Park is still under construction, and a wire fence can be seen along Cottage Grove and 39th Street, put there to keep pedestrians from entering the park grounds while construction is going on. We have now circumnavigated Beat 213, and have passed the areas where most of the narcotic violations, robberies, and batteries occur.

The interior section of Beat 213 is much like a small residential village. The buildings vary considerably in condition. Some residential structures, such as the Paul G. Steward homes located on the 4100 block of King Drive, and several other private homes and three-story apartment buildings are in immaculate condition. It is not uncommon for buildings in excellent condition to be located next to abandoned houses, vacant lots with overgrown weeds, or poorly kept homes. Several private homes in the area have been there for more than one hundred years and are occupied by longtime residents, often senior citizens with little income and no children successful enough to share the costs of home repair. This phenomenon of intergenerational failure will be discussed in chapter 5. Many other residents take pride in their homes and make considerable effort to prompt their neighbors to do the same. The strongest evidence of such efforts is on the 4000 block of Vincennes Avenue, where volunteers have planted extra flowers along vacant lots.

Only a few commercial properties are located on blocks other than the external boundaries of Beat 213 covered in the video tour. These other businesses include a struggling corner store which is about to close on the 500 block of Bowen Avenue, a school on St. Lawrence Avenue between 42nd Street and 42nd Place, the Ritz Hotel and affiliated businesses on the 3900 block of King Drive, Centers for New Horizons on the 4100 block of King Drive, and a thrift store on the 300 block of 42nd Street across from Centers for New Horizons. With the exception of about eight churches, all of the other buildings on the interior of Beat 213 are owner-occupied or rented residential structures in various states of repair.

FOUR

Perceived Sources of Neighborhood Disorder

The Importance of Understanding Perceived Sources of Disorder

The next three chapters place broken windows and collective efficacy theories under ethnographic scrutiny by presenting offenders' statements about the relevance of certain variables to their criminal activities. However, to understand fully the working capacity of broken windows theory, we must first understand how various participants in neighborhood life explain perceived sources of neighborhood disorder (Figure 4.1).This foundational knowledge is critical because broken windows theory relies heavily on offenders' interpretation of neighborhood disorder. I contend that understanding offenders' perceptions of the sources of disorder will set a good foundation for comprehending how they interpret its presence or absence as relevant to their criminal activity. Such discussions will also help us to know whether drug dealing came first, for unrelated reasons, then neighborhood disorder followed, or the other way around. Furthermore, exploring the perceived sources of neighborhood disorder will help us to understand why, for offenders such as street drug dealers and robbers, the meanings associated with neighborhood disorder often depend on how the disorder came into being, where it is situated, who

Figure 4.1. Block club sign, near trash, 39th and King (2004).

owns the relevant property, and whether or not the disorder is a signal of construction or destruction.[1]

Since most drug dealers and robbers are quite familiar with the neighborhoods in which they conduct business, they are aware of the circumstances that caused an area to deteriorate. They are quite aware that many of the factors that have contributed to neighborhood deterioration have little or nothing to do with whether residents care about their neighborhood. For the most part, they do not interpret neighborhood disorder to mean that no one cares about the area, and that therefore it costs nothing to sell drugs there. Offenders' interpretations of neighborhood disorder

1. For instance, whether a pile of dirt or overgrown grass on a property are present because a building is being renovated, constructed, or demolished, and whether or not the work seems to be progressing on a reasonable time schedule.

Figure 4.2. Gutted building on Oakwood (2004).

will be discussed in chapter 5; in the meantime, we will explore local perceptions of the sources of neighborhood disorder.

Perceived[2] Sources of Physical Disorder

When offenders, other residents,[3] businesspersons, and city agents including police officers were asked why so many buildings in the neighborhood were either abandoned or kept in poor condition (Figure 4.2), two responses were prevalent: poor property management and disruptive tenant stock, and *intergenerational failure* —a term many residents use to describe the higher incidence of economic failure among the younger generations than among the older ones. These failures are largely blamed on the disappearance of work from the area and the impacts of drug addiction, especially to crack cocaine.

2. Although most of the quotes used in this section were derived from individual offenders, the expressions were selected because they communicated beliefs that were widespread among all offenders.

3. On some occasions drug dealers were also residents of the block.

A cautionary note: neighborhood experts offered several statements that express their perceptions about neighborhood change. It is important to stress that this study does not present these perceptions as if they are reliable facts about the forces chiefly responsible for neighborhood change. Instead, these statements indicate how informants perceive changes that have occurred in their neighborhoods. Forces of neighborhood change appear to be more deeply entrenched in past histories than the informants report. For example, some neighborhood experts identify the era around 1986 as the period when neighborhood change became most pronounced. It is likely that forces of neighborhood change began long before that period; however, few neighborhood experts make references to factors that occurred long before that time period.

Poor Property Management and Disruptive Tenant Stock

When asked to explain the chain of events that resulted in the abandonment or current dilapidated condition of properties in the neighborhood (Figure 4.3), many informants told stories about what they considered the poor social habits of tenants and poor property management. As the

Figure 4.3. Ritz Hotel in deterioration (2004).

narratives suggest, on some occasions poor property management seems to have led to property decline and a departure of "good tenants," who were replaced by "bad tenants." On other occasions, according to some residents, the bad tenants came first, and then the quality of property upkeep declined, leading to the prevalence of irresponsible tenants and to further decline in property management. Offenders such as Flashy, who has spent time in prison for several crimes including drug dealing, robbery, assaults, car theft, and burglary, believe that slumlords are the source of neighborhood disorder:

You have many people who own property in this area and do not live here. They inherited the property from their relatives who moved out or died, and they rent them out but do not repair them. Now what sort of tenants you think you will have if you are not taking care of the property? Many of the people who live there are hardworking and honest people who want to do good in this world but they have to put up with this mess. So they move out and the rent must be cheaper if anyone will rent it. Now who you think will rent a shitty place. . . . Mostly people with huge problems and unstable in their life. They then tear the place down.

Mr. Flo[4] is a longtime resident of the neighborhood who has had extensive experience with the banking industry. He believes that discriminatory banking practices led to poor property management and high physical disorder among many multifamily rental buildings:

The biggest thing influencing the poor condition of buildings around here is the reluctance of banks to provide financing to property owners in this area. As a result, property owners are not able to conduct necessary periodic changes on houses, and the buildings go to ruin. I am friends with people who own multifamily units in this neighborhood and since the redlining began, they are having a hard time with doing even routine repairs. This has affected the quality of management that they can employ and the type of tenants that they can attract and keep. When good tenants—I mean people who do not cause any trouble, do not tear up your place, people who try to maintain order in the building and the neighborhood, people who pay their rent regularly—when these people are disgusted because the building is not being maintained, they move. When these good tenants move, there are empty

4. All birth names and street names in this study have been changed to protect the anonymity of the informants. I have assigned aliases to all of the informants; in most cases I do not know their real names. Most of the aliases were assigned to particular individuals because of some frame of reference in my own mind. For instance, Icepick is one of the six people I interviewed who carries a sharpened and concealed ice pick as his weapon of choice. Throat, a former offender of many crimes, claimed that his preferred technique while committing robberies was to hold a knife under the throat of his victim.

Figure 4.4. Ritz Hotel in transition (2004).

apartments. These apartments need to be occupied if the mortgage is to get paid. At that time, the property owner has to find tenants as quickly as possible. Sometimes, they are no longer so careful with the screening of tenants, and a few bad ones slip in the crack every now and then. There are good tenants, and there are bad ones, you have to believe that. . . . Sometimes the economy is bad and the tenants themselves cannot pay. But their economic conditions were questionable in the first place. But since the property owner has to fill the empty apartments as soon as possible because good tenants are moving out, he has to take what comes [Figure 4.4]. Bad tenants tear up the place; they often have bad company and cause hell in the place. Sooner or later, the property owner no longer is able to keep the place as clean as it used to be because it becomes too costly. Instead of sweeping the hallway once a day as used to be done in the past, now he has to sweep it at least twice a day because people are throwing garbage all over the apartment. They simply have bad living habits. It is hard to evict them. They keep tearing up the property, and the property owner cares

Figure 4.5. Dilapidated apartment building, 4000 block of Calumet.

even less. Then at some point, it is too expensive to repair the building, and there become more vacant apartments. Things are going downhill after that [Figure 4.5].

Ms. Hat is an employee at the Ritz. Recently, the owner of the building was assessed a $10,000 fine from the city because of failure to respond promptly to multiple demands by the city to repair code violations. The owner projects that it will cost approximately five million dollars to repair the building to the point of compliance. Ms. Hat explained how the building arrived at its current physical condition.

Traditionally, the Ritz has always been the spot for the undesirables. During segregation, Duke Ellington and his crew stayed here because they were not allowed to stay downtown among the white people that they played for. After segregation, the hotel was still thriving [Figure 4.6].

What has happened recently is that [this hotel] has continued to be a comfort zone for other undesirables: people we call the residentially challenged. . . . These are people who do not have a stable place to live. Most of them now are produced by the restructuring of CHA buildings. The city is closing up the buildings over there on State [Figure 4.7], and the people, most of them have no set place to stay. Some of them are able to get placement because they are legal tenants. But many of them are just squatters. Squatters have no rights. What has happened recently, over the last three years or so, is that they come over here for a short stay, and never move out.

Many of these people check themselves in, and never check out. Some of them are mentally challenged; they are really sick and need help. Others of them are simply up to no good. You should see what they do to this building. . . .They remove the fire alarms and use them as ashtrays. They kick the doors in when they cannot find their keys. They burn the beds and furniture. They dump garbage all over the place. They

Figure 4.6. Wide view of Ritz Hotel (2004).

Figure 4.7. Stateway Gardens building, now demolished. Such buildings are a source of squatters in Grand Boulevard.

fight and cause trouble. You will never imagine what these people will do. Some of them are professional tenants, too. They know exactly how to buy time at your place. They know exactly how hard it is to evict them, so they do not pay and remain there. Then they get hostile toward you. The bank does not want to finance to have the place repaired because it does not consider it a good business.

Bike was born on Chicago's South Side and has lived there all of his life. He is disabled and spends most of the day drinking and socializing with his friends in an empty lot whenever the weather permits. Bike believes that the decline of property is largely associated with poor tenant stock, particularly drug addicts. He explained how blocks in the neighborhood changed, and described the demise of the building next to where he was being interviewed on the street.

You would go to sleep under the hedge and don't nobody mess with you. Now they want to mess with you just for sleeping, telling you to wake up. Since the hedge was cut all went to hell. You go to sleep then nobody mess with you, you go to sleep now, they knock you on the head. . . . This used to be like a rooming house. People that came from the South used to room there and work in the area. They had lots of rooms and recreation there for them. . . . Then there was a fire in the building, and then another fire. They fixed it after that first fire, but it was not good anymore after the second fire. They had those crackheads in there smoking that pipe. They were smoking that cocaine, and caused a fire in there, and then they closed it down. People come by and try to buy it, but it is a lot of work to fix it. If the person has the money, I can tell you it is worth the investment because it has a good foundation.

When asked why there is so much trash in some of the vacant lots, Bird, one of Bike's friends, said that it is pure laziness.

Lazy. Lazy. You see that garbage can sitting up over there, they too damn lazy to walk over there and put the garbage in the garbage can [Figure 4.8]. That's what it is, and it don't make no sense. It don't make no sense. We have garbage cans sitting right up here in the front here. All you have to do is take it, put it in the garbage can, but you know what they did, they get through drinking and throw it right there by the garbage can, just lazy. I know one time, me and that brother over there, we were here until three o'clock in the morning picking up bottles, there were bottles all over this part here all through the lot. We fill up this garbage can, and another garbage can, all through the night, picking up the bottles, cleaning up the lot. They just lazy.

Figure 4.8. Sometimes, there are no garbage cans, as at this bus shelter at Pershing and King.

Bike interjected to explain why they cleaned up the area.

We did it because Bud Billiken was coming, Bud Billiken Day, a parade day. We did not have to clean it up; the city would come there and do it anyway. But why we did it is because we did not want one of them kids to come down here and fall down and cut theyselves on one of them bottles, broken glass, and stuff. That is why we did it.

Like I say that daytime crew that come in here, the daytime crew, me and him, we clean up stuff. That afternoon crew, and that NIGHT crew, forget it, they ain't cleaning up nothing, they junk it, they sit there and drink that wine and whiskey and throw the bottle right back behind them, or throw the bottle over here. One of them babies come through here and fall on one of those pieces of glass, and cut the shit off theyselves. We don't want that to happen to them babies.

After cleaning a large empty lot and taking a break in the shade under a tree, a group of city streets and sanitation employees expressed their opinions about the sources of physical disorder. One city employee thought that physical disorder is due to poor property management and the careless practices of tenants.

Many landlords are slumlords. Simply put. Many tenants are nasty people, simply put. When the two of them come together, they can tear a whole place down. You will not imagine some of the habits people have. Many of the landlords do not want to hire a janitor because they want to save money. Or for that same reason, when they hire one, they hire him part-time, and they hire one that is not a good worker so they do not have to pay him much money. What effect do you think this has on a property? When the building is not kept up, the better tenants who want a decent place to live move out and then worse tenants come. Then they deface and destroy the apartment until people cannot live there anymore. They break the sink, toilet, stove, and even the floor, the cupboards too. Eventually they are evicted or have to leave. Then the landlord cannot afford to repair the place because many of the tenants are not paying rent and it is a legal battle to evict them. Some of the landlords get the money but do not do the repairs because they are just after the money. It is a cycle most of the times.

Another streets and sanitation employee who is also a resident of the area said that the problem of poor property management is not restricted to large buildings, as many seem to suggest.

Too many people seem to think that the big apartment buildings are the ones with most problems with property upkeep and building upkeep. But you have to remember that there are many houses that look like single-family houses and are not. There are a lot of houses that look like multifamily houses with all relatives and are not. They are small rental properties. But there are some with multifamilies too, and they are as much a problem as the ones with tenants. I think the biggest problem around here is related to work. A lot of people do not have work and must find a place to live. Or a lot of people have a place to live and then lose work and do not get another job right away. Many of them did not grow up in a house and do not know much about caring for property. Yes, there are some nasty ones who hardly clean up after themselves, but most of them are not this way. It seems like when people get out of work they just get depressed and don't act right.

Another streets and sanitation employee believed that commercial properties were in worse condition than residential properties—and for some interesting reasons:

Some of the buildings in the worst conditions around here are not the rental and private homes, but the commercial properties [Figures 4.9 and 4.10]. Many of the liquor stores, grocery stores, barber shops, fast food joints, even motels in this area are all in buildings in poor condition, except for a couple. There are also rental places with bad landlords and tenants. Remember that.

Figure 4.9. Grocery, Bowen and Vincennes (1999).

Figure 4.10. Gas station, Pershing and Rhodes (1999).

Other residents expressed concerns about the condition of commercial properties and consider them the biggest eyesores in the area. During a block club meeting, one resident said:

The biggest eyesore in this neighborhood is the commercial buildings. Think of [the store at 43rd and Cottage Grove], for example [Figure 4.11]. It is operated by a group of Arab men who do not own the property. The property is owned by a Jewish man who lives in the suburbs. The Arab men sell to African Americans in this area. Mostly poor black folks. Now follow this logic. The customers complain about the condition of the building to the storeowner. The storeowner says that if they ask the landlord to repair the building, the rent will increase. When the rent increases, the price of the products will increase. Now these are already bad quality products. Stale oranges, lettuce, tomatoes, but many are packaged goods. The upstairs of the building is abandoned, really ugly. The inside of the place is filthy. The floors are not clean, the

Figure 4.11. 43rd and Cottage Grove (2000).

walls need repair and painting. The outside is very dirty with litter. They do not clean the outside and you have to wonder about the inside. But the point is everyone seems to get a deal. The Arab men get cheap rent for their store. They are not interested in buying the place because they can leave any time, plus the Jewish landlord does not want to sell the building because he can collect rent with almost no repairs. And he is waiting for the neighborhood to change so he can make bigger money. The customers do not get very good products but they get it for cheap. Besides, the liquor sells quickly and it does not get stale. Fixing the building is the last thing that seems to be on the agenda.

When asked what would required for the dilapidated commercial buildings to be repaired, another resident said:

The word is out that the landlord for some of these stores is about to convert the abandoned upstairs into condos. Gentrification is on the way. The yuppies are coming in. The area will have to change soon. There is little that we can do about it. Many of these landlords are what we call speculators. They are waiting for the price of the properties to increase, to know when to sell. So they will keep the property and charge whatever rent they can and do as little repairs as possible. They will repair the building either when the city forces them to do so or when they want to convert to condos, or something else. But the change is coming.

Figure 4.12 provides an example of the sort of neighborhood change residents anticipated. This picture, taken in October 2004, shows considerable changes made to the same building depicted in Figure 4.11, which was abstracted from video footage (video photography) captured in December 2000.

Figure 4.12. 43rd and Cottage Grove (2004).

Figure 4.13. Well-maintained property, 4100 block of Calumet.

But of course, not all properties in dilapidated condition in Beat 213 are rented for residential or commercial purposes. Many of the abandoned or dilapidated buildings are owner-occupied single or multiple-family units. Figures 4.13 and 4.14 depict properties in the beat that have been consistently well-maintained.

Residents and city agents have pointed to what some have labeled *intergenerational failure* to explain the sources of physical disorder among owner-occupied residential properties.

Intergenerational Failure and the Demise of Private Residential Properties

Ardy has lived on one of the blocks in Beat 213 for more than forty-five years. Her children were raised in the same neighborhood and went to neighborhood schools. She is proud to refer to her children as "successful people." But raising children in this neighborhood has not been

Figure 4.14. Well-maintained property, 41st and King.

easy, Ardy says. Many families have not had the same opportunities and results as Ardy and her husband. Ardy indicates that many families have suffered from what she and some others in the neighborhood have termed *intergenerational failure*. When asked why many of the houses in this area were in much worse condition than others, Ardy responded:

Are you serious? Are you serious that you do not know . . . ? Most of the single-family houses around here that you see in bad condition are so because the younger generation has not done as well as the older generation. They have failed their families. It may be because of involvement in drugs—be it crack or cocaine, or something else; it may have been lack of aspirations or hope; it may have been being too comfortable, or what have you. But if you trace back most of these homes here, you will find that the younger generation has somehow failed to have the things that the older generation got for themselves. In some cases, not only have they not replicated what was done by their older relatives, they have done much worse. Some of my friends and I call this intergenerational failure. Intergenerational failure because one generation failed the other. . . . Let us take this house across the street here for example, and in fact the two abandoned-looking houses that you see down the street, and many others. But let us begin with this one here. The parents both worked for the post office. They had good jobs. They got their jobs after desegregation and the activities of the '50s and '60s. . . . The children got caught up with the wrong people and the wrong things and could not maintain the house after both parents died about ten years ago.

Ardy said that a few other houses on her block and on adjacent blocks had deteriorated because of similar reasons. She explained the circumstances that led to the abandonment of one house and the demolition of another.

There used to be a nice brick house here on this lot. It belonged to [a particular family]. One day [the wife] came back from work and saw smoke coming from the building. A neighbor called the fire department. Some neighbors went inside to help because the fire was not so strong yet. They got inside and found one of the kids was strung out on drugs and had caught a bed on fire. Now this was in the middle of the day. . . . By the time the fire department got there, the building was fully up in smoke. By the time they got done with it, it was not good no more. The family moved to the next block. This happened six years ago, and the building was just demolished about four months ago. The other building next to it was left in a will for one of the sons of the family. He had a job but could not fix the property for some reasons. He had some drug problems too. The city took the building because of back taxes. They just boarded it up about a year ago because there were squatters inside of it. . . . This is what I mean by intergenerational failure. Many of the younger people are not doing as good as the older generation; they do not take care of the properties the way the older generation did, the properties become in terrible condition, they get code violations, do not pay the taxes, the city takes the buildings, does nothing with it for a while, and then things get worse until somebody is about to buy the building from the city.

Ziggie is one of the persons Ardy refers to when she speaks of intergenerational failure. He inherited a building from his parents and has not been able to keep it in good enough condition to satisfy people like Ardy. Ziggie spoke about his current situation:

I be under pressure by these people over here to fix this property, but they do not understand my story. They don't wanna hear it. The building got this way because the bank will not lend me money to fix it. I cannot get money from the bank because there is no insurance on the building. . . . Why there is no insurance? Because I cannot afford it. Work is scarce around here. It is not that I want this house to look like this, but I cannot help it. They will have to understand. And I am not the only one like this. There's many people like me in this area, all over the city I imagine. I am talking about people who inherited property but cannot keep them up because the bank will not lend you money.

When I told Ziggie that it is understood that money is needed to repair the roof and the stairs, but that may not explain why there is so much garbage in the yard and the grass is not cut, he replied:

Well, this is demoralizing. If you cannot get money to repair the house, you feel like you don't care. Besides, I have a lot of kinfolks who come to live up in here. People I am helping out because they don't have nowhere to stay. When a house does not belong to them, they don't care, and throw trash all over it. I am tired of cleaning up after them. I know that the city will take the building. It is only a matter of time. But I am tired of the frustrations. . . .

Others did not use the term "intergenerational failure" to explain the demise of owner-occupied properties, but they offered similar explanations. One city police officer said:

A lot of these houses in poor condition belong to older folks who cannot afford to keep up the property. Their Social Security and retirement checks are too little. Their children are often of no help, too. They are either on drugs, away, in prison, or too preoccupied doing their own thing. But it's mostly because their children are not in the condition to help them.

One other longtime resident said something similar:

The younger generation just has not kept up the property as the older generation did. The drug epidemic and the loss of work in this area is what prevented most of them from doing so. But the parents did much better than many of the children that are now between twenty-five to fifty years old. Some of the parents had to be placed in nursing homes and left the children to take care of the property. Some took care of the property if they had good jobs, and others just let the property deteriorate until the city took it.

As the above statements indicate, there are many sources of physical disorder. Residential properties follow different pathways to deterioration. The demise of residential rental properties has been associated with poor property management and poor tenant stock, while intergenerational failure has been blamed for the dilapidation of most owner-occupied private homes.

Poor property management and disruptive tenant stock have also been blamed for the demise of many commercial buildings. However, the dilapidated condition of rented commercial properties sometimes reflects a compromise among landlords, tenants, and customers. Landlords are able to obtain revenue from the buildings without the costs associated with major repairs, storeowners (or other tenants) receive "low rent" because of the condition of the buildings, and customers receive inexpensive products. Many storeowners claim that when they complain to landlords that the building they occupy requires major repairs, they are threatened with rent increases. Therefore, in order to maximize their profits, tenants often refrain from demanding that buildings get repaired unless the problems drastically affect the daily functioning of business. The physical condition of such buildings is likely to continue to decline unless the landlord is forced by the city to make repairs, to avoid (or respond to) code violations, or unless the landlord decides to participate in neighborhood redevelopment initiatives. But whatever the forces may be that cause physical disorder, what does it really mean to drug dealers?

FIVE

Where's the Dope At?

The Need to Understand Drug
Dealing from the Ground Up

This chapter presents ethnographic research about street drug dealing. This qualitative data will explain the puzzles presented in Appendix A, where crime statistics were used to test the relationship between neighborhood disorder, collective efficacy, and the crimes of drug dealing, robbery, and battery. Those statistics were cross-checked with results from a neighborhood experts' survey and field notes to be sure that the hotspots observed in the statistics were accurately reflected in the knowledge of persons actively involved in neighborhood change (reformers), neighborhood patrol officers, and offenders themselves. It was concluded that although the police statistics did not account for every incident of crime that took place in the neighborhood, they were a dependable source for identifying where most of the crimes tended to occur (the hotspots).

It is clear from the statistical results that for both 1999 and 2000, high physical disorder had no significant relationship with high levels of street drug dealing (see Table A.5). Social disorder and collective efficacy, however, were found to be significant, although the relationships were not straightforward. While low social disorder was strongly matched with low drug dealing (76 percent and 80 percent respectively), high social disorder was not predominantly matched with high drug dealing (only 26 percent and 35 percent respectively) (see Tables A.12 and A.13). Therefore, the statistical data say more about what happens in the *absence* of social disorder than about what high social disorder actually causes. These statistics highlight the need for other sources of data to better understand the complex relationships between physical disorder, social disorders, and street drug dealing.

Collective efficacy was also found to have a positive and significant relationship with drug dealing in both 1999 and 2000. That relationship, too, was not straightforward. Few blocks (19 percent in 1999 and 6 percent in 2000) were high on drug dealing when collective efficacy was high. However, when collective efficacy was low, only a small proportion of the blocks (29 percent and 35 percent respectively) were drug dealing hotspots (see Tables A.18 and A.19). The question remains, why? These complex relationships demand a search for the missing *active ingredient(s)* needed for high drug dealing even in the presence of high physical disorder, high social disorder, and low collective efficacy.

To begin solving this puzzle, Geographic Information Systems (GIS) maps were used (see Appendix A) to show where the various drug dealing hotspots were located in relation to levels of physical disorder, social disorder, and collective efficacy. The maps showed that the stable hotspots were situated mainly in the northwestern and southeastern corners of the area. The video ethnography presented in chapter 3 already identified these hotspots as the major business areas of the beat. However, some important questions still remain. For instance, chapter 4 outlined perceived sources of disorder, but how exactly does the presence of disorder influence where drug dealers decide to conduct business, or where robbers select targets? How do participants in social disorder episodes—such as panhandlers and public drinkers—select locations, and how does their presence relate to opportunities for drug dealing? Might panhandlers and public drinkers choose to be in certain locations for the same reasons that drug dealers frequent them? Or is it, as broken windows theorists contend, that panhandlers are the "first broken window"—they invite more serious crimes? What is it then, about those locations?

Perhaps more importantly, how do street drug dealers actually go about selecting locations for business? In doing so, how are they influenced (if at all) by dilapidated features of the location (physical disorder), patterns of social interaction within it (social disorder), and the capacity for collective action against crime (collective efficacy)? This information is very important if we are to better understand the complex relationships among neighborhood disorder, collective efficacy, and street drug dealing. This chapter allows drug dealers and other participants in everyday neighborhood life to "speak for themselves" on these issues.

Drug Dealers' Interpretations of Disorder in Reference to Business Opportunities

The strategy in this research was not to simply ask drug dealers what neighborhood disorder meant to them. Instead, I sought to determine what factors they considered most important for initiating and succeeding in their business, and how and to what extent neighborhood disorder served as a market cue in reference to each important factor. Keep in mind that according to broken windows theory, neighborhood disorder is a cue to offenders that no one cares about the neighborhood, and that therefore there is little to no cost for committing crimes there. I contend that understanding the meanings drug dealers make of neighborhood disorder will be one milestone in further unraveling the neighborhood disorder and crime dilemma. Drug dealers have identified three factors as most important in their business: (1) working within an area of *high demand* for the consumption of street drugs, (2) close proximity to a *high supply* of bulk or wholesale drugs along with high access to a supply of potential street workers to peddle the drugs, and (3) *high exchange opportunities* between dealers and clients—opportunities for quick and secure transactions. Locations are mostly described to the extent that they offer drug dealers these ecological advantages.

Drug Dealers' Interpretations of Neighborhood Disorder and Cues for High Drug Demand

Illegal drugs are in great demand in American society, and in the city of Chicago, Beat 213 is no exception—many drug users and addicts live within and around it. In this section of Chicago, various forms of cocaine (including crack cocaine) and heroin are the major drugs demanded by clients. The products change from time to time as dealers experiment with different products that arrive on the market, but the clients mostly remain loyal to their usual choices. Many street drug dealers view themselves as providing a service to clients who rely on them daily, and in some instances several times a day. For other dealers, it is simply about earning money in an environment where work seems scarce or unmatched with their skills, especially if they have a prison record. In a real sense, drug dealers view themselves as entrepreneurs engaging in economic exchanges that provide money to meet many of the same needs that others fulfill through legitimately earned income. Most street drug dealers are more concerned about how money is spent than how it is earned. Therefore, they feel less guilty about their work when the money is spent to support, feed, shelter, and clothe themselves and their families. In this area that is home to many former felons and few businesses, opportunities for legitimate work are few. Therefore, street drug dealers view their activities as a necessary evil in an area characterized by high unemployment, depression, isolation, and the consequently high demand for street drugs as a form of self-medication.

The drug clientele is very diverse. It includes unemployed street hustlers and addicts, participants in the underground and informal economies, blue-collar workers, college students, and professionals. Some of these clients live on Grand Boulevard, but most reside in other areas and travel there only to purchase drugs. In a neighborhood that is predominantly African American, many white clients can be seen making drug purchases, and then heading back to the Dan Ryan Expressway, north toward downtown, or south toward Hyde Park.

Like their clients, the dealers are also quite diverse, albeit in different ways. They range from flamboyant, unstable, and short-lived users to discrete, steady, and disciplined businesspersons who do not use their own products. The first group of dealers see themselves as making quick money for a short time period. The second group takes street drug dealing more seriously and views it as a steady business that serves desperate people in high need of their products.

One of the most important factors to all street drug dealers interviewed for this research is working within or close to an area where there is a high demand for street drugs among residents and visitors. Drug dealers who are familiar with local social processes know from experience exactly where such neighborhoods are located. Consequently, they do not have to seek out cues in the physical environment to find attractive sale areas. Instead, dealers are often assigned to "leasing[1]" neighborhoods and are offered protection within them by their bosses, friends, or relatives. Occasionally, dealers stumble upon lucrative locations after a process of trial and error.

It is important to distinguish between the wider neighborhood, such as the twenty- to sixty-block radius within which a street drug dealer works, and the exact micro neighborhood location, such as a street corner or a section of a building within that broader neighborhood, where the drug dealer actually "sets up shop" and conducts most or all transactions. While the drug dealers who are not familiar with the area and not

---

1. Some bigger bosses claim monopoly over certain areas, and dealers must pay them a fee to use a location if they want to avoid violent confrontations.

well connected with locals scan large deteriorated areas of the city as potential ideal places to establish a drug dealing business, they use different cues to select precise neighborhood locations from which to conduct sales. Such micro location selection strategies are determined based on the ecological advantage a space offers (discussed below). Here I explain how dealers report that larger neighborhood locations are selected, and when and how neighborhood disorder serves as market cues.

Quick is a self-proclaimed drug dealer who brags about evading the police. When asked what a "run-down building" means to him and other drug dealers, he said that it means poor folks live there and cannot afford to repair it:

Sometimes, a run-down building as you call it, or an abandoned building, some people think it is a haven for selling drugs or prostitution. But not all run-down buildings are the same. You have to know what is the story behind the building. Sometimes you pay no attention to the building itself, but what is happening around it. It depends on where the building is. Like this building down the street. It is a run-down building, windows are missing on the top, garbage is all over the place, people throw it there, and others do not pick it up. A little business is done there, but it is not about the building. This is just the place where it happens. It is not about the building, the way it looks. It is just a sign that poor folks live there and they cannot afford to repair it.

Stash's comments were similar to other drug dealers', echoing a view that properties in poor condition serve as cues for high drug demand. This is a signal that the city does not care about the neighborhood; many residents are poor and depressed, and desire illegal drugs to ease their pains.

Which building? We do not care about what the building looks like. Most of the buildings get in terrible condition because people could not continue to pay their rents or mortgages, with no jobs, or with many personal problems. So to us, the condition of the buildings tells you of the struggles the people are under. This is a place that the city does not care about what happens for now. In areas like this, there are many people who want to ease their pains of a depressing life with no jobs and lots of problems. There are many of these types of areas in Chicago. So you find a spot that you comfortable with, somewhere where you familiar with because of the people that you know and know you. They will come to you. Sometimes you will go to them. You find an angle where it is easy for them to come to you. They know where you will be at.

Flash shares that view, arguing that large deteriorated sections of the city suggest a ghetto environment where many people use drugs or come from other areas to buy them because they know that police response is generally slow in such areas.

I'll tell you like this. More drugs are sold on the streets in dilapidated neighborhoods in general, but not on all dilapidated corners. Why? The trash, boarded up windows and all that you talk about tell you that you in the ghetto, you are in that part of town. This is a forgotten part of the city. How you choose a location in such a place is another issue that I will explain to you later. . . . This is a place where people have a lot of problems and will medicate themselves to deal with the pain. And this is the place where people who live in other neighborhoods and are depressed come to get their fix if they cannot or do not want to get it close to where they live, and have the means to ride over here to get it. It seems that all neighborhoods that look like this one has the same sort of thing going on. I mean many depressed people trying to deal with the problems themselves. So we the so-called drug dealers are their hope, not to say that it is right. . . .

While Flash admits that a large deteriorated section of the city indicates that illegal drugs are most likely in high demand and that the services of the drug dealer are needed, he denies that such deterioration is a signal that residents do not care about or have no control over what is going on in their neighborhood. He suggests that some people in such neighborhoods do not intervene against street drug dealers not because they do not care, but because they regard it as unavoidably necessary because of employment and addiction problems.

One week after my interview with Flash, I was interviewing a neighbor on a street corner when we saw Flash get arrested. The neighbor appeared very upset over Flash's arrest, but then said, "oh well, this may be for the better." When I inquired what that statement meant, she revealed that she had a heroin habit that was on the verge of becoming an addiction, and admitted she was one of Flash's clients. This was firsthand confirmation of what Flash had attempted to explain in our interview the previous week.

Now you ask why people do not chase us out of the corners. Well sometimes, some of them do. But what you must understand is that to many of them, we are giving a service even if they will not admit it. . . . It makes no sense to link the condition of the neighborhood with whether we dope dealers believe people will chase us out or not, as you asked me a little while ago. People in all neighborhoods, even the ones like this one, will step up and come forward against what they do not want to deal with. They do it here all the time. Again you have to remember we are delivering a service to many in need to calm their pains. So if they are not calling the police on us, or telling us to move, it is because they, someone they know well, or someone they heard about has a drug habit and buys from us. . . . We are doing them a service. To me, when you ask what makes us know where we can get away with selling, it is knowing how much we know the people around us need the service and benefit from the money that we spend around here, not if they have boarded-up windows, cut their lawns, or something like that.

These statements by Quick, Flash, and Stash are, in part, consistent with the broken windows theory assertion that neighborhood disorder is a signal that "no one cares." However, to drug dealers, disorder does not signal a universal lack of care about the neighborhood. Instead they attribute lack of care to city government, not necessarily area residents. While drug dealers and residents alike interpret large dilapidated areas to mean that the city does not care, city agents such as the police and streets and sanitation employees interpret the same façades to mean that residents do not care about their neighborhood. These opposite attributions of blame for lack of care create additional opportunities for disorder to accumulate, as city and non-city agents point fingers at each other in their quest to explain who is responsible for neighborhood deterioration, neither side can agree about who should correct the problems.

These testimonies also highlight an important distinction not identified in previous work on broken windows theory. Although neighborhood disorder on the micro neighborhood level such as a street corner is seldom a direct invitation to sell drugs, at the macro neighborhood level physical disorder is interpreted by street drug dealers as a market cue: it says "this is an area with many depressed people and high illegal drug consumption." This interpretation of disorder serves as an invitation to "set up shop" within such a space. Drug dealers know that local addicts welcome them, and addicts from other parts of the city travel there to purchase illegal drugs because they know that such locations are not on the city's priority list. Many drug dealers share this view but insist that neighborhood deterioration does not mean that residents do not care about their neighborhood. Rather, the dealers have their own theories about what drives demand for their product. They believe that large neighborhoods are populated both by people who consume illegal drugs, and by people who resist their sale in the neighborhood. In addition, many residents who do not use illegal drugs are sympathetic about the high demand for illegal drug use in American society and the massive unemployment faced by many inner-city residents that "legitimizes" drug sales in their communities. Drug dealers also believe that residents are not primarily concerned about the use and sale of drugs *per se,* but are worried about the violence and neighborhood deterioration that often accompany it. It is also clear that within such broadly defined macro sections of the city, the micro location drug dealers select for sales is not necessarily determined by the level of physical disorder.

Cash Money expressed this view. He was born in Grand Boulevard but has not lived there much for the last eight years because of several incarcerations, including some for possession of narcotics with intent to sell. He claims that Grand Boulevard has always been his place of business because most of his relatives and friends live there. Cash Money insisted that physical disorder does not mean that people in that neighborhood do not care about what is going on around them. Instead, he said, it means that because of their current situation, people cannot do much to change things. To prove his point, Cash Money invited me to join some of his friends in a volunteer march organized against prostitution and drug dealing in the area. At the beginning of the march, a police officer addressed the crowd, giving the police perspective of the problem:

We need to come together to get rid of the slumlords, abandoned buildings, and boarded-up properties that are at the roots of the problems that we face in this neighborhood. These places are attractions to drug dealing, prostitution, and other crimes that occur too often around here. It gives them the impression that you do not give a hoot about what is going on in your neighborhoods. Please join us in this march against prostitution and drug dealing in your neighborhood. We need to clean up one building at a time.

Cash Money walked most of the route with other residents who chanted slogans to express their intolerance for drug dealing and prostitution in the neighborhood. It appeared clear that residents cared about the problems and the chants were quite convincing: "Yea, yea, we say no, drug dealing has got to go," and "yea, yea, we say no, street prostitution has got to go."

It was puzzling to see some prostitutes and drug dealers, including Cash Money, among the protest participants. There were also a few people I knew to be cocaine and heroin users, one claimed by Cash Money as a regular customer. Cash Money had made his point by exposing me to the complexity of neighborhoods and street drug dealing. As he explained it, the protest was not against drug dealing in general, but against the violence associated with it and in favor of keeping the neighborhood clean. He said that because he is not violent, the protest was not against him. He was convinced that residents were actually protesting against slumlords and neighborhood physical conditions because of resident concerns about potential violence and the decline of their property values, rather than calling for the complete elimination of drug dealing in the neighborhood. This, to Cash Money, was a sign that residents cared about their neighborhoods but also tolerated the presence of certain drug dealers because they know there is a high demand for illegal drugs. Moreover, drug users, nonusers, and dealers are often part of the same dense social network.

To me, the residents are protesting against slumlords, owners who live in other areas and do not keep up the rentals they have in this area. That causes buildings to fall apart and make the neighborhood look bad. They are tired of feeling that they are living in the ghetto. There were many new homeowners in the crowd concerned about their property values. Prostitution is ugly in a neighborhood, and drug dealing too, I guess. . . . But my point to you was that just because the neighborhood looks the way that it is does, this does not mean that people do not care what is going on. . . . They care, but cannot do something about everything. For example, what can they do about drug dealing when there are not a lot of jobs and so many people use dope? Many people do not use dope but the people who use it use it a lot, and they are related to the people who do not use it. . . . If they wanted to, they could be aggressive against dope dealers who were in their march. But they said nothing to us, why? They were speaking to the crowd and no particular person. This is because they know what is going on. They care, but cannot do much about it because so many of them and their family and friends have drug problems. It is like you have to remove all their family to get rid of it. It would be like shooting themselves in the foot. That is not going to happen. . . . So you see we are a part of the neighborhood, part of the community as I told you some time ago. We care about the abandoned buildings, the slumlords, the prostitutes, and the violence involved in the dope dealing. They cannot do much to stop dope dealing by itself altogether because it serves a secret purpose for too many people in this neighborhood. . . . People who come hereto purchase are victims of big drug addiction problems in the United States.

The data presented in this section reflect meanings street drug dealers associate with the physical deterioration of neighborhoods (physical disorder). To them, physical disorder is not necessarily an invitation to sell drugs with no resistance, but rather an indication that such areas are populated with many depressed people seeking to self-medicate with street drugs. As a result, it becomes a very complex issue when a vast section of the population is expected to mobilize against drug dealers whom residents themselves regard as fulfilling a function that is necessary to many in their community. Instead, drug dealers believe that residents' concerns are aligned more with the violence that can be associated with drug dealing than with stopping drug dealing altogether. Nonetheless, to street drug dealers, if anything serves as an invitation to sell street drugs, it is not how properties look and are maintained, but real knowledge about the nature and extent of demand for and use of illegal drugs in particular areas. Of course, knowledge about a potential customer base and drug demand is only one ingredient for successful drug dealing. Street dealers also need easy access both to higher-level drug dealers from whom they purchase in bulk, and to a ready supply of lower-level workers who help coordinate the sales. The role neighborhood disorder plays in these business needs is explained in the following section.

Drug Dealers' Interpretations of Neighborhood Disorder and Cues for High Supply

The second most important factor in the success of street drug dealing is to the ability to work where wholesale or bulk drugs can be easily obtained for retail. The hierarchy of dealers ranges from various types of street dealers and middlemen to big-time controllers. Street dealers were the majority of subjects interviewed for this study. Middlemen often work out of local residential or business structures, providing street dealers with bulk products that can be subdivided into smaller packages for street sales. This is done when retail street dealers operate independently of the middlemen. In other instances, street dealers are employed by middlemen who are employees of the big-time controllers. Under those circumstances, street drug dealers receive drugs prepackaged for street sales. Big-time controllers seldom reside in the neighborhood where the street dealer works. They are mostly mysterious figures who are often the subject of speculation, even by the middlemen.

To the street drug dealer, two sorts of supply are important: bulk drugs from middlemen; and workers such as hypes,[2] lookouts,[3] and errand boys[4] to help coordinate sales. Blunt explains how he and other street

---

2. Hustlers who are often themselves drug addicts.
3. These are people who steadily observe the perimeter to determine if police officers, customers, or other questionable people are approaching the location where drugs are being sold.
4. People who run errands or engage in petty hustling for drug dealers.

drug dealers obtain this information and the relevance of neighborhood disorder to this pursuit.

If I understand right, you asked how we know where the big stash is and how we know where we can get help in the business, right? Well you know where the bigger man is because you already connected with what is going on. You do not just begin right off the street like a stranger and get in. You find out about the connections after months or years of knowing people who know, or knowing for yourself. But the big guys want to set up in an area where they can be protected from the police, to be in disguise without much resistance against them. If you do not know too much about an area and notice that it is a run-down part of the city, you know that there is some underground life there so you try to tap into it through connections. . . . But when you look at certain well-kept neighborhoods you know that you don't stand a chance unless you know the people there for sure. Police in those sections like Hyde Park be all up in your business, and the people too. But in run-down areas you get a sense that the people may be up in your business if they not your customers, but the police will be slow to come unless they on a raid or a sting. So you will stand a better chance in neighborhoods like that. You know that the bigger man will be close by so you can take a chance 'cause you know it [bulk street drugs] will be coming steady and the police be moving slow in them areas. They ain't gone come by themselves. They need to plan it out first and that will take some time.

Blunt explains that a similar logic holds in terms of locating a steady supply of workers to participate in conducting sales.

If you already connected in the neighborhood you already know who will be willing to make a little money on the side dealing dope. You know in the ghetto there always be a whole bunch of young guys without work and without much to do, looking for opportunities like this. They see the fancy clothes, fast cars, new sneakers and all that, and they want it. Many of them ain't got much going on for them at home. If the police rolls up on them they face little penalties because they minors. So you want to be rolling where you can find them a dime a dozen. Now to go back to what you was asking about what the place being run-down and all that have to do with it, I think it is more to do with what you know about the ways of the people that live there. If you notice a bunch of kids hanging out at late hours and during times when they should be in school, this is your hint that they will be willing to do this to make some money. So you make your move to enlist them. Again, that is only if you new in the area. If you already connected, you already know them and enlist them anyway.

Other drug dealers, like Big Money, expressed similar views that loitering signals that many idle youths may be tempted to get involved in
selling drugs. Furthermore, loitering is sometimes regarded as evidence
that drug dealing is already in progress among some of the youth. Or it is
sometimes an opportunity to recruit workers among the youth involved
in loitering but not yet in drug dealing. Big Money draws parallels between recognition of African American adult male street congregations
as spot markets for drug dealing labor and as opportunities to recruit
daily scrap workers.

If you see a bunch of young kids hanging out on the corner when they should be in
school or when it is too late for them to be out anyway, you know that they done
gone wild. You know that they up to no good. At least that is how many drug dealers
think. You need bodies to peddle the stuff so here is your opportunity. Sometimes
you see them hanging on the corner like in front of a liquor store, a vacant lot or a
house, and you already know that they be dealing there. But you see not all of them
already be involved. Some of them are looking for that chance. You give them the
opportunity because you may have a different product. I see it this way. When the
men with the trucks who collect scrap metal want a worker for the day, he knows
that he can drive by somewhere like the corner of King and 43rd St., next to the el
train on 43rd and Calumet, or on the corner of 43rd and Cottage or spots like that
and find an idle middle-aged man who ain't got nothing to do and give him a day
of work by taking him along. In the same way, a drug dealer can pick up young
guys on the street corners because they be standing there waiting for something to
happen, waiting for an opportunity. So that is how you get them. But it is only in
certain neighborhoods this be going on. In some other neighborhoods, the youth
may be hanging out but they be just passing time, not looking to deal dope. So you
must know the difference and make your move. But you can tell the difference if
you been doing this for a minute [or for a while]. . . . Other times, when you see the
certain way that they hanging out, you know it is dope dealing that is going on so
it is not your chance to recruit them because they already spoken for, they already
employed, so to speak.

Purse was one of the few female street drug dealers I got to know. She
claims that most of her customers are other women, especially street
prostitutes. As a result of socializing with them, she has been arrested
on police sweeps aimed at reducing prostitution, but she says that she
is not a prostitute nor has she been charged with drug possession. She
began selling crack cocaine and heroin five years ago after losing her job
because of failing a random drug test. I asked Purse to explain how she

makes sense of the way people congregate or socialize in public space, and if this means anything in her efforts to sell drugs.

People have to socialize, everybody socialize. . . . I don't have to look at where people socialize to know where I can make a sale. I already have my customers. They know where to find me. When I see people hanging out I figure that's their own business. That is what they have to do, and they have the right to do it. I got no time paying too much attention to all that. See, but to me, it is about making the money and safety thing. I been robbed a few times so I don't want to be too much on my own. I hang with my friends and take care of ma lil business that way.

Similar to Purse, Pipe claims that because he has regular customers, loitering is mostly irrelevant to his business. However, loitering does sometimes give him the opportunity to blend into the crowd and remain in disguise.

I do not look at where people are hanging out to know if I can get away with what I want to do there. I already know where it flow. My folks know where I be at. But I be where the action is at. There always be fellers hanging on the corner. This the place where they hang out. That's they spot. But when I am in with a little crowd, I can blend in 'cause there be a special way to do my thing. I hang with my friends and avoid being too much in the open. It is harder to detect me that way if you don't know ma flow.

Cash Money's comments were consistent with how the other street drug dealers I interviewed said they make sense of loitering and panhandling. This is the idea that street corner congregations are not the same, and that panhandling, public drinking, and loitering tell about the different ways people socialize and deal with the pressures of life. In fact, contrary to the "disordered" assumption about street congregations, in some instances persons who appear to be loiterers actually help to maintain security and order in the neighborhood.

As I told you before, you cannot make judgments of people hanging out on the corner if you don't know who they are and what they are doing. . . . People who do not live in this neighborhood and see people hanging out believe that it is always about dope dealing. But when you know the ins and outs of the neighborhood you know different. And if you are a dope dealer, you know that there are some crowds you just cannot blend into because the folks won't be having that. They may be security against you because they know what you be about, and they do not want that in the neighborhood even if they may be sitting there with a bottle of wine turn up upside their head, or carrying on with a bunch of noise on the streets.

Panhandling is often viewed as a form of work for those who may be unemployable.

Now panhandling is a way of life in some parts of every city. It is a job without a job. . . . I am one to think that there is a place for every person. Some people be down on they luck and that is what they do. . . . They cannot keep a job for some reason. . . . Now you ask what it means to be selling dope? Sometimes they can be your customers since they may be trying to make money to support their habit. But not all of them. I think what it means is that this is an area with people who are facing a hard time in their life. That's about it. That's how me and the fellers think about it.

Drug dealers such as Bling Bling insisted that public drinking should not be interpreted as a sign that residents have no control over their neighborhood. Instead, they view it as a way of life among people who are attempting to cope with the challenges of life in yet another way, through drinking. In some instances the street-corner drunk is regarded as an active participant in social control, which includes discouraging drug dealing.

The wine-heads who drink in the empty lots like on the 4200 block of King Drive and near Pershing and Vincennes make the place look more run-down than it already is. These are men and women who been down on their luck and drink together to pass time. It is like their own world to them, but they look out for the neighborhood too. Most of those wine-heads want nothing to do with dope and dope dealers because they been there, done that. They been down that road before and know that this shit can bring a whole lot of problems. Some of them ended up on the street corner because of dealing with drugs when they were younger. Some of the younger ones still experimenting with both worlds. But the older ones want to get the dope dealers and the dope out of the neighborhood because they know about the problems firsthand. Plus they do not want all that violence around them because it will cause the police or the landowner to chase them out of where they congregate. So you find that they try to keep some order where they are and a dope dealer will avoid trying to blend into where they are because they are on another program and will most likely chase you away before you ruin the thing they have going on.

Interviews with the men that Bling Bling refers to as wineheads confirmed that they see themselves in a similar vein. Although such men

Figure 5.1. Hangout, 43rd and King.

participate in social disorder by public drinking, frequent public urination, loud speaking, and laughter in the vacant lot on the 4200 block of King Drive (Figure 5.1) and elsewhere, they view themselves as adding security and order to the area. For instance, Cadillac, one of the men who hang out on the 4200 block, argued that they played an active role in getting the city to board up several nearby vacant buildings to prevent them from becoming drug houses, sites for prostitution, and other illegal activities:

I will not sit here with this half-empty bottle of Wild Irish Rose in my hand at 10 A.M. on a Tuesday morning and tell you that what we are doing is totally right. Me and my buddies sit there drinking all day. We must go to the bathroom after a few drinks so we go up against the wall. The women do it too. We speak and laugh loud, sometimes play a little music from a car, and all that stuff. The homeowners say at the meetings with the police that it does not look right, and we believe them. The police asked us to keep it away from the front of King Drive and we be doing that. But what many do not know or care to say is that we keep order here too. For example, you see this vacant boarded-up building next to us here? We marched with the local people to get the city to get on the owner to board it up so that no drug house can become there, no prostitution can happen inside, or someone cannot burn it down by accident or by being evil-minded. We keep out the dope dealers, look out for rapists, and if someone wants to burglarize one of these homes when the people are not home, guess what, we got an eye on them and they cannot do it. Many of us are disabled or retired and this is our socialization so people have to know who we are before making judgments.

Bike and Bird are two other habitual wine drinkers who congregate in that area. They express particular concern for the safety of school children as they cross the busy street, and worry that they might be prey to sexual predators.

The abandoned buildings, they can't get in them. They can't get in them. First of all we complaining about them around here, board these damn things up. Too many kids coming through. The kids have to come through here. They go to that school over there, that school here. They have to cross the busy street and the crossing guard is not always there. We get there early, and leave late so we can always keep an eye out for them. We know their parents and their relatives. Sometimes we are their relatives too. We want no one to harm them by running them over or by sexual ways or something else. We care about them and look out for them.

These two drunken middle-aged loiterers and their friends complained to the city so that the doors and windows of two abandoned buildings in their neighborhood could be sealed to stop them from being used as crack houses. But Bike and Bird are equally concerned about the safety of children. Two years ago, Bike's niece was kidnapped, sexually assaulted, and murdered, then her body was chopped up and thrown in a dumpster in front of a nearby abandoned building. Since then, he and his drinking buddies have vowed to be vigilant for the safety of children in the neighborhood.

These interviews with street drug dealers and public drinkers indicate that street congregations can easily be inappropriately labeled as criminal opportunities. Although these gatherings may appear to be disorderly in the sense that they look unappealing to many residents who complain about them, they also serve as a form of security and order in the neighborhoods. The testimonies by drug dealers and others reveal both consistencies and inconsistencies with the assumptions of broken windows theory. Data from these interviews establish that knowledge about local social processes and connections to social networks are very important for understanding drug demand, as well as potential drug and labor supply. However, drug dealers are cognizant of the role that neighborhood disorder plays in the process, especially on the broader neighborhood level. Widespread physical disorder, such as abandoned and dilapidated buildings, overgrown lawns, and vacant lots, signals to drug dealers that the area is depressed and is in a non-prioritized section of the city, and that therefore abuse of illegal drugs is expected to be high as residents attempt to self-medicate. Middlemen in the drug-dealing hierarchy find such areas to be suitable business locations partly because they anticipate law enforcement response to be slow in areas where their products are in such high demand. This is consistent with broken windows theory. However, unlike assumptions implicit in broken windows theory, measures of neighborhood disorder do not necessarily signal to drug dealers that residents do not care about or have no control over their neighborhood. Dealers understand that there are different types of residents in these areas, some of whom are their clients, others of whom are their constant opponents.

Measures of social disorder such as loitering, panhandling, and public drinking signal to street drug dealers high unemployment and a consequently large pool of potential recruits with few employment alternatives. These public displays also suggest to street drug dealers that middlemen may be operating nearby because middlemen often rely on idle young persons to peddle street drugs. As a result, the drug dealer who is not very familiar with the area can test out whether such a location might be lucrative for his business. This is also in support of broken windows theory, which suggests that neighborhood disorder will attract the criminally minded to seek opportunities in such locations.

On the other hand, local drug dealers indicate that it is a mistake to interpret every episode of loitering, panhandling, or public drinking as an opportunity to sell drugs or an expression of social disorder. Although drug dealers can sometimes blend into street-corner crowds to conduct sales, in many instances they are forbidden from interacting with certain street-corner groups because group members are concerned that drug-dealing activities will attract unnecessary attention from the police. More importantly, while measures of neighborhood disorder serve to signal high demand and high supply in a broad section of the city, it is not very important in the decision-making process by which dealers select small neighborhood units such as street corners to conduct sales. So if neighborhood disorder does not inform drug dealers about the best micro spaces to conduct business, how do they select such locations? The following section addresses this question by chronicling how street drug dealers select, stumble upon, or are assigned profitable locations to conduct business.

Drug Dealers' Interpretations of Neighborhood
Disorder and Cues for High Exchange Opportunities

As long as street drug dealers are within a general area of high demand for street drugs and have a high supply of bulk product and available workers, the next challenge is to find opportunities to sell the product. Aside from sometimes selling drugs wherever they are, street drug dealers seek out specific locations that offer the best opportunities for their business to flourish. Opportunities are best found in locations that are ecologically advantageous. In the street drug dealing business, there are three major components to such ecological advantage: (1) secure transactions; (2) deniability; and (3) the presence of enablers. Transactions are most secure when they can be quick and secretive and can allow for easy escape from the police if secrecy is compromised. Deniability refers to the ability to deny that one is in that location only to sell or purchase illegal drugs. Enablers are people who in one way or another aid and abet drug dealing by helping to protect the dealers and their supplies from police detection or confiscation. Street locations such as blocks vary considerably in their ability to satisfy these three criteria of ecological advantage.

To be successful in the street drug dealing business, the dealer has to find and keep ecologically advantageous locations, since this plays a major role in determining the extent to which transactions might be secure. As Broker, a serious, steady and discreet drug dealer insisted in 2000, it is all about location.

Similar to the business of real estate sales, it is an issue of location, location, location. Now, not all locations give you the same rewards for your time and the effort that you put into your business. You must know the right ones, or the better ones. You got to have a good spot, and once you have it, you need to take care of business to keep it and make it profitable. It is all about the location that you can have because all sorts of people are out there wanting your product. . . . No I really mean that they need your product. It is a matter of how to hook up with them. This is what I mean when I say that location is key. Location is really key. . . . How well the location is being kept up is not so much of a big deal as where it is at and what is already the what it is known for. You need a prime spot, somewhere where the action is at.

I refer to those right, better, or preferred locations as being ecologically advantageous for street drug dealing. Drug dealers explained how these locations are discovered, assigned, or stumbled upon. The relevance of neighborhood disorder as cues to high opportunity is explained in the process.

To street drug dealers, a location is ecologically advantageous when, simply because of where it is physically located, transactions can be steadier and more secure compared to other locations. Transactions are steadier when there is a pool of drug addicts who live, work, or socialize in close proximity or can get in and out quickly by driving on a major route or by using dependable public transportation. Transactions are more secure when they are quick and secretive. Within the research site, a prime dealing location offers opportunities for quick transactions when it is at a major business intersection with foot and vehicular traffic flowing from several directions, and when it already has a reputation as a place where exchanges are done quickly. However, sometimes drug dealers prefer quieter locations, such as one-way streets where traffic travels in a controlled and predictable direction, or locations where they are imbedded in sympathetic networks. Sympathetic networks allow drug dealers to hide their larger supply of drugs and replenish them when necessary without having to travel too far. Sometimes drug transactions occur quickly in housing complexes staffed by disguised lookout personnel, who serve as dealer security to prevent police interception. Often this is in or near the location where the street drug dealer, relatives, lovers, or friends reside. In any case, for a location to work, aspects of the physical positioning of the locality must help make transactions quicker, smoother, and more predictable for the client. Regardless of how well or poorly kept such locations might be, they are the ones sought out by drug dealers for business.

When asked why he selected a particular corner to sell drugs, Quick replied, "This always been the spot. If you have the connections, this is the spot." What sort of connection is Quick referring to, and how is that established? Interviews with dealers suggest that most locations are either obtained through connections (or networking) or simply stumbled upon. Otherwise, the freelance street drug dealer must test several potentially lucrative locations to determine which works best. Whatever process enables a street drug dealer to occupy a lucrative location, that location is kept as long as possible because it typically offers the three components of ecological advantage: secure transactions, a close proximity to enablers, and deniability.

Neighborhood Disorder and Cues for Secure Transactions

Street drug-dealing transactions are most secure when they are secretive, quick, and allow for easy escape from the police when secrecy becomes compromised. Quick summarized this during a SSO video ethnography group interview with three other drug dealers and himself.

Once you located in the hood, you need you a spot where you can take care of your business right quick. You don't need too long a procedure to get this over with. That's what your customers be looking for, the opportunity to get their stash and keep moving. Many of them may be on their way to work. If they are not working, they in a hurry too. So you need deliver quick. When you quick you also reduce the chances of being hassled by the police. 'Cause to be quick you have to be secretive. I mean you want you customers to know exactly what is the set-up, but you want no one else to know. It has to look like a regular interaction. But you need to be able to escape the police right quick if your secret plan does not work. That happens every now and then.

Equipped with SSO data of the research site and a paper map outlining each street, I asked Quick and the other drug dealers to identify the locations most favorable to this sort of secure transaction. Then while reviewing the SSO movie, which simultaneously showed both sides of each street in Grand Boulevard, these drug dealers identified the exact features that made each location attractive. I also asked them to explain how the physical condition of the location (physical order) and the patterns of social interaction within it (social order) relate to secure transactions. Hot Spot spoke first.

When we look at this map that you have here, the best spots are along King Drive, Pershing, Cottage and 43rd. There are a couple locations on the inside that are pretty good too, like along Vincennes and down on 42nd near the park. But the outside borders of this map be where most of the actions at. . . . The intersection of King and Pershing, King and 43rd, Cottage and 43rd and little spots in between. Now if you go out of this map and further north into Ida B. Wells, then you work mostly out of the buildings. If you go further west across Calumet towards Michigan, on the way to the projects on State Street, a few spots be popping along the way. In this area, though, I already pointed out the main spots.

The other drug dealers agreed that these are the main drug dealing hotspots in Beat 213. Their characterization of the drug hot spots is further supported by GIS analyses of Chicago police narcotic data, as was outlined in the previous chapter.

Excited about seeing the maps and videos of the area, Quick used the SSO data to explain why these locations are hotspots, directly addressing my questions regarding the relevance of neighborhood disorder to drug dealers' activities:

When we look at the map that you just had us write on, and the movie showing both sides of the streets, it is easy for me to answer your questions about why these spots and not others have more activities. . . . Now take me to the corner of Pershing and King. . . . See, this is a main intersection, the buses go by every 5–10 minutes at the most so you can be quick, easy come, easy go, bam bam. You have folks from cross the street at Ida B. Wells going to the grocery and liquor store, Atlantic. The fast food joint, the stores on the other side of King, all bring people together. This is a major business junction even though it is not as busy as say, King and 47th or Cottage and 47th. You can see the police from any direction if they appear. Your customers can get to you from any angle and you can see them. You can disguise because although it is a wide open area, not too much people be able to get up in your business.

"So tell me," I asked him, "how does the way the that the intersection looks, and the way that people interact within it, affect this quick transaction, escape from the police, and secrecy that you talk about?"

As we said earlier, you pay no attention to what the place be looking like, the condition of the lawns and buildings, if people be throwing trash and such. Although if you look at King and Pershing you see lots of trash on the bus stops, in the parking lot of the liquor store, plenty people be hanging out in the lot and on the corner. Many of the people be on their way to somewhere, or waiting on the bus or a person. You know that this is the spot because of the activities going on in it, the reputation it already got for many and many years of its own life. Plus, it is a busy intersection. If you have a spot with this much traffic in a neighborhood like this one, that's what dope dealers will move on, 'cause that's what they be looking for. The trash that is there tells you that the city is slow to service the roads in these parts. It does not mean to me that this is a good place to sell for whatever reasons you asked me about what it makes me think of how people will respond and if I think I can get away with it. That is what you ask, right?

Paps, another drug dealer present, asked to view the SSO data depicting the corner of 43rd and Cottage so that he could explain why some spots there are more lucrative for drug dealing. The video data were gathered in 2000 when the large brick building on that west corner of 43rd and Cottage was in disrepair. A grocery store, fast food outlet, and check-cashing place were among the businesses located on the first floor of that building. All of the windows on the upper two levels were broken and were either boarded-up or left wide open. But Paps argued that to associate the looks of the building and the trash on the corner with why this is a popular corner to sell drugs would be a mistake. He points instead to the ecological advantage of that corner.

Okay, show me that corner again. What do you see? First, there is one bus on each of the streets even while you took this video shot. You see people going in and out of the bus, and you see traffic. You see the brown brick building with the Jamaican grocery store, although it is a Arab store. People going in and out, and the same is with the check-cashing joint, the hair salon and the food place. This is where the action's at. You can take care of business in little time, you can get out and come back with more supplies, or have it dropped off with no one notice. Your customers can feel not too exposed and you can almost guarantee they will get no drama. Now don't let the boarded up window on the top fool you. This is not why dope dealing happens there. It is because of what I tell you. Forget the trash. It is on every corner, even more on some other areas on the interior of the area you showed us. It is not the trash, the windows broken at the top of the building . . . it is as I explained to you. It is kind of funny that you would ask what the building conditions mean for selling drugs. . . . Do people really believe that?

Other drug dealers, like Icepick, believe that the physical condition of a location may be relevant to selling drugs in a particular location. However, Icepick does not suggest that neighborhood disorder is an indication that one can sell drugs there with anticipation of no resistance. Rather, he sees indicators of disorder such as trash as possible tools street drug dealers can use to help facilitate their activities.

See you pick a spot, wherever it look like the place not being kept up clean, grass cut—that's my spot, that's my spot. So much trash and stuff out here, I can hide my stuff up in here. You got so much junk you are not gonna want to look through every bag up in here on this ground. You do not have enough time to do that. If you don't keep these buildings up, if you do not keep the grass cut, if you don't keep it clean and put your little sign up saying, "Warning, stay away, we will call the police," you be something to somebody selling.

"So," I asked, "do you mean that you go sell drugs there because the trash is there or because the building is not being kept up?"

No I do not go there because the trash is there. I go there because as I told you before, there just be some spots that be kicking. The man may pass one down to you. Somebody may be shot or done been to jail and the spot opened so you move in if it is not a gang thing and no body moving on it. Or you may create the spot yourself. I mean you discovered it by yourself, and you build it up to make it prosper. . . . Once you decide to be in the spot for whatever reason you think it be good for your business, if it has a lot of trash or not being kept up, you use it in your favor to hide your drugs, not clean up after yourself, hide in the building. Even if the place be all clean and well kept up, you still use it to your advantage because in this case you can hang out like a regular person and have respectable customers that ain't gone be hassled. Either way, you work what's there to your advantage once you decide to be there. That's what I mean.

Wanting to pursue this line of questioning, I asked, "You seem to be saying that the trash and dilapidated buildings may not attract you to the spot but once you are there, it may help you be productive and stay there?" He said that was right. "So if the trash and dilapidated buildings do not attract you there, what does it?" I persisted. "What is the most important thing in finding a good location?" Icepick explained that the amount of foot and vehicular traffic in a location and to the chance of operating in secrecy or disguise are important factors that are sometimes found in the least obvious places, at least insofar as broken windows theory is concerned—such as near a school. Such places are sometimes selected, not because of some obvious disorderly feature, but because of the possibility for networking: building a clientele there, making it a place of business. "The most important thing," Icepick told me, "is how much traffic comes through." "Do you mean walking traffic, vehicular traffic, or both?" I asked, to which he replied:

Both. How much traffic coming through. See, this is what I am telling you, it's a network, it's a network. If I know that you got something. Let me see, for instance, what a perfect spot is. Oh, it used to be by [a particular street], by the store, by the church, right across the street from the school. [Interviewer; "So why here, why across the street from the school?"] Because everybody figuring out that it not going to go on, they done respect the church, they done respect the school, 'cause the kids gat to come out at recess. . . . That's a prime spot! 'Cause it is busy, it is a productive business. Ain't nobody be looking for nobody selling here, you got to be out your mind to be selling here. But you see, that's the type of atmosphere I want to bring you. I gats to be crazy to be right here selling drugs. This is a public school. Now the penalty for you to get caught one hundred yards in front of a school, it carries from one to seven years in the penitentiary. See the time be increased especially if you like me, you are a felon, every case you catch, the time increases. Like if I catch a robbery, it was from four to fifteen, now it jump from four to fifteen to fifteen to thirty. And somebody just can say I done did it, ain't gat to be done it, once you go to the county, they looking at your background—this is what you do, yea, you did it—you know what I'm saying.

Icepick suggests that finding a good spot also involves trial and error and taking chances on locations that appear to have potential as a lucrative spot. Sometimes those locations are passed down to dealers by their bosses or other interpersonal connections. The sorts of places that were once prime can change, can become no longer lucrative, and dealers move on to other sorts of places. So dealers must be creative and alert enough to recognize and respond when they stumble on good spots.

When a newcomer stumbles on a good spot, he or she must invest time, energy, and resources to make it lucrative. Icepick explains how this is done:

They look around, set up shop, like it used to be right here in this building, standing up, selling drugs. But I guess the police got to shutting them down so much. But they might come to check out an area, they might start standing out in a certain position, posted up somewhere, and somebody will come pass, you know, looking for something, and here you go, just like network. [Interviewer: "But how do they know how to set up? How do they know where to stand first?"] They pick a spot. [Interviewer: "How do they pick it?"] They look at an area, like this area for instance, right here, right open, I can run, I can get away from the police, quick. Okay, I hide my drugs in that pipe or whatever and I stand out here and wait on peoples to come pass.

Icepick indicated that if the location seems comfortable to stand but business is flowing slowly, the drug dealer can use some techniques to accelerate the activity, such as passing out free samples to build a clientele.

Okay, now if that don't start picking up the business, what I would do is I would start passing out freely. . . . Yea, but I would not give you a whole lot. I would just give you some. . . . Rocks, blows, whatever—that is how you pump up the spot, you know, you let them know you gat it—I ain't go sell it to you; just come back about an hour. You see, you want this drug so you gone come back, and you gone bring two of your friends back with you, "Well we ain't losing nothing, let's go 'round there and see, he give you each a piece, you all go tell somebody else." Now here they all come . . . pass it all out free, bam! You have it potent enough where they will want to come back. So when they come back, you let them know that you in this spot and know we be doing this, passing this out on certain days. They all get to come; now you got a drug spot.

Although it is a secretive business, drug dealing also depends on networking, advertising, and investing. For example, Icepick explains the paradox of a dealer giving away drugs for free when he is selling those drugs for someone else. The drugs given away for free are purchased with the dealer's own money so that he can get clients dependent on his product. It is his way of investing in the location so that his activities can thrive there, enhancing his own reputation and building his clientele. He explained:

No, I go take my own money, like a quarter ounce for $200, I might know somebody who throw me a little extra in there so I bag up my work, bag up my money that I paid for and take some more out of it for samples. . . . I'm not gonna cut this . . . I'm gonna leave it potent like this. . . . I pass this out as strong as it is to get you to me, to get you hooked. . . . Right . . . you know what I'm saying . . . now I'm gonna get you hooked on a potent bag and when you come back to me, it's not gonna be as potent as what I gave you first. Then you gonna have to keep coming back to get more. Right . . . right 'cause you hooked. That's the fruit/freak test with anything . . . you know where there is something free there is a lot of people. So I hook you in . . . you in the net now. . . .

While we were sitting in the car, conducting the tape-recorded interview and reviewing the SSO movie, Icepick illustrated how drug dealers stumble upon potentially lucrative locations. A known prostitute and drug addict approached the car to solicit sex and/or purchase drugs. The tape recording captured that moment:

Like, her coming here, a particular drug addict, a particular prostitute, she needs her fix, so she's gonna do what it takes to get it; she wants some heroin, she wants her a rock so she will do whatever. See, they pick these spot; everybody don't go in the house no way, you standing out looking, all you have to do is stand around, this all you have to do.

As the woman tapped on the glass, I asked Icepick, "What is she looking for?" He replied,

She's looking for a trick . . . she wants a date. "Ah, we okay." [The drug-addicted prostitute solicits us while we are sitting in the car. Icepick and I both tell her that we are fine.] Yep, and that's how they come—just walk up on you, and this particular spot could be your mark. Say you had your pants down, sucking your thing, hands in your pocket and everything. That would be the spot.

Icepick said that from this moment on, this could have been his place of business. The location begins to feel like he owns it, so the next steps would be to build his clientele and to employ some people, preferably the young and impressionable who will then take the neighborhood on a downward spiral.

Now, if I sit right here on this block and worked it, worked it myself, ain't got nobody selling for me . . . worked it myself, police ain't been bothering me, people know what I'm doing, now my clientele increase . . . more peoples get to coming . . . now I need somebody else to sell my work now . . . because the police goin' come any minute, so I need some fall guys . . . okay, I gonna get you such and such . . . okay. I'm gonna give you a 35 pack, but I'm gonna give you $60 off. Now you know kids, when they younger, I think they wild and all of that . . . ain't straight in their head because they still trying to find their way out in life, too . . . man, $60 . . . I give them two of these . . . go give me some new jumpers, got get me a new jacket, go buy me all this FUBU and all this stuff, yeah name brands, okay . . . I can make that right here . . . if I sell five what they call them? Jabs. If I sell five jabs . . . I can go get this coat I want, I can get this little car. . . . A jab is a 35 pack. Yeah . . . you call them jab. See, it's a different terminology from this side of town to that side of town, to all up the streets you hear different sayings. Well anyway . . . man that's when everything go to turn down. Now you look down, and say I know you like having these little gym shoes, name brand this, okay . . . now I gonna use Shortie . . . you got his cut and man when customers come you serve them . . . okay? Now Shortie selling drugs. Now Shortie don't want to listen to his momma, dad, or nobody . . . I don't need you . . . now Shortie staying in the drug house . . . Shortie don't wanna go school any more . . . the money is the hook, line, and sinker . . . we keep you looking good because that's all they competing about now . . . what I got and what you got . . . just they don't know they destroying the neighborhood.

These data suggest that in their quest to select locations in which to conduct drug sales, street drug dealers seek opportunities for secrecy and disguise. The level of neighborhood disorder in a given location does not reliably provide dealers with cues for secrecy. Instead, dealers depend on their knowledge and experience about how the place functions. Only when it is determined that a location may be productive do drug dealers capitalize on other features of the space to help conduct business. The features of both orderly and disorderly spaces are susceptible to manipulation by drug dealers in order to facilitate their business.

Neighborhood Disorder and Cues for Deniability

The ability to deny that one is in a location solely to sell or purchase drugs is the second ecological advantage drug dealers seek in micro locations in which to conduct sales. Such locations are often at or close to busy intersections, commercial strips, bus stops, corner stores, liquor stores, barber shops and beauty salons, fast-food outlets, housing complexes, parks, playgrounds, and school yards. The crowds in these locations sometimes provide opportunities for drug dealers to blend in and conduct secret transactions. However, if the dealers seem suspicious and are approached by the police, they can tell a convincing lie about why they are there, since those areas have other, legitimate purposes. As some of the following quotes will show, instances of neighborhood physical disorder such as abandoned and dilapidated buildings, overgrown lawns, and litter play no important role in providing drug dealers with cues about finding lucrative locations.

Indicators of neighborhood social disorder such as loitering, panhandling, and public drinking are also unimportant to drug dealers in their quest for deniability. Instead, the business establishments themselves, regardless of their level of upkeep, are the cues for deniability. Because these establishments attract a constant flow of people, drug dealers and their customers can easily pretend they are there to patronize local businesses rather than to participate in the purchase or sale of street drugs. Stash explained how this is done.

The corner stores, fast food joints, check cashing joints, and bus stops are all places where people be for a purpose. So how you gone tell me that I have no reason to be there, or that I am here to sell dope. You don't know that. I may be here to wash my clothes, buy a bottle of water or something else from the corner store. I could be hanging out waiting on the bus to get here, or waiting for my bossman to pick me up for work. But I can only convince you about this if the businesses are there. So you see, this is why we hang out in these parts because ain't no telling exactly that you here to get or sell dope.

Another drug dealer explained how visiting a parent or going to the store can be a basis for deniability.

I do not live in this neighborhood but this is my place of business. When the police come up to harass me, I tell them that I am here to visit my mother. Other times I say that I am on my way to the store. If they follow me in, I get some pop or some munchies, nothing too expensive if this is not what I wanted to do. They may shake me down but because I can back up what I say they will less likely do it unless someone call them on us. [Interviewer: "So how do you know which spot to go to, considering the fact that there may be several choices to choose from? For example, when you choose a spot to frequent, do you consider how well it is kept up, the sort of people hanging out there or anything like that?"] Ain't too many choices 'round here. What you got, Pershing and King, 43rd and Cottage, over by the el on Calumet and 43rd? It is not too many businesses around here so you go with what you got. In other neighborhoods like Hyde Park, there are more options so you can question which one as opposed to another one. But you go close to where you live or where you and the fellers be hanging at. . . . It is nothing about how well the place kept up but whether or not you have options of places to be. It is whether or not you can show other reasons why you are hanging there so you can deny when they accuse you of being there to deal dope.

A veteran police officer explained his experience with this sort of behavior.

Now a good place to sell it is where people know and frequent . . . like [a particular liquor store] is a good place, for example. There is a store right there. People come to the store, people leave the store, they always have an excuse; they are coming to the store or they are leaving the store. They have a reason for being there. Because nine times out of ten you pull up, you jump out, he is going to go to the store. He is going to buy a pop, buy water, he is going to buy something. "I'm just going in there going to buy a pop."

In the quest for deniability, the drug dealer does not seek out signs of neighborhood disorder. Instead, he or she is more interested in observing how places function in terms of routine and legitimate activities. Whether such commercial sections of neighborhoods that are imbedded within high drug demand areas of the city are well maintained or not, they offer drug dealers and their clients the opportunity to deny that their presence there is exclusively drug-related. Therefore, the cue for deniability is not neighborhood disorder, but rather, knowledge about the routine activities of a micro neighborhood location and the ecological advantage that preexisting businesses provide: a place to be for a variety of reasons.

Neighborhood Disorder and Close Proximity to Enablers

The ability to keep the larger supply (stash) of drugs in a safe and disguised location close to where transactions are being conducted is another important consideration for street drug dealers. This is particularly true for those involved in the more sophisticated operations who desire to reduce direct risks. The less sophisticated street drug dealers encounter more direct risks because they keep all of their supply on their body, sell it, and then go to middlemen to purchase more for resale. The more sophisticated operations involve multiple players, with those on the lower end of the hierarchy taking the risk of actually making the street transactions while those higher up acquire, secure, and replenish the larger supply or stash. The stash must be secured somewhere. Sometimes that secure location is the home of what appears to be a law-abiding person who may receive financial or other compensation for his or her role. In some instances, the stash is kept at the nearby residence of a dealer, a close relative, lover, friend, or acquaintance. I refer to those persons as enablers. These locations used for stashing are selected by drug dealers not because of some reference to neighborhood disorder but because of where they are strategically situated in reference to the location where most of the direct dealer-client exchanges occur. Stash, a local drug dealer, explains how this works.

You always need somewhere to keep the larger stash because there is no telling when somebody may get jealous of your operations and want to rob you, or when the police is on a raid and pull up all of a sudden. There always be someplace to keep it. If you new to the area you get connected but most of the time this is where you know. You do not want the stash too far from where you doing your operations. You want to save time as the business keeps on the flow. [Interviewer: "How do you know where the best place to keep the stash is, and who you should leave it with? Also tell me, in making that decision, how do you think the way that the neighborhood is kept up affects who you may contact to keep your stash?"] Most dope dealers who do not know a neighborhood too well will have to figure their way in if they do not have much connections. So it like this, if they see the place not being kept up, like the grass be overgrown, people homes need major repairs and there is a lot of trash on the streets, old tires, abandoned cars and such, they figure it is helpless people, poor people that live there. The same way I told you earlier that you figure out you in this part of town and you figure people here use drugs, it is the same way you figure a couple people may not mind making a little extra money to pay their bills by looking out for you. Think about it. They live here in a depressed area. But you cannot trust then too quickly and you may want to begin by hiding it somewhere under the trash or in a wall until you get to know who you can trust to leave your shit with. So when you do not know the place well you may think that people in a run down building need the extra money but you do not know for sure because they may want nothing to do with dope dealing and may actually be the ones fighting against it in their neighborhood. As you get more connected you get to know who you can trust, who will not turn you in, steal or use your shit. I mean who will not tamper with it. You get to know that after a while and work out of that information rather than looking at the condition of the neighborhood to figure out who you might test out. Do you get what I mean? [Interviewer: "Are you telling me that if you are not connected to people in the neighborhood and do not know who to trust, you will try to know who may be most tempted to make some extra money by hiding drugs for you by looking at how well the property they live in is being kept up, so you can test them out? But if you already know them you will know exactly who are more likely to hide it for you, so you pay less attention to the condition of the property?"] Exactly. . . . Yes, that is what I mean. . . . Remember though, that most dope dealers already know where they can hide the larger supplies because they usually work out of an area they or their friends grew up in, or they know people who know people there. So you do not make judgments about them because the slumlord ain't taking care of the property, you make judgments based on what you know. The real deal about who is who, and who is willing to do what. Sometimes people owe you and this is how they can pay you back. If you know the neighborhood well you already have all this information and do not have to go figure it out.

One veteran police officer explains how this aspect of drug dealing functions. Responding to the interviewer's question "Based on your long-standing experience working in this area, what is the logic for picking a spot to sell narcotics? What are the drug dealers looking for in a place for their operations?" the officer replied:

Somewhere where they are comfortable. They have to be comfortable and it cannot be far from where they can hide that bigger stash. It has to be somewhere where they can go to get it quickly. Because they will not bring everything out at one time. If they have a 30 pack, say thirty rocks or thirty bags of heroin, they will not bring that out at one time. They'll sell that, and then go get another one. [Interviewer: "So it seems as if they hide it somewhere. What is usually a good place to hide the stash?"] Usually in a house, someone's house. And they know who to talk to, like they will not ask [Mr. J], who works from nine to five, he does everything pretty much by the book, the only thing he might do is drink a few beers on his porch. They'll ask [Ms. C], who does not do anything all day, just waits for her checks, once a month, someone who will not mind a couple of dollars, or a girlfriend. A girlfriend's house. [Interviewer: "So how does the physical order of a place, how the place looks, relate to where a drug dealer goes to sell, or hides the stash? Also, besides being close to hiding the stash, what else makes a place advantageous? What is a good location?"] What do you mean by a good location? To sell it, or to stash it? Stashing it at a place where it is by someone they can trust will not take it, call on them, or cheat them. If they are going to stash

127

it, it is going to be at a girl's house, or [Ms. C's] house. Somewhere where they'll pay but they must be sure that she is not doing it, because if she is doing it, then you are taking a chance with stashing it. Now we are talking about a big bundle here, not what they can sell on the street. They get hypes[5] to sell it on the street for them sometimes. But they will not give them the whole bundle. [Interviewer: "So it is a place where people already are for a reason that is a good place to sell."] Right, but not always; for example, on [one block], even if they do not live there, they say, "We grew up around here." There may be one or two guys over here visiting [a particular person], or visiting whomever. Because on [that block] they do not sell it themselves; they have a few hypes out there. They will be out there, but they will not sell it themselves. And I am quite sure that one of the houses where they are holding it is right on the corner, right there, easy to get to. And one of the guys lives there.

As Stash has indicated, when a drug dealer is unfamiliar with an area, neighborhood disorder may serve as a cue to where potential enablers live because some people desperately need extra money and may be tempted to obtain it by assisting persuasive drug dealers. However, the more familiar the drug dealer becomes with the area, the less he or she relies on physical environmental cues to know what is possible. Instead, locally knowledgeable dealers focus exclusively on their knowledge of the functioning capacities and trustworthiness of social networks. This finding partially supports broken windows theory, but it highlights considerations in dealer decision-making that are not incorporated in that theoretical framework.

All of the drug dealers I interviewed indicated that they did not interpret neighborhood disorder to mean that no one cares about the neighborhood. Instead, they regarded it as a sign that the city does not care about developing or servicing that part of town. Dealers familiar with the neighborhood reported several instances when residents intervened against their activities. However, residents' resistance has little effect in the face of slow police responses, high rates of drug addiction, and the constant influx of people visiting the neighborhood to purchase illegal narcotics.

These findings suggest that drug dealers' interpretations of neighborhood disorder have some association with their business decisions. If efforts are made to reduce significantly the number of abandoned and dilapidated buildings, abandoned cars, unkempt lawns, and vacant lots that are concentrated in certain sections of the city, drug dealers who are unfamiliar with the area will have a few less cues for detecting poten-

5. Street drug addicts.

tially slow police response, high drug demand, and high supplies of bulk drugs and potential workers. This would, then, make business decisions difficult for nonresident drug dealers. However, drug dealers who are familiar with the area and who know the nature and extent of local drug use will not automatically withdraw their business simply because the area is being cleaned or developed—unless, of course, the buildings out of which they operate are demolished or otherwise become unavailable to them.

Repairing dilapidated buildings on street corners and elsewhere may have some effect on the newcomer's perception of opportunities to sell drugs, but not much impact on the longer tenured drug dealers who understand how the local area functions. This will depend, in part, on whether the building in question was being used as a drug house. However, if the building is located in a busy intersection that offers several ecological advantages, merely repairing its external façade will likely have little or no effect on drug-dealing activities. In fact, to the extent that a more attractive façade increases trade, it might actually have the reverse effect, enabling a higher level of drug activity as legitimate customer traffic increases.

Aggressive enforcement of panhandling and loitering laws may reduce drug dealing in a location in which these activities are themselves actually instances of drug dealing in progress. In the absence of panhandling and loitering, drug dealers unfamiliar with the area will be less likely to "test out" the location as a potentially lucrative spot. However, those familiar with the area who do not rely on panhandling and loitering as cues for drug dealing opportunities would be unaffected, since they will continue to conduct business in their usual ways. In any event, it is practically impossible to eliminate street congregations since they are part of everyday life and are often unrelated to criminal activities.

Aggressive enforcement of public drinking may reduce drug dealing activities and help improve the image of the neighborhood in terms of how depressed it appears, especially to newcomers and outsiders. However, since many public drinkers also provide direct and indirect security to the area, their absence may create opportunities for criminal activities such as drug dealing, robbery, and burglary.

Finally, the data suggest that the relationship between neighborhood disorder and street drug dealing is not as straightforward as broken windows theory postulates. Data reported here both confirm and disconfirm tenets of broken windows theory, particularly the assumption that drug dealers will inevitably use disorder as a cue for their activities. As the interviews with dealers and others reveal, the core of drug-related activities in the neighborhoods is rooted deep below what is publicly visible. Street drug dealers insist that their business can only be understood in the context of the high demand for narcotics in American society and the specific problems of lack of employment and opportunity, particularly in inner-city areas. As a result of those larger problems, drug dealers construct notions of themselves as local heroes who provide segments of the population with goods and services they need: they provide one category of people with medication to calm the pains associated with the pressures of everyday life, and another category with income when legitimate work opportunities appear to be too scarce.

As long as there is high demand for narcotics that are not legally available, and as long as jobs in concentrated sections of cities remain scarce, drug dealing will persist notwithstanding levels of neighborhood order or disorder. As drug dealers have revealed, as long as such conditions persist, as areas around corner stores, bus stops, busy intersections, and housing complexes in such neighborhoods will remain attractive locations for dealing, not so much because of neighborhood disorder as because they are ecologically advantageous. They offer drug dealers with market opportunities in the form of secure transactions, deniability, and the proximity to enablers.

Collective Efficacy and Street Drug Dealing

One of the major findings of Robert Sampson and Stephen Raudenbush (1999) was that collective efficacy, defined as mutual trust and solidarity among neighbors combined with willingness to intervene for the common good, was strongly related to low crime. Collective efficacy, they argue, influences both crime and neighborhood disorder. Findings presented earlier in this chapter indicated that although high collective efficacy seems to help produce low crime, low collective efficacy is not sufficient to produce high crime. Therefore, I have sought to understand and explain these processes through analysis of ethnographic data. One key issue of concern was to understand how street drug dealing began in the neighborhoods, and the relevance of collective efficacy in the process. In so doing, I sought to comprehend the extent to which residents and others had mutual trust for each other; the extent to which they demonstrated like-mindedness about standards of behavior in their neighborhoods (shared expectations for actions)—especially as this relates to drug use and sales; and what influenced their willingness to intervene against drug dealing.

I began by gaining a sense of how citizens understood the notion of trust and how it relates to criminal opportunities or crime reduction. They understood trust to be a degree of confidence that people would not act against the best interests of others whether or not that person was present. The notion of trust[6] was best articulated by Ada:

Trust is a strange thing. It can hurt you, and it can save you. When people around here say that they trust each other they mean that they are confident that they will not do anything to harm them—in their presence, or at their back. I say it is a strange thing because sometimes trust allows bad things to happen. Like most of the child abuse that happens is because someone trusts a child to be with another person. Many young people got hooked on drugs because their parents trusted them to go play next door with the children of the neighbors that they trust. You trust your girlfriend so you allow her to give your man a ride, then she takes the opportunity to make a move on him. But when you trust somebody, you believe that they have your best interests at heart.

In order to understand the complex ways that trust, solidarity, and the willingness to intervene relate to street drug dealing, I asked drug dealers and other participants in neighborhood life to explain what life has been like for them, to explain how and when street drug dealing became a conspicuous problem and how citizens have responded in the process. Razor, a repeat offender with multiple crimes on his record, including drug dealing and robbery, and a longtime resident in Beat 213, began the explanation.

Researcher: What was it like growing up in this neighborhood? I mean, what were people like—did they trust each other, did they know each other well, did they help each other?
Razor: This side of town right here? Peoples got along together, they tried to help one another. . . . I do something to you, your momma be able to come over and sit down and say something to my momma. . . .
Researcher: What street was that?
Razor: . . . That's right down the street . . . we used to just like go to one another's house, sit down and try to do our schoolwork . . . everything was real nice out here, man, it was beautiful out here . . . you know had the little parks and everything all fixed up . . . oh you could just walk down the street and everybody would be so friendly. . . . People could trust their children to play together and trust the adults not to hurt them and to correct them. You could also trust that

6. Also see chapter 2 for findings on trust as it relates to collective action against crime.

people who came over would not steal from your house, not even use bad language in it.

Researcher: Are these people still here?

Razor: Some of them are and some of them ain't . . . everybody now scared about some of the things that are happening . . . you know. . . .

Researcher: No, I do not know; what do you mean? What happened?

Razor: From what they seen in the neighborhood . . . how they seen people starting to change . . . you know . . . I might ha knew you . . . now I don't know you . . . I'm treacherous now . . . I'd do anything to you . . . you know but if we grew up together, you ate at my house, you slept in the same bed with me but now you want to kill me. . . . I don't know . . . I try to understand what makes peoples change like that . . . why do . . . why do we do the things we do . . . you know but . . . who am I to say though, but like I said with this neighborhood everything was real nice, but you start seeing a bunch of shooting. . . .

When asked who threatens to kill who, and why, Razor responded,

Razor: Shooting yeah! . . . killing right out in the front of you . . . right in front of your door step . . . this lounge right here . . . everybody used to come party over here . . . I used to sneak in there when I was younger . . . then after it turn out . . . everybody go to fighting. . . . It would be over small stuff among the people that you grew up with. It would start all of a sudden and sometimes you do not even understand why.

Researcher: Where did this all begin, and what did people do about the changes?

Razor: . . . Everybody . . . round up in here, they used to respect the elders and everything, but now, nobody have no respect, and that made the elders cringe, go back into theyselves—just wave they hand. But when they see you coming they just go in the house because as you start growing up I guess you feel like—we as the teenagers felt—man, you can't tell me nothing, I'm grown now. So the elders started staying in their house. You used to see people sitting all out here having their little snowball stands and everything—now it seem like a wave came through everybody.

Researcher: About what year you think these changes happened?

Razor: Umm . . . 1986–87, everything started flipping over—guys started breaking in stores. . . .

Researcher: What happened around '86?

Razor: '86, that's what I'm saying, neighborhoods, flowers everywhere, buildings up, you know, but it seem like everything . . . you see . . . the younger peoples that was coming up, they gat to tearing everything up, selling drugs; you see when the tidal wave came, when the crack came, people just lost the love. When everything started happening, when the crack came, everybody just changed, they didn't care about nothing else, they didn't care about the elders, they didn't care about where they slept at, what they done, so something that was pretty now ruined, you know a lot of these buildings—like I said, there used to be one right here, too, you used to be able to sit out in the front, but you can't do that no more.

Researcher: What brought the crack into the neighborhoods?

Razor: It started, you know, when different people started moving around out the neighborhood, stretching out, going to more areas, they found out about this, and they brought it back to the neighborhood, and test it. So you got strung out, and you got your friend that you grew up with, you know you all have done everything together so I trust you, I'm a try it too, now I'm hooked. Now I'm stealing from Moms, now I'm fighting Moms; now I am fighting my brothers and sisters, now I'm stealing out the crib, I'm getting mad because I can't get none; I'm busting the windows down; I'm doing, now I got to move. Now somebody else done move into where you just left, start selling crack out the building. Now they gat into the fight with the guys on the next block that they knew all their lives; it is a competitive thing now; you taking my customers, you you, like they really own something, like I own this block over here, I sell my drugs here, you can't come over here and sell your drugs. And, everybody just went crazy, man, I just don't understand why peoples don't like for each other no more, don't respect each other no more. I walked down here, I was just speaking to people, "How you doing," you know, you used to be able to get a "How you doing"; now they look at you like "He must be crazy or something. . . ." Peoples I do know, and peoples I don't know. You know, just trying to have a friendly good morning, like old times, the way we used to do it, "How you doing," that's the way I was growed up.

Several other residents echoed Razor's observation that 1986–1987 marked a clear period of change in the neighborhood. They also suggest that the drug market began in the close-knit community, which still remained close-knit as the drug-dealing problems escalated but changed considerably in the purpose for which they were close-knit. Ms. Bank is a self-proclaimed middle-class resident who grew up in this beat and has lived there all of her life, more than fifty years.

I remember it was about 1986–1987 that the neighborhood started changing rapidly. I guess there were some secret changes going on but the shit hit the fan, so to speak, between '86–'87. I think it was the drugs. All of a sudden, in this nice neighborhood, young people started experimenting more with the use and sale of crack. Before that, I knew people who used cocaine and heroin. But when the crack hit the streets, it became a big business where anybody could afford to try it because it was cheap. Now here is the problem. You trust your child to go by the neighbor's for an overnight or to spend some time, but do not know that the neighbor's child is messing with crack. Your child trusts them because they always play together.

Now you know kids, they like trying things out. They try the crack with the neighbor's friend, and then they are hooked. Once they have an addiction, it is downhill from here. You have a relationship with your neighbor, and you do not want to insult them by telling them that their child got your child on crack, so you leave it for a little while until you figure out how to tell them. Then it is too late. Other children are already involved, in worse ways. You no longer know where it started. Now that affects your relationship with your neighbors because your children are stealing from them or doing bad things at their home. You were once a close-knit community to protect your children from cars speeding, or from being on the streets, but now you are a close-knit community to keep your children from going to jail because of the drugs that they have gotten involved in. . . . It is not that you are no longer close-knit; I think it is that you are close-knit in a different way. Remember that when you live in an area for a while, you have neighbors who are also relatives. So when your child does drugs with the neighbor's child, it can often be a relative. . . . What do you do in a case like that?

You act as if you do not know what is going on, but you do. You are close-knit, but it is to protect your children. The irony is that you are not protecting them at all. Because it is this very attitude that causes the problem to escalate. Many people stay behind their windows and do nothing about the drugs on the street. Some people think that they do not care, and sometimes this may be the case, but most of all, it is because they feel as if they cannot do anything that will make a difference, because they know the kids well. They feel sorry for them because of job situations and other reasons. But they still stay close-knit, but do not use this relationship to get the drugs out of the neighborhood.

Statements from various residents have also indicated that trust has a complex relationship with narcotic violations in a neighborhood. As some of the narratives suggest, part of what makes a place attractive to certain drug dealers is the opportunity to hide "the bigger stash" at a trusted location. One drug dealer explains this importance:

A good spot is one where you can keep your stash where it cannot be detected and is protected. You gat to know, you gat to trust the keeper with your stash. You gat to know that they will not turn you in or tell the police about your business. . . . There is always a person you can trust to protect you that way because they be sympathetic about your situation with no jobs around here and all.

While trust sometimes helps to facilitate drug sales in the area, it is also an important component for building capacities for keeping street drugs out of the area. Residents explain that a failing local economy and the entrance of crack cocaine caused severe drug addictions among residents, and this ruined trust among those who were informally tasked to maintain order in the neighborhoods. The main problem has been that some of the persons tasked to help reduce drug dealing face a severe conflict of interest because their children, relatives, or children of their friends are involved in the problem. As Ms. Ram explained, this drastically affects residents' capacities for action against drug dealing.

Understand that before the crack epidemic arrived in this area, you could be sure that your neighbor was not part of the problem, and their children were not part of it. You could tell the heroin addicts and many of them were employed so they did not have to be dishonest to make money to buy their drugs. The problem ones were strangers to this neighborhood. Now you are expected to work with your neighbor to reduce drug problems but it is their children that are the problem. Sometimes they work with you just to be able to protect their children. Therefore, you cannot trust people in those situations, and it affects what you can do about the problem that concerns both you and them at the same time.

There are also complex relationships among solidarity, the willingness to intervene, and neighborhood dealing. One of the most important issues to consider is that these neighborhoods are characterized by high unemployment and poverty. Many people need a helping hand and a few are willing to make certain compromises in order to meet their basic needs. Many of the residents have lived on their blocks for considerable lengths of time and know the major players quite well. They have cross-cutting relationships and conflicts of interest as a result of the various affiliations with their neighbors. These conflicts of interest that exist within their bonds of solidarity sometimes impose limits on their ability to intervene against drug dealing. One neighborhood expert explained how solidarity among residents has not helped to facilitate collective action against crime:

People around here have lived here for a long time, some for over fifty years. They know exactly what is going on. But it is their sons and daughters, or friends of their sons and daughters, that are causing the problem. What are they going to do? They will intervene, but it is not just whether or not they will do something, but what will they do? Sometimes they will intervene and take sides, and make a fight even worse; sometimes they will intervene and tell the police that it was another guy with black pants and a blue baseball hat that was selling the drugs, not this guy here. They will intervene to help if a person needs some help because somebody is abusing them.

They will even intervene when dope dealers are selling drugs in areas where they really do not want them to sell. They will push the dope dealers from place to place, until they are tired. But they may never get to the bottom of the matter, and get these guys jobs, schooling, or something else so that they can spend their time doing something else. It is not about how well you know your neighbors and if you will intervene. It is about what you know about your neighbors when you know them well, and how you will intervene. As a matter of fact, it is not even just whether or not you intervene and how you intervene, but whether you follow up on the intervention. Some people tell dope dealers to move on all day, but they never take the next step to know what is really needed to move them on, calling the police, making the guys see that they are serious, and even helping them. It is the follow-up that matters, not just the knee-jerk reaction. . . . But many people cannot follow up because they know the people so well that they know their limitations. They are fearful of retaliation. Retaliation that may cost them a friendship, some sort of benefit, or even some physical harm. This is a catch-22. . . . Most importantly, they will have to intervene against their own close kin folks and they just cannot do it, especially as they have no trust in the criminal justice system to rehabilitate them.

A former drug dealer further explained the complexity of solidarity and the willingness of residents to intervene against drug dealing.

The real dope dealers that was out here paid you money. . . . I mean they helped out the people because they knew them. I'm talking 'bout they might give you somethin' to make $500. They'll tell you keep $200 give me three, you know what I'm saying? Now you getting some money and . . . is like this. Plus they help out the peoples in the community; they'll see them, you know, "How you doin' today, Miss Matty O?" "I ain't doing so good." "Tell me what wrong," pull up, get out and talk to 'em. "My rent need to be paid." Okay, pay the rent, they pay the rent for 'em, don't look for nothing back; I'm talking 'bout the real dope dealers. These guys out here now ain't nothing but lil ruddy puddies. Lil punks hangin' out, that's all, playin' games, 'cause see when those guys was out—I'm not making them out to be heroes or nothing, I'm not parading them on—but they was trying to do something legit after they get whatever they get out the community. . . . People would not do much against them because sometimes they felt at one with them.

A current dope dealer suggests that those days are not gone. He claims that dope dealers still play some "street politics" to keep their business going by helping some residents:

We gat to give a little every now and then. People up in here in a down-and-out situation most of the time. Somebody always wants something. It may be because they just want more, or because they ain't gat nothing much. They might need some help with some groceries, they rent, looking out for they children. There is always something that you can do to be on they best side. And they will look out for you. You gat to show them some respect and they will look out for you. That is the way it is. You will never imagine which little old grandmamas make a lil change here and there, looking over some products every now and then. People in they house doing nothing, and they check too small. They can make a little change, you do a little business. But you have to look out for them and help them out so you can continue on they good side. You gat to do a lil street politics . . . and help them out with whatever you can.

Residents seldom succumb to this street politics. Many times, residents intervene when drugs are being sold in an area and in a way that they consider very distasteful. Sometimes they are successful, other times they are not. The following statements tell about the successes and failures.

Not all people around here can be bought. Some simply say, "Get away from me, I want nothing to do with you." Others will curse the fuck out of you, sometimes with some humor, sometimes seriously. The main thing is that people get upset when you sell dope in some areas, and leave you alone when you be in some other areas. If they approach you with respect, you will move on, but if they try to be too hard on you, and you been selling there for a while, and you pissed off about losing your business, you retaliate. But some of them succeed because they know how to approach. They know the approach.

A drug dealer was asked to explain the situations in which residents retaliate against their activities.

Researcher: Do residents ever fight back?
Dealer: Yes, some of them fight back.
Researcher: When do they fight back, under what circumstances?
Dealer: When they get tired . . . okay when they going out, buy stuff, newly make their place of residence look new, like these people with these homes. But if I start letting you or if I'm at work and you start to come and sit on my porch and I tell you to get out, you going say, "That bitch or that nigger, they always saying something, man, about what the fuck I'm doing . . . man, I don't need to talk to you" . . . okay. You might see them again. . . . This time you might call the police, some of them might go to jail because of it, now he ain't gone do nothing to you, but he'll have his guys to come back and get you. You might be minding your own business, but you already know. . . .
Researcher: Sometimes, dope dealers might move out, sometimes they might stop, and sometimes they might resist. When do they stop, and when do they resist?

137

Dealer: When they don't want to go to jail anymore . . . they will stop. You know when you let them know that "I'm not playing, I'm not scared, I'm going come out and I'm gonna tell you about my place, you don't pay nothing here." See what it is with some of them, if you come out and talk to them, respect them, don't come hostile, talk to them, you might crack a little sense of humor in there, you know, you might say I understand, I understand. But if you come saying . . . with aggression, they going get aggressive too, you know what I am saying? Now if you see they don't wanna hear what you want to say . . . now it's time for action. Okay, I'm calling the police. I'm doing what I have to do to get you away from down here. They may leave.

Researcher: Because they were asked respectably first?

Dealer: Right, I talk to you, that's when those goes to fighting back. I'm tired, I talk to you, I live here, I've been living here for years, I'm not gonna let you run me out. . . . See that's what a lot of them try to do . . . and a lot of them if they ain't mentally stable will come back and throw something in your house.

Researcher: If you chase them away, they will throw something in your house—what do you mean?

Dealer: Yeah!

Researcher: Throw something like what?

Dealer: A Molotov cocktail.

Researcher: What is that?

Dealer: It's like a bomb.

Researcher: What is it made from?

Dealer: It's made from gas, sand, dirt, gum. Put gum in, when it hits the fire it's gonna splatter; once you throw it through the window and the bottle break it's gonna splatter . . . it has like a stem on it with fire. Like a fire bomb.

Researcher: Do you know of any instances when that happened around here—when people tried to chase dealers away and they did that to them?

Dealer: Yes, yes, right down there on [a particular street]. . . . Yes, used to be an old building right there on the corner . . . it was like a mansion, you know. . . . Nope . . . I'm saying they knock that down now. It is torn down. Used to be that they gave clothes and everything up out of there, used to give food from the back, it's just people there who were trying to keep it up . . . trying to help the neighborhood.

Researcher: What happened to them?

Dealer: The people went out of town to visit somebody and they come back one day and guys just hanging all around their home. They told them, "Why don't you all move away from the house?" The older neighbors try to tell them, "You all leave them peoples alone, they helps the neighborhood, you all tears it down." They throw a Molotov cocktail in there and burnt it up . . . they did not burn it up bad, but the peoples that was living there, they did not want to stay around anymore because they saw the change coming on and what they did . . . they just left, they left all the furniture and everything in their house. I know because I got the furniture . . . a ten-piece black leather pit set. I was staying right across the street, I walked it from their house. They had antique lamps and everything. They still had covering over everything, the pictures and everything, we got a lot of stuff from out of there. And you see when you tear a building down . . . you see the movie where the animal is killed and then come a clean-up crew and another clean-up crew . . . well that's how it is . . . humans act just like animals at times. Okay, now we got the furniture, they come they take the pipes, they take the vanity, toilet stool . . . they take everything . . . copper out the house, they just strip it . . . just strip the building . . . those are the scavengers.

Researcher: Did anybody move in afterward?

Dealer: No, they stop using the house because the peoples, they had somebody that could help them, but they did not want to go into all that; they just shut the building down and boarded it up.

Researcher: And eventually what happened?

Dealer: The city tore it down, yeah, they tore it down.

Researcher: So how did neighbors and people in the neighborhood respond to that incident, and afterward, did they try to intervene again?

Dealer: Some talked, some do a lot of talking, but you know it will be a bunch of them around that gather so that they might jump on a few of them. A few moved on. They took on another spot because the police was on they toes over there. You had to move the operations because it was not worth the hustle by the police. The neighbors kept up the pressure too. They did not back down, and the guys had to move.

Another drug dealer explained that they are more likely to resist collective action against them when working out of a lucrative location.

Dope dealers will more put up a fight when they already set up shop in a spot that is profitable. If they in a spot where business is slow, and you ask them to move, there is no big thing in that. But if they on the corner with most of the traffic, the little business places where people frequent, or another location that be jumping, you know they not about to move for nobody unless you really put on the pressure. Even when you succeed and get them to move, they will come back to test it out later because that is a good spot that their customers know to come.

Collective efficacy theorists contend that residents are less likely to intervene when rules seem unclear —when norms of unacceptable behavior are not well established. I explored this claim in the field and found support. However, this matter is also more complex than it appears on the surface. Residents and others are more likely to intervene against actions perceived to be problematic—such as drug dealing—when they are clear that it is not acceptable. However, they also believe that not all unacceptable behaviors are equally harmful, especially when other problems are considered. And they are more likely to intervene when they believe they have the capacities to follow up on initial actions. In this particular instance, they are more likely to intervene against drug dealing in their neighborhood when they believe that offenders will be brought to justice, and more importantly that offenders will be provided with assistance so that they can earn income through honest and legal means. Broker explained his encounter with such a situation:

Yes, folks agree that dope dealing is bad for the neighborhood and those who use it, especially the younger ones. It is clear to everyone that dope dealing should not be going on. But what is the alternative for many of us? Although someone may be sure that you should not sell drugs in the neighborhood, they also consider that you are out of work, been out of prison, and cannot find decent work as you are a felon. So they sympathies with you and as long as you not causing too many problems and taking care of your little business like supporting your children, they may not approach you so hard as the guy who is causing problems, shooting up the place and such.

I have observed that although residents are often clear about what the acceptable norms are in their neighborhood, they realize that coordination and resources are necessary to obtain results. Therefore, when these are scarce, they question the potential for successful action. For instance, during community policing meetings, block club meetings, and private conversations, residents expressed a great intolerance for drug dealing in the neighborhoods. However, this anti-drug norm clashes with another very prominent and perhaps higher-order norm: every person has a right to eat and feed his or her family. When resources for the latter seem scarce, and when drug dealing appears to fulfill the basic needs of individuals and families, residents who are willing and able to intervene are often forced to reconsider the consequences of their actions. No one wants to feel as if they are taking away food, shelter, and clothing from others, especially from children in desperate need. Therefore, they have been more likely to intervene against drug dealing when their efforts are coordinated with those of others who offer hopeful alternatives for those who peddle drugs as a form of work.

We are still left to answer one of the main questions that made this field research necessary. Why is it that high collective efficacy helps to produce low levels of drug dealing, but low collective efficacy is not sufficient to produce high drug dealing? It is clear from the data that certain forms of collective action against crime help to reduce both criminal motivation and opportunity. Residents who united to supervise each other's children, to assist them with school projects, career planning, and career opportunities appear to have been successful in reducing criminal inclination among young persons who otherwise would not have been as enthusiastic about their future. Many of those neighborhood young persons are enrolled in prestigious high schools and universities. When they return to the neighborhoods during school breaks, they sometimes become involved in neighborhood initiatives and I have had opportunities to engage them in lengthy conversations about their future. They express great desire to remain out of trouble so that they can later enjoy a prosperous lifestyle. Young persons who have less investment in their future have tended to be more doubtful about whether they will engage in crimes such as drug dealing as a means of earning income.

Collective action also helps to reduce neighborhood disorder. Mention has been made of several instances when residents, through the institution of community policing or by other means, have united to force city officials and slumlords to perform necessary repairs to neighborhood properties. While the presence of dilapidated structures may not be as much of an invitation to commit crime as broken windows theorists contend, such structures are often harmful to neighborhoods because they turn away many potential decent and productive residents who interpret dilapidation as a threat to home investment. Residents on certain blocks in Beat 213 have been successful in demanding and receiving the city services necessary to remove such threats from their neighborhoods so that desirable tenants—rich or poor—can feel welcome. Residents' collective action has also been successful in reducing social disorder. For instance, during beat meetings, citizens and their police designate certain issues as priority problems. Loitering and public drinking are often on the list of priority problems. Both police officers and residents leave the meetings with assigned tasks for which progress reports are to be presented at the next meeting. I have witnessed several instances when loiterers and public drinkers have been displaced or assisted. In one instance residents decided that they did not want the middle-aged and elderly men and women who socialized and drank alcohol in public on the 4200 block of King Drive to completely vanish from the neighborhood. They acknowledged that many of them either lived in the area or had grown up there, and that they sometimes helped to deter crime. The compromise that resulted was for the police to instruct the drinkers to clean up after themselves and to congregate in the remote section of the empty lot that was least noticeable from King Drive. Field observations, then, strongly support the notion that collective action is effective at reducing neighborhood disorder and crime.

Low levels of collective efficacy are not sufficient for high levels of drug dealing mainly because drug dealers do not select spaces to sell drugs based primarily on perceived levels of collective efficacy. Rather, they do so because of the *ecological advantages* the space offers for their operations. To street drug dealers, where the neighborhood block is positioned in the neighborhood and how the space is being used provide more opportunities than perceived low levels of collective efficacy within it. Therefore, blocks that are in the interior or remote sections of the beat and are frequented by fewer individuals are less attractive for business. Unless a neighborhood block can offer drug dealers the ecological advantages they seek, it can continue to enjoy low levels of drug dealing because other, more desirable locations are still available. Therefore, the *ecological challenge* a block is under simply by virtue of where it is situated in the broader neighborhood spatial network is the missing active ingredient on blocks that are low on collective efficacy but also low on street drug dealing. For the same reasons, *ecological challenge* is also the missing active ingredient on blocks that are high on social disorder but also low on collective efficacy.

Summary and Conclusion

Ethnographic data in this chapter support, challenge, and explain the statistical finding outlined in chapter 4. The data explained why high levels of drug dealing did not correlate significantly with high physical disorder. Furthermore, when physical disorder was relevant, it was not primarily explained by the claim of broken windows theorists who assume that physical disorder is a cue to motivated offenders that they can commit crimes in that place with little or no cost. Instead, drug dealers interpret physical disorder as a sign that the city may not care about the neighborhood, although the residents might. High physical disorder in a broad section of the city suggests that one is in a dilapidated area where street drugs may be in high demand among some residents who are depressed and who self-medicate with illegal drugs. High physical disorder in a broad section of a city also suggests that there is a willing and able supply of young unemployed persons who may be willing to peddle drugs as a source of income. It is also a sign that city services are slow in that section of the city, and that bulk drugs may be readily available for purchase from wholesale drug dealers. However, to drug dealers, physical disorder is not important when selecting a small neighborhood location such as a street block from which to conduct sales. Instead, such opportunities are found in locations that offer the ecological advantages of secure transactions, deniability,[7] and the presence of enablers.

The ethnographic data also suggest that the physical condition of a block may gradually or rapidly deteriorate as street drug dealing transactions increase. The residential stock of neighborhoods frequently changes because narcotic transactions are often accompanied by violence, property damage, and concern for personal safety. Less stable tenants often replace the fleeing, more stable populations. Management of rental properties often becomes less efficient as less revenue is raised because of the presence of the newer, disruptive population. Drug dealing may persist, but this is not simply because the physical disorder of the place is increasing. Instead, it is often because of the reputation the place has gained as a site for quick, secretive, and secure transactions, quick and assured escape from the police, close proximity to enablers or enabling locations, and the opportunity for deniability.

Ethnographic data provided insights that explain why social disorder had a significant positive association with narcotic violations for both years, as well as why the absence of social disorder is significantly associated with low narcotic violations while high social disorder is an insufficient condition for high narcotic violations. As the narratives from various drug dealers, police officers, and other neighborhood experts indicated, low social disorder is matched with low narcotic violations because many of the locations that are low on social disorder are also situated in locations that are not of interest to drug dealers. Such locations are isolated from the main transportation routes in the beat and are not in the business sections where many people congregate for various reasons. Such locations provide drug dealers with an opportunity to

---

7. The ability to deny that one is in a location for the sole purpose of selling or purchasing narcotics. This is why certain busy commercial streets with liquor stores, grocery stores, barber shops, laundromats, and bus stops are often considered favorable locations. They offer multiple reasons for being there other than participating in narcotics sales. However, not all ideal drug locations are on busy commercial streets. For example, certain locations between State and Federal Streets are havens for drugs but are not busy commercial locations. However, such places still offer what some consider relatively secure transactions, easy escape, high opportunities for concealment, and deniability (the ability to claim that one is visiting a friend, lover, or a relative who resides in the buildings).

"blend in" with the crowd[8] and disguise their reasons for being in that location should they be approached by the police.

High social disorder is insufficient to produce high narcotic violations because although social disorder is sometimes an important ingredient for drug dealing, what is more important is *where* the social disorder is taking place. Recall that most drug dealers are interested in locations because of what is in and around where they are situated. Therefore social disorder is only useful when it is matched with an appropriate location that is also characterized by the presence of certain fast food restaurants, grocery stores, furniture stores, check cashers, and hair salons—locations of *ecological advantage* to offenders.

Knowledge of who participates in producing the social disorder is also important. For example, some empty lots are frequented by *oldheads*[9] or *wineheads*[10] who have a strong dislike for drug dealers, many of whom are younger than themselves. Often, when younger drug dealers attempt to "blend in" with these men (who sometimes panhandle, drink on the public way, push buggies, and loiter), they are often chased away or somehow made to feel unwelcome. Many oldheads perceive the younger generation of rock sellers (their term for crack dealers) as the biggest threat to a neighborhood. Some oldheads are former heroin or cocaine dealers who have become too battered for the profession. They often display no tolerance toward the younger generation of drug dealers (rock sellers), whom they perceive to be involved with the sale of a more devastating drug. Many oldheads have retired from legitimate jobs in the steel industry or service sector. Some are on disability from having been injured on the job. They spend many long hours socializing in empty lots and other uncontested public places, drinking, loitering, playing music out of their vehicles,[11] and socializing in other ways. These men often discourage drug dealers from socializing with them because they do not want to be bothered by police officers who may wrongly perceive them as aiding and abetting their unwanted guests. Sometimes, these men select locations that they know are unattractive

8. It is important to note that drug dealers do not want to blend in too much, as they want their customers to recognize them with relative ease, and they do not want to be mistaken for others who may be targets of the police or of rival gang members. Also, drug dealers are not able to blend in with all street-corner groups; most middle-aged and elderly public drinkers despise them, viewing them as vampires who drain the life out of the neighborhood.

9. A term often used by residents and police to describe middle-aged and older men who frequently congregate in uncontested public spaces.

10. A term often used to describe public drinkers, usually unemployed or underemployed persons who socialize in empty lots in the research site.

11. Often Buicks or Cadillacs.

to drug dealers so that they can avoid the conflicts that might otherwise ensue.

There are many other instances when the location of social disorder and the actors involved in the activities are not inviting to narcotic dealers. Some of these include regular roadside picnics during the summer and socialization after athletic events, after school, or among neighborhood children, teenagers, and adults playing on the streets. More important than the level of social disorder is where the social disorder is taking place and who the actors involved are.

Appendix A also tested the theoretical claims of collective efficacy theory against the distribution of drug dealing offenses in 1999 and 2000. Measures of collective efficacy were derived from a survey of neighborhood experts who were asked questions about levels of trust, solidarity, and the willingness of residents to intervene against actions perceived to be wrong in their neighborhood.

Indeed, this complex relationship between collective efficacy and narcotics violations is reemphasized by the ethnographic data. These data indicate that trust, solidarity, and the willingness of residents to intervene have rather complex associations with narcotics violations. On several occasions, trust is the social capital (the enabling factor) that facilitates drug dealing in particular locations. Many street drug dealers do not carry their entire inventory to the streets for sale. Instead, they keep the larger supply at the residence of a trusted neighbor or in hidden locations guarded by trusted eyes. Such locations must be close to the spots where smaller supplies are sold. The trust between drug dealers and their enablers facilitates smooth and quick transactions. On the other hand, residents who desire to intervene against illegal street drug transactions in their neighborhood must trust in each other that they will not reveal their identity and strategies to drug dealers. A break in this trust often results in acts of retaliation against neighborhood reformers. Trust, therefore, inevitably entails risk.

Furthermore, since drug transactions in a neighborhood are often accompanied by other illegal activities such as violence and property crimes, neighbors are required to trust each other to watch over their property and their children, to protect them from victimization. However, this very trust of the neighbor is often used against them. As narratives from Razor and others suggest, young persons in these neighborhood often get introduced to drugs by trusted neighbors, friends, and relatives. Parents often allow their children to visit with neighbors and relatives because they trust those people to look out for their best interests. But the trust extended can facilitate opportunities for secretive experimentations with the use and sale of illegal drugs. Therefore, trust has an ambivalent relationship with narcotics violations. As a form of social capital, it may facilitate as well as suppress opportunities for involvement in the narcotics violations. Trust cannot always be trusted.

Solidarity also has an ambivalent relationship with narcotics violations. In this study, solidarity was conceptualized in objective and subjective forms. Objective solidarity referred to length of residence, while subjective solidarity referred to the extent to which residents felt as if others who lived there were "like themselves." Ethnographic data indicate that length of time in a neighborhood is sometimes not positively associated with a higher level of knowledge about local activities and relationships. Many residents who lived on some blocks for long periods of time knew little about what happened there, while others who lived there for shorter periods of time but were more socially active had better knowledge. In addition, the length of residence in an area is not always associated with positive sentiments about the place or with a desire to improve it. Residents who have lived in an area longer may not be more likely to intervene. The willingness to intervene often is associated with the ties between the perpetrator and the other.

Ethnographic data also suggest that the willingness to intervene is not always matched with actual acts of intervention. It is what people *actually* do when they perceive that the safety of their neighborhood is under challenge that really makes a difference, not what they *think* they will do. In several instances, persons who have little experience with intervening against crime in their neighborhood express high willingness to do something should anything happen. On the other hand, several neighbors who express high reluctance to intervene have actually intervened frequently. This is because they do so reluctantly. They are often placed in situations in which they have to choose the lesser of two evils: obey their inclination and do nothing out of fear that offenders may retaliate, or disobey that inclination and take action, and see what happens. It is important to keep in mind that there are different costs to intervening against perceived wrongful actions committed by different populations of youths in different neighborhoods. Reactions may be driven by more hostility on certain blocks as opposed to others. Residents and businesspersons are quite aware of those differences.

Even more importantly, as the quotes from residents in this chapter suggest, different strategies of informal intervention yield different results. In some instances, informal intervention has led to acts of retaliation and further victimization; in other instances perpetrators have surrendered. Therefore, what appears to be important is not simply the willingness to intervene, but the ability to intervene in particular ways and to follow up on previous actions. Over time, these follow-up actions are likely to change the structures of opportunity a place offers motivated drug dealers and their clients.[12]

Since the research site and its general surroundings are characterized by highly concentrated disadvantage, there will be high motivation among some of its residents to consume street drugs and to become involved in street drug entrepreneurship as a form of economic innovation.[13] However, street drugs must be sold somewhere, and not all places are equally attractive. Places that are attractive to drug dealers offer certain structures of opportunity. These opportunities include (1) secure transactions, (2) deniability, and (3) the presence of enablers. Over time, patterns of narcotics violations will change as either structures of opportunity or offense motivations change.

As the ethnographic data indicate, trust, solidarity, and the willingness to intervene (shared expectations for action) serve to both inhibit and facilitate narcotics violations. It is true that the presence of trust facilitates action. But what determines the actions or ends toward which trust will be used? It is also true that solidarity among neighbors is likely to facilitate action. But again, how will the actions toward which solidarity is used as a means to an end be determined? Furthermore, the willingness to intervene facilitates action, but what determines what neighbors are willing to intervene against, and how will they decide to take action and even to follow up on their actions in this regard? Stated otherwise, under what conditions will forms of collective action be used to produce public goods (such as neighborhood safety programs), as opposed to being consumed as a private good (such as drug dealing for personal financial gain)?

The answers to these questions are related to, among other things, the broader socioeconomic conditions within which neighborhood actions are imbedded and the conditions under which residents are called upon to take action. The ethnographic data suggest that under conditions of concentrated disadvantage, as far as narcotics violations are concerned, trust often facilities aiding and abetting (conspiracy), solidarity

12. Assuming that the motivation to offend has not been reduced by other factors in the life course.

13. Again, this study does not focus on variations in the motivation to offend during these years. This is assumed to be a constant based on the defined socioeconomic characteristics of the research site and its immediate surroundings.

often facilitates secrecy and protection, and the willingness to intervene is often a smokescreen for personal gains. Stripped from those broader neighborhood socioeconomic constraints, these components of collective efficacy are likely to yield results more closely associated with the production of public goods than with the production of private interests. Future research needs to consider such analyses across neighborhoods.

"I Want It, I See It, I Take It"

The Robbery Hotspots

Understanding Robberies from the Ground Up

How do robbers determine *where* to go to find people to rob, *whom* to rob once they get there, *how* to rob them, and *when*? Moreover, how do the assumptions of broken windows and collective efficacy theories relate to these decisions? Discussions in previous chapters and crime statistics outlined in Appendix A highlight the need to further explore the relationships among the physical and social façades of neighborhoods, collective efficacy, and robberies. As with drug dealing, which was discussed in chapter 5, robbery was found to be strongly related to both social disorder and collective efficacy, but not with physical disorder. Why is physical disorder almost irrelevant to robbery hotspots? How can the complex relationships among social disorder, collective efficacy, and robbery be further explained? Why is it that low social disorder is strongly associated with low neighborhood incidence of robbery, but high social disorder is insufficient to produce robbery hotspots? What does neighborhood disorder really mean to the motivated robber?

Regarding the relationship between collective efficacy and neighborhood robberies, how exactly are issues of trust, solidarity, and neighbors' willingness to intervene associated with robbers? Why is it that fewer robberies occur on blocks with high collective efficacy, but low collective efficacy is insufficient to produce high neighborhood incidence of robbery? This chapter gets closer to answering these questions by presenting ethnographic data about how robbers select (or stumble upon) their targets and how physical neighborhood appearances (physical disorder), social neighborhood appearances (social disorder), and residents' perceptions of the capacities of collective action to reduce crime (collective efficacy) are related in the process.

Before discussing in detail many of the processes involved in robberies, it is important to note that, as one seasoned police officer indicated, "not all crimes reported as robberies are actually robberies, and not all robberies are reported." For instance, robberies associated with the use and sale of narcotics tend to be unreported. In some cases, for example, drug addicts purchase drugs on credit from dealers. When those customers do not pay the dealer at the end of the month or whenever the payment is due, the drug dealer or his/her associates may capture the customer and "take" the payment from him or her. Sometimes, neither the assailants nor the victims define this as robbery. Other times, one labels it robbery while the other does not. Some victims perceive this as justified as long as they are not hurt too badly. Drug addicts who have obtained street drugs on credit have told me, for example, "He gonna have to rob me to get his money because I ain't gat none," or "He gone have to get it hisself." Drug dealers have said to customers in my presence, "I'm 'a rob you if you ain't get me ma . . . money first of the month", "Now don't let me have to hold you up to get ma money," or "I ain't gat to do it to you again to get paid, right?" Police officers and residents may know of these instances, but they may not become part of official statistics because no reports or complaints are made. According to local police, most of the robberies actually reported occurred in instances other than those just described. Most are cases in which the offender and victim may know each other but the offender is not robbing the victim as a form of collecting a debt.

Staging Robberies: Finding Locations and Targets

Swift reports that on different occasions he has spent time in prison for armed robbery, aggravated robbery, assault, weapons possession, and battery. At the time of our interview, he had recently obtained an early release from a ten-year sentence for his part in three armed robberies. Swift was asked to explain how he and other robbers selected a location in which to conduct robberies and how they decided exactly whom they would rob at that location.

Researcher: How does a robber select a location to rob people and determine which people to rob?

Swift: It depends. Sometimes you go to where you know the action at, sometimes the action brings itself to you. You know you out there to rob somebady because that's what you and the fellas be doing, or you do by yourself. You know where the spot be at. You know where they be at. Mostly it be somewhere where you find the right kind of people. You know what I'm saying?

Researcher: No, what is the right kind of place? What is the right kind of person? For example, is there something about the way the space looks, or about the way people relate to each other in that space? What is it about the space where you go to rob, and the people that you choose to rob? Tell me, exactly."

Swift: Again, it depends. . . . It might depend on where you live and where you want to go. It may be just where you feel comfortable. It might depend on where you been doing this for too long and want a break because you feel you 'bout to be caught. It may be that you had a good take there sometime before. It may be many different things. But generally, you rob where you be at for whatever reason if you have the chance. It is where you feel comfortable, or where you get the chance. Or you may go out looking, hunting. Trying to hit a lick.

Researcher: Give me some examples of places and examples of the kinds of people in those places.

Swift: Most of the time you don't want to rob nobady. You would just want to get the money and go. But it ain't that easy all the time, so there be some resistance. So you go to a spot where you can escape easy. Like in this neighborhood it may be a currency exchange, a grocery store, a fast-food joint, outside a bank in another neighborhood, a store downtown, a gas station. This is all a place where people be at with money. [See Figures 6.1 and 6.2.]

Researcher: Yes, people are there with money. But many people are there with money. How do you choose which one to rob?

Swift: There always be somebody distracted. There always be somebody not paying too much attention to what they doing. You want to get it quick. The situation presents itself. You may have a strategy and then again you may don't have one. You see the money, you take it. You know where the money at, you go get it. To make it quick you pull a gun. If they resist, you must show you mean business. It depends on who it is [Figure 6.3].

Researcher: So does the way that the place looks have anything to do with all of this?

Swift: It ain't really matter what the place be looking like. Like I said, you go there because of what happens there, not what it looks like, because there's no telling. It depends too on what you out to get. Ain't nobady 'round here gat lots of money and valuables walking around. You may find that in the suburbs out west, or at

Figure 6.1. A robbery hotspot where robbers taught me to see opportunities beyond neighborhood disorder, as Swift explained.

Figure 6.2. Another robbery hotspot, across the street, in the same intersection with Figure 6.1.

Figure 6.3. Looking for potentially distracted pedestrians in a preferred location.

a grocery store, gas station, or currency exchange. But what it look like ain't gat nothing to do wit what be going on.

Researcher: More specifically, does the way that a place looks—based on the condition of the houses, trash on the street, graffiti on the wall, badly kept buildings—have anything to do with you robbing people?

Swift: You mean a run-down neighborhood? I live in a run-down neighborhood. Basically, most the places 'round this way gat something run-down 'bout them. For example, last year I caught a robbery [on a particular block] with some abandoned apartments upstairs and a closed liquor store next door. But this my regular spot of business. I ain't gon hit there because of the things you ask about. I already explained to you that it depends on the movements in the spot, not the other stuff you ask me about.

Researcher: What do you mean by the movement in the spot?

Swift: I mean you know who be in the spot, what they gat, and how they carry theyself. If I show you, you will know what I mean. You ain't gone go where nobody be hanging out, going to get some fast food, the corner store, doing they lil business . . . 'cause that is the place you most likely to do a quick hit [Figure 6.4].

Researcher: So what about the way that people relate to each other. Do you go to a place where you know people trust each other less, where they do not know each other well, and where they are not willing to stop you?

Swift: What do you mean . . . ? No, you go where the action be at. There be some of the places with security guards and the police be hanging out there. I mean some of the gas stations, grocery stores, and currency exchanges, depending on what time of the day. But some of the spots gat people who look out because there be so many robberies be happening 'round there. But when you hit a lick in a spot where you don't be going too often, there is no way to know how people will react. But if you have a regular place, you have a sense. It all depends. . . . But

Figure 6.4. Another robbery hotspot where robbers search beyond neighborhood disorder for potential victims who are doing regular business, and are distracted in a quick getaway intersection.

if you know that there be people looking out the window, you may think twice about this person right there unless you want it real bad. . . .

Demoute is a self-proclaimed crack addict and street hustler who has also served time in prison for robbery, aggravated assault, theft, and battery. Although he claims that it has been about one year since he robbed someone, he is not sure if he has lost the habit. He explained how he has selected robbery targets in the Beat.

Researcher: Tell me how you prepare for a robbery; I mean, how you choose where to find someone to rob and who to rob.

Demoute: I gat a few regular spots 'round here.

Researcher: Tell me more about these places.

Demoute: Just my regular spot, 'cause I know some of the people 'round there and what they do.

Researcher: What do you mean?

Demoute: Ain't nothing special 'bout this spot other than it is down the street.

Researcher: There are many spots down the street, so how did you come to choose that one? Is there something about the way that it looks, in terms of the condition of the buildings, trash on the street, graffiti, anything like that?

Demoute: No, actually, this spot don't look too bad like some the places 'round here.

Researcher: Well, is it something about what the place looks like in terms of who hangs out there, how many people hang out there, drinking in public, panhandling, or something like that?

Demoute: There be some of the fellers hanging out next to the liquor store next door, and the laundrymart, is that what you mean?

Researcher: Yes, but I want to know if there is something about them being there that encourages you to rob people there.

Demoute: It depends on which robbery you mean. I caught a robbery on this block over here because they wanted to get me back. I been robbed by [name] some time ago.

Researcher: Who is that person?

Demoute: He is a dealer out here. Sometimes they seem to be jealous and rob other dealers who seem to roll harder than they do. They got me, I got them back.

Researcher: How do people here respond to all of what is going on? I mean, how do they respond to robberies, and how do their reactions affect your willingness to continue robbing persons here?

Demoute: I do not pay too much attention to what the folks do around here. I know they call the police when somebody gets robbed, but then again, that is what I would do myself—call the police or get them back. I know some people 'round here that involved in the neighborhood, saying they looking out against dope dealers. . . . The point I am telling you is that when you want it, you take it whenever you see it. If I want it, and I see it, I take it. It is as simple as that.

On several other occasions active or former robbers who had selected victims in the beat explained that their target selection was mostly associated with a habit, observing people, having had some experiences there, and knowing what they could get away with.

Icepick has also served time in prison for various types of robbery and other crimes. He, too, explains how robbery victims are selected.

Researcher: You told me how the drug dealer picks a spot, but what about the robber? How do you choose a good person to rob?

Icepick: Watch'em; watch'em; you have to watch'em; you have to watch'em; you have to watch'em, there's certain things about them. You have to watch, you have to watch they every move. You, you clocking they every move. You trying to wait until a specific spot and when it comes, then you make your move.

Researcher: What do you look for when you watch them? When you say you watch them, you watch them, what are you watching for?

Icepick: I'm watching to see they body language, see is they paying attention, watching they pockets. 'Cause see the money in and out the pockets, you know. And it really doesn't matter some of the time. Now some of the time, you might just go all the way out. I might just say forget it, you know what she looks like, how much money. I might just go ahead and take care of my business.

Researcher: So it just happens randomly, just who happens to be there at the time?

Icepick: Right, right, sometimes. If I want it now and it is here, I have it.

Researcher: What is the specific spot?

Icepick: Okay, you might come where there is not too many peoples, and you make your move.

Researcher: You mean in a remote area like in an isolated alleyway where there is no one to see what you are doing?

Icepick: You may catch a few robberies there too but this is not what I mean. I mean you go where many people go, but you go there when many people are not there.

Researcher: Tell me more of what exactly you mean, and please give me an example.

Icepick: I mean like 43rd and Cottage, a busy intersection where people always go to do their little business and they have money on them. You go there, but not when too many people are there [see Figure 6.4].

The interview data from Swift, Demoute, and Icepick indicate that while there is some loose planning involved in the robbery event, much of the robber's success depends on spontaneous opportunities within active places of interest. Police officers have also attested to the role spontaneous opportunity plays in robbery scenes. As the following narratives indicate, robberies are often associated with spontaneous events that sometimes relate to intention to commit other crimes, such as theft.

Researcher: From your experience, what have you found to be the main issues involved in staging a robbery?

Police officer: It is usually opportunity. If somebody is slipping up, you take advantage of them. If you see somebody, out alone, like, the Chinese place right down the street from the Ritz. A lady went to get some food. These guys went to get some food, then they saw her money. When they came out, they stuck her up. They put a gun at her and told her to give up her money. Then they drove off. They got caught because they went bragging about their own crime.

A neighborhood expert tells of how the attempted theft of an acquaintance resulted in robbery:

Neighborhood expert: Sometimes you know who is robbing you. Like one guy on 39th and King Drive, he used to sell cigarettes, he was an old guy, seventy-seven years old, he sold weed too, marijuana. But every time [the police] searched him, he never had the marijuana on him. [The police] never sweated him for selling cigarettes. So two young guys robbed him, in broad daylight, in the middle of the street, near the Ritz, because he would not let go of his bag. Now the wineheads kind of stick together, because the wineheads caught one of the guys, and [the police] knew the guy, and then [they] went to the house and got the other guy. He was at home with the bag with the proceeds.

Researcher: They were robbing a man they knew with no mask on their faces. Why no mask?

Neighborhood expert: I think what happened is that it was going to be a plain old snatch the bag and run. "Let's snatch his bag and run, what is he gonna say, we stole his cigarettes and leave?" And what happen is that the guy did not want to let go, they hit him and he still did not want to let go, they hit him and he still did not want to let go, so they picked up a brick and hit him on the head. They hit him and it became a battery, and when they hit him with the brick then it became aggravated battery. They stole the bag and that became a robbery, which is often a battery and theft combined.

A resident explained how she became victim to a robber:

It was the end of the month and I went to change my check 'round the corner at [a particular check-cashing store]. I know that people be getting robbed 'round there but you never think it will happen to you. One guy came up and asked me if I had any change as I was entering the door. I said no and the other one who was with him came into the check-cashing place. He was still in there while I changed my check. I made a phone call and he went outside. I went back to my car and they approached me. I said I had no money and they said, "That ain't right, we know you gat it." One grabbed my purse. I said, "Get your motherfucking hand off me." The other one slapped me upside the head, pulled out a gun, and said, "Let go the bag, bitch." I let it go and they got off. But I had placed my money in my bra while making the call. I knew it was 'bout to come down from the way they were watching me. But they do this every now and again around here.

As one robber explained, sometimes other crimes lead to robberies, but on other occasions, the intention to commit robberies results in other crimes such as murder.

Throat: You know, we was down there, trying to rob, trying to rob a guy, but my cousin cut his throat and I wasn't . . . I really didn't, I really didn't want to be involved but I got in the car anyway, but the man wasn't dead. So my cousin he got out his car, the man that he cut his throat, he got out his car and my cousin got a jack out the man's trunk and hit him in the throat. They give us fifteen, well, we got thirty.

157

Researcher: How old were you guys?

Throat: I was, I was what . . . nineteen. But I got mines cut down because they saying "You was just like an accessory. You ain't actually do the murder." So they
gave me fifteen.

Researcher: Why were you guys robbing people?

Throat: [Laughing] That's the way we grew up. That's the way. . . . If you know . . . I'm
a tell you like this. It's a lot of us kinfolks that's all we do. . . . Kinfolks. My, my . . .
my cousins, my family. We just hung together, drank. 'Cause that's the way we
grew up, around our family. Everybody in the household didn't always . . . wasn't
none of them productive. Ain't none of them have no job. All we do is drink
all the time and get out here and hustle. . . . And yeah, in the household and
that's the way it's going on right now. You know, we used to see our uncles and
things do it so, we felt like that. Everybody walk around the house with knives on
them. . . . My mama said at age twelve we had to put food on the table if we had
to live there, so we took it to the streets.

Several neighborhood experts said that most robbers in the area
are repeat offenders who have acquired a habit. Some robbers work in
teams while others are loners. Some specialize in robberies while others
engage in other crimes such as drug dealing. Nightlife, a former robber,
said that some of the most dangerous and successful robbers only work at
night and frequently engage in different types of crime. Nightlife believes
that understanding the life of the "night peoples" is very important if one
seeks to fully comprehend the dynamics around robberies in Chicago.

Researcher: What do you mean when you say we need to understand the night
people to understand robbery?

Nightlife: Because robbery is part of hustling. There are many people out there that
this is all they do, hustle. There are different kinds of hustlers, and a group of
them do robberies very often, but only or mostly in the nighttime. I used to be
one of them, hustling in the night, getting me mine and so on. . . . That's the way
it is with the night peoples, they hustle all the time and sleep in the day.

Researcher: Tell me more about these people and what they do.

Nightlife: Nightlife peoples, say you know you don't see too many peoples out [in the
daytime]. You know it's all different categories of peoples. You got the working-
class peoples that come out in the daytime, and you got the people that do drugs
come out at night. . . . Naw, take that back, it's three types of peoples. . . . You
got the alcoholics, you got they come out in the daytime 'cause they know ain't
gon be too many drug dealers out you know and they ain't gon have too much
problems. They can drink, they can stagger and you know talk to people, laugh
loud and you know feel good about themselves amongst themself. When it go to

getting dark they go home. It's like, it's like vampires comin' out and they know what the peoples that come out at night, they know what they gonna do. We call it, we call it getting some money out here hustling. It's hittin' the lick.

Researcher: What is hittin' a lick and hustling all about?

Nightlife: Yeah, we hittin' the lick, we goin' out tonight and hit a lick so now we waitin' fo somebody he, he ain't gotta be robbed. We can just talk to'em outta our mouf, you know talk to'em sell'em a good story, walking wit'em, talk to'em. Then before you now it, man you been then come up wit something. Okay, the other flip side of the knife...

Researcher: So you walk with them and rob them?

Nightlife: Naw. No. . . . They just talk to 'em they call it game. . . . Yeah, good game, talking, talking, you got peoples that talk real good can sell you something. . . . Yeah, they can sell you something, they, I mean, can talk real good. [They sell you] a conversation.

Researcher: What else do they do?

Nightlife: Okay, these are the night peoples, the night peoples stay out all night. . . . Yep, and the ones that want the drug, they stay out all night. They drive to them stores out in the suburbs; they call it boostin', they go stealin'. . . . Yeah, they go stealin', they get the money. Well they sell the clothes or whatever, they boost the alcohol . . . or whatever, you know. They have on girdles, they have on girdles, the men. The mens have on girdles so they can wrap a lot of stuff around they waist. They might go wrap some expensive clothes around they waist and they have on, you know, long coats and everything around theyself. They consider theyself as not being a low-class drug user.

Researcher: "What are their ages, and what else do they do?"

Nightlife: From fourteen on up to seventy. . . . Yeah, you got'em out here just that old and they think they real slick so they call theyself players. . . . Yeah, and they pickpockets too, they dress real nice, keep a newspaper up under they arm and always have a woman wit'em well-dressed 'cause she, she the one who sticks, yeah. She might walk up on this side and bump you and she holla "Excuse me," he then, he then got ya wallet. Okay, it's gone be a third man that he gone drop the wallet off to, so if you catch him he ain't got nothing. "What is you doin', I don't have anything." Shake'em down, they can't charge'em wit nothing, you know, so here go da middle class. They call themselves middle class too, night people, they rob, they sell drugs . . . for the dope dealers. They been then woke up, but they sell drugs so they can get they sick off.

Researcher: Sick off, what's that?

Nightlife: Yeah, sick off. They might want them a blow, you know what I'm saying or a rock, so he might give'em a pack and say I'll get you a blow this morning and I'll get you a rock at night. You know, you then got yo sick off. So when you come out here hustlin' and sell my stuff I guess you can get you some somewhere else. But see what they do is take the bags, he might give'em some fat bags, they'll break'em down to lil bags, long as he get his money it doesn't matter. So, you know they double jugglin'. That's what they call double jugglin'.

Researcher: Double juggle means to make from big bags to small bags?

Nightlife: Right, you know they break'em down so like here go what they call the low middle-class crackheads as they say, crackheads, they lay here and get the lil money thangs that's left behind. They might go get a bike, steal a bike you know give'em bout six or seven dollars you know, sell it to get'em a roc hook up wit they buddies, they buddies might got a lil money, he might been done got his check today you know, they go spend up, smoke up the money or drank it up whatever they want to do wit it. You know now they broke, they stay out all night everybody now stay out all night hustling, doin' this just keep put drugs in 'em, now daylight come they ain't got a dime or a cigarette or nothing and they hungry and when they eat, you ever seen that movie, uh, the *Lion King,* when them, what was them laughing hyenas went through there and ate up everything. When they showed when the big king died, how it wasn't nothing left, that's how they do, they come home and they don't wanna hear no noise, they just wanna sleep and eat, sleep and eat all day. . . . As soon as night comes they gotta get out there and have enough energy to get out there.

Researcher: That's why you say they're vampires?

Nightlife: Yeah, the vampires they have to recycle all over again, and they constantly do this. They constantly do this until they either die or they go get 'em some help, you know it's sad to say only a few of 'em make it. But they do robberies too, some special kinds of robberies to support their habits, for a thrill, or just something that they do. They are all over the city but you will find most of them in the areas where there is not much work and there is mostly hustling. It is a lot of hustling out here.

Some neighborhood experts have indicated that there is another form of robbery that is often unreported to the police: instances when drug dealers rob each other. As one police officer said:

Most dope dealers don't stick up. If they are going to stick up somebody they are going to stick up another dope dealer. They will know what he has; sometimes he talks too much. Sometimes he will have a stash out. . . . They will have a stash out, they might throw dice, this guy may not be doing good right now, and this guy might be rolling. So he might find out where he lives, or he might have someone else open his crib, get into the safe, get it out.

Although many drug dealers who are also robbers select targets among themselves, there are a few that seek other types of victims. A neighborhood expert described an instance when a former drug dealer turned beauty shop owner and part-time robber:

We did have this one dope dealer that was on our beat, on [a particular street]. . . . He had opened up a beauty shop, and it was not doing too good, he was working his way up. Now from what I understand, he had killed three or four people and had gotten off on all the murders. He had a beauty shop on [a particular street]. I guess when you live a certain way, you get used to it. So what he started doing was he started sticking up currency exchanges. But the way he would do it is that he would stake them out, see who locks up. Because whomever locks up the currency exchange is someone the owners trust to lock up. This is the person to lock it up [the majority of the time]. So he would follow them home and when he gets to their house he would pull a gun on them, take them into the house, into their own house. They would hold guns on the family, and they would take the person. One of the guys would take the lady back to the currency exchange to open it up, disarm the alarm, clean it out, and then they would call and say to let the family go. [Researcher: "So did they call the police? How did they eventually get caught?"] Yes, and they got caught. Everybody would call, but they did not know who he was, they did not need a mask, they had no mask. If you don't know them, you don't know them. And you see, they did not have him on profile as a robber. When she looked at the mug shots, she was looking for robbers, through the robbery pile, but he was not known as a robber; so that may be why she could not pick him out of the book. So he got caught because he kept doing it. So of course, the police stake out the currency exchange, and that is how he got caught.

Many robbers eventually get caught because they approach the same victims repeatedly or return to the same areas where they have had success. Some robbers operate in areas where they are well known, but many travel to other areas. One robber explained why he did not commit robberies where he lived. He described it as simple stupidity:

Robber: I had a guy to come right up to my house and said I robbed him. I never seen the guy in my life. Because when I was doing robberies, I was on the West Side. I never been on the South Side doing nothing.

Researcher: But you lived on the South Side. Why did you go to rob on the West Side, not the South Side?"

Robber: See, 'cause we just that stupid. Criminals are stupid. Now I figure that they ain't gone catch me right here on the West Side but they will catch me on the South Side. I went to the West Side to do the robberies but I come back home on the South Side.

Researcher: So you go to the West Side thinking that it is harder for them to identify you? Why did you go there?

Robber: No, I go there looking for to do what I'm gonna do, rob people.

Researcher: So why don't you do it here?

Robber: Because this is right around the neighborhood. A few peoples knows me 'round here.

Researcher: So you had to go somewhere where you are a stranger?

Robber: Yes, right. But don't I know that there is polices on this side too, and they do network. See that's stupid. That is what I'm saying, stupid. You go on one side of town, do something, and go on this side of town. Don't you know they done gat a report out to describe you, what you look like, and they gat a printout. Here you is walking, erk, erk, pull up. "No I ain't do nothing." They take you to the station, here go a person behind the glass talking 'bout, "Yea, that's him." Stupid, stupid. . .

The above quotes indicate that there is considerable variation in the way robbers select their targets. In some instances they select a location that will allow them to be anonymous; on other occasions anonymity seems less important. Robbers sometimes rob the same target multiple times because such targets present predictable opportunities. However, in some instances, they function based on spontaneous opportunities. There is no evidence that robbers intentionally select their victims or locations based on cues of physical disorder. Instead, they primarily select people in or around grocery stores, currency exchanges, fast-food restaurants, and liquor stores. These are locations that robbers have claimed offer predictable and spontaneous opportunities—places of *ecological advantage*. They are places where robbers anticipate several people to be walking around in a state of distraction with money or other valuable items in their possession.

Robbers pay some attention to issues relevant to collective efficacy because they claim to avoid robbing people in certain locations if they know they are being watched, and that those who are watching them will take action to see that they are brought to justice. However, there are instances when the temptations of spontaneous opportunities are so strong that the robbers ignore the presence of capable guardians or eyewitnesses and proceed with their activities anyway.

I have witnessed instances where collective action against crime has led to reductions in robberies. One good example is on the 4100 Block of King Drive, where residents of senior citizens' housing have become victims of robbery and car theft. Through the institution of community policing, residents, business owners, and local police united to provide more visibility on the streets and advised residents of precautions they could take to avoid becoming a victim, and police conducted swift arrests. During subsequent meetings, there were declines in the robbery statistics as well as increases in residents' sense of safety in their neighborhood. These collective actions against robbery also led to reductions in criminal motivation for two young men who had committed robberies in this area. After their friends were caught on a nearby block for the robberies they had committed, the two young men realized that the residents were serious about getting robbers caught and that they would most likely be caught next. So they changed their habits and finally accepted the invitation of one of the community members to become active in a neighborhood organization designed to assist young people to obtain legitimate employment. As a volunteer, I assisted those two young men with their GED assignments. One year later, they obtained their high school equivalency certificates, and they are currently enrolled in a Chicago area college. Both of them obtained employment through the reference of one resident who is actively involved in anti-crime initiatives in the Beat and who has strong connections with several Chicago area business owners.

I witnessed several other instances of collective action against crime leading to changes in both criminal opportunity and criminal motivation. This is especially the case when residents are simultaneously sympathetic and firm. Participants in collective action against crime are more successful when, in addition to collaborating with the police to have wrongdoers warned or arrested, they also help wrongdoers to gain access to legitimate economic opportunities.

The missing active ingredient between social disorder, collective efficacy and robberies is indeed *ecological disadvantage*. Blocks that rank high in terms of social disorder but do not contain people who are distracted in public with valuable properties in their possession are not attractive to robbers. Robbers are interested in being able to randomly select a victim out of a pool of many potential victims, such as can typically be found on blocks where business establishments are situated. They are not interested, for example, in robbing a random person selected out of a group of middle-aged and unemployed men who can frequently be seen socializing in vacant lots. Robbers perceive that the chances of obtaining a considerable amount of money or other valuables from any of these men are quite slim. Therefore, although social disorder is high on such blocks, few robberies will occur because the ecological advantage robbers are seeking is not present.

Low collective efficacy is also insufficient to produce high robbery rates if the block in question does not additionally offer robbers the ecological advantages mentioned earlier. Since robbers do not primarily select locations in which to seek victims based on perceived levels of community trust, solidarity, and willingness to intervene, the absence of such factors is almost irrelevant to them. Therefore, residents on blocks that are ecologically disadvantageous to robbers can enjoy a life relatively free of robberies in spite of the fact that they are not engaged in collective action against robberies. Indeed, residents have less urgency to organize against robberies if none are occurring on or around their block. However, if their block offered ecological advantages to robbers, robberies would occur there, and this would trigger them to organize to reduce or eliminate the occurrences. More often than not, crime is a precursor to collective action against it. In turn, such collective action is often effective in keeping crime at a minimum. However, the crime is there not because of inaction on the part of residents, but because of broader forces that are often beyond their control. Such forces include the very positioning of their block in reference to the broader spatial, social, and economic structure of the city. Neighborhoods within broad areas of concentrated disadvantage are placed under greater challenge to organize against crime.

However, within concentrated disadvantaged areas themselves blocks are not under the same degree of challenge. This is because not all of them contain or are next to the sort of businesses that certain motivated offenders consider sought-after criminal opportunities. The motivation to commit robberies, like the motivation to peddle illegal drugs on the street level, is associated with efforts at economic gain with a perception that legitimate sources are not sufficiently available.[1] Many residents consider it unfortunate that local businesses that were established to serve the needs of their community simultaneously attract entrepreneurial and predatory offenders. This is a persistent predicament of neighborhoods characterized by concentrated disadvantage.

Summary and Conclusion

This chapter began by indicating that the statistical findings presented in chapter 4 raised the urgency to use field research to unveil the "missing active ingredient" that explains the associations among physical disorder, social disorder, and collective efficacy. Ethnographic data were

---

1. This is true even though several drug dealers and robbers have told me that they have selected their profession because it is a form of self employment, it is exciting, and they pay no taxes. However, most low-level dope dealers and robbers are simply attempting to make sufficient money to feed themselves and their families, to have some money for recreation, and sometimes to feed their drug addictions. On several occasions, they earn less than minimum wage.

presented to explain these complex relationships. Testimonies from robbers, police officers, and various residents explained how robberies are commonly executed. While staging robberies, robbers pay almost no direct attention to physical disorder, find differential opportunities among places of high social disorder, and take heed of factors relevant to collective action against them.

Most notably, robbers thrive on spontaneous or predictable opportunities that are available in spaces mainly because of where they are located and what business activities occur within them. They often select locations where persons are likely to be busy and distracted, with money in their possession. Sometimes robbers carefully select their victims by "clocking" their careless actions and ambushing them with appropriate timing. On most occasions, they carefully select a location and haphazardly select a victim from a group of people that all seem equally vulnerable. Based on these data, I conclude that the ecological advantages a place offers to robbers is the missing active ingredient that explains why the incidence of robbery is not high in most locations of high physical disorder, and why it remains low even on blocks characterized by low levels of collective efficacy.

SEVEN

"That's the Way We Grew Up"

The Battery Hotspots

Understanding Batteries from the Ground Up

Ethnographic data from residents, police officers, and the researcher's direct observations indicate that most batteries that occur in the neighborhoods fall under three broad categories: (1) domestic batteries,[1] (2) acquaintance batteries,[2] and (3) batteries associated with other crimes. Most domestic batteries are related to efforts at establishing domination and control over others for revenge as a result of unresolved conflicts, either spontaneous or long-standing, that escalated. Very often, these conflicts ensue when drug or alcohol use is involved. All of these issues relate to both domestic batteries and acquaintance batteries. However, in addition, acquaintance batteries are frequently associated with delays in the repayment of outstanding debts, such as borrowed money or credit extended for illegal drugs. On other occasions, batteries occur in the process of committing other crimes such as robbery, assaults, gang intimidation, rape, and murder.

---

1. Batteries among persons who reside in the same household. They may be spouses, siblings, other relatives, or roommates. The actions may take place behind closed doors or in public view, in private or public places.

2. Especially when alcohol, other drugs, and the borrowing of money are involved.

Throughout the ethnographic component of this research, considerable effort was made to understand why batteries occur more frequently on some blocks than on others, and what roles physical disorder, social disorder, and collective efficacy variables[3] play in the process. Why is physical disorder almost irrelevant for high incidence of battery while social disorder and collective efficacy matter considerably? More specifically, why is it that few batteries are observed on blocks with low social disorder, but high social disorder is insufficient to produce high incidence of battery? Similarly, why is it that fewer batteries are observed on blocks with high collective efficacy, but low collective efficacy is not sufficient to produce high incidence of battery? As the narratives that follow indicate, batteries often result from what offenders, residents, and police officers refer to as "stupid and petty stuff," "over nothing," or "just to do something." Perhaps most importantly, batteries are most common under conditions of intensified interaction, when disagreements are met with desires to dominate by inflicting bodily harm to prove a point. That point is often related to gaining respect in one form or another.

A Close Look at Domestic Batteries

Offenders, law-abiding residents, and beat police officers were almost unanimous in their belief that domestic batteries are the most common type of batteries occurring in Beat 213. Domestic batteries usually involve injuries inflicted by fist, knife, firearm, or another dangerous object. After identifying the blocks perceived to be battery hotspots in the beat, a beat police officer was asked to explain circumstances that usually accompany batteries and why there were more batteries in some blocks than others:

Police officer: It is really a question of who lives there, how they spend their time, who they interact with, who's got a beef with who, and what they are doing about it. Some people are always fighting wherever they go and if they are in your neighborhood, you will always be called to where they live. Some of the business places have a lot of batteries too because people get into it with each other there, over something petty. But the majority of the batteries we get in this area are domestic batteries. Husbands, wives, uncles, parents, and children—just people living together. But mostly live-in partners.

3. Trust, solidarity, and the willingness to intervene.

Researcher: What is most common about batteries when they occur in this beat?

Police officer: It is almost an everyday occurrence; it is also a lot of kids, parents who sometimes get involved and take it a little further than it should go. But most of our batteries in terms of arrests come from domestic batteries. Because this is the hottest thing going on now.

Researcher: What do you mean it is the hottest thing now? Who is most likely to beat who, and why?

Police officer: There is almost always something else involved in a battery; if it is not drugs, it is alcohol. A lot of them have too much time, they both may have too much time together; maybe they are not working. So I am home with my girl and . . . you know . . . you know. Something little turns into something big. So drugs, alcohol, and too much time because of unemployment, maybe they need a hobby or something. They sit at home with not much to do, argue over something petty, and then somebody gets beaten up.

Researcher: Does this imply that only unemployed people batter each other? Are there batteries among people with jobs?

Police officer: Are you talking about legal or illegal jobs? . . . People who have legal jobs beat up on their wives and family members, too, and these are reported sometimes, too, or you may know about it on the streets. But the majority of full-time working people around here are not as actively involved in domestic violence than those not working, just sitting at home. We get more calls, and I know more instances when it is among people that are unemployed. There seems to be more frustration among them, and they have the time with each other whereas the working spouse or couple has less time together even though they are frustrated with each other, too. And around here, they are just as likely to call in, or somehow, you get to know about it through the grapevine.

Researcher: So what do neighbors do about domestic batteries?

Police officer: There is not much that neighbors can do, unless they know the parties well, and they know that they will respond favorably and not with hostility. As I said before, there are many times that people get involved when others are fighting and it is seen as if they are not minding their business. Even the victims are ready to beat up the neighbors sometimes for coming to their aid.

So neighbors may try for a while and then just call the police when a fight begins because they feel it is not worth it for them to get involved. But that again depends on the history of the fighting and the way that those involved respond, generally. Sometimes, even the police do not want to do anything unless they must; because some people, that is they thing. That is what they do. And as a neighbor you may find yourself in a situation that you do not want to be in because of saying something to them. So again, it depends on who are involved. Sometimes you learn that the best thing is to leave them alone. Then eventually, someone might end up dead and the other in prison. Either that or they will get hurt badly and somebody will finally realize that they cannot live together.

Many residents also expressed belief that domestic batteries are more frequent among the unemployed than among the employed. One businessperson explained her perception of why:

Most of the batteries I know about in this neighborhood are domestic. I mean among people who live in the same apartment. Now there are some of them that you will not know much about and they are rare. Like a professional couple down the street that argue and every now and then there is a push or a punch. I know them, so I know about it. But most of the people that beat up on each other actually have drug and alcohol problems, are not employed, and mostly stay at home. This seems to force some insecurity among the men and they beat up each other, or their women. Many domestics do not involve couples, but brothers, cousins, uncles, sisters, and so on. A lot of it has to do with the drugs, as I said. When people are not in their right mind, they act strangely. Lots of time, plenty of drugs and alcohol and no jobs equal lots of people getting beaten up. I think it is really as simple as that.

Some residents believe that domestic batteries are most prevalent among disruptive families.[4] Therefore, there will be a considerable number of batteries wherever these families reside:

The [block name] is higher with batteries because of the families that come to live there. There are some people that fight wherever they live. Some families are just trouble. They will bring it where they go. They often cannot get to rent good locations because either (a) they cannot afford them or (b) they have bad references because they tear up each place they go. They go to the cheap and run-down places because this is all they can get. And they can squat in the vacant rooms or apartments there, too.

Another resident explained the troubles disruptive families can bring to a neighborhood:

We lived out west and were neighbors with a family that now live one block from us. I do not understand how we got so lucky, or unlucky. But the whole family is a

4. In this study, disruptive families were identified not based on surface variables such as marital or socioeconomic status, but by their known actions. A family was considered to be disruptive when at least one member of its household was known by the researcher (either through direct observation or based on information from reliable neighborhood experts) to engage habitually in neighborhood disruptive behavior such as blatant child abuse and neglect, partner abuse, noisy activities, frequent fights, robberies, or other criminal activities.

mess. If it is not alcohol abuse, it is drug abuse, if not drug abuse it is verbal abuse. Now they fight with each other, and they pick fights with other people. So you have a double effect: people who fight with each other, and pick fight with others on the street. You can see them fighting in the yard. About six months ago, one of the boys stabbed his cousin because of some arguments over drugs. The mother is a drug addict, the father is in and out of prison, the kids are getting old enough to be trouble too. The twenty-one-year-old one has already been to jail and out. Just problem families.

One resident who had recently spent time in prison for several crimes including battery, assault, and multiple robberies said that batteries are more prevalent among some families because this is the way that they learn and teach others how to resolve conflicts:

And you know, that's the way we was growing up in the household seeing them. Didn't nobody really have no love for one another, because if you say something wrong to me, I'm 'a hit ya in the eye and we go to fighting, I'm 'a stab ya, cut ya, do whatever to ya. We saw our uncles do it. We carried weapons on us in the house. [Researcher: "I imagine that they made a lot of noise while fighting. What did neighbors do about this?"] Neighbors? What could they really do? It is best to stay out of they business, especially if you don't know what be going on. I say they ready to hit they own family, cut them, stab them, and they often do. What do you imagine they will do to neighbors for butting in? They neighbors were family too, and they was doing the same thing. . . . You cannot be in your house beating up your woman and children and then turn around and tell the neighbor that they cannot do that because it is wrong. They will turn right around and ask you who the hell you think you is to be lecturing them about something that you do too.

Other residents expressed belief that many of the persons who commit batteries were themselves victims of battery or witnessed physical abuse in the household for extended periods of time. One motivated offender, who at the time of the interview claimed to have been wanted by the police for battery, robbery, and parole violation, explained some of the violence he witnessed as a child:

When I was little, I always used to wonder why my family stayed in it so much. Because that is all I used to see when I was little. My uncle cut his mother from earlobe to earlobe. Yea, we all jumped on him with force. . . . Because his mama was in him and his woman business. He said she ain't had no business telling her to do nothing, or telling her nothing about him. She said something, he cut, hit her from ear to ear.

My cousin said something to him, he hit him with one of those ball pin hammers, hit him in the top of the head. My other cousin looked across, got to talking; he slapped him, but he had hit him with that knife. And he told him, "Shake your head," and when he turned his face, skin opened up like that, seehu, skin opening up like that. . . . I saw the white meat and everything in his cheek, ooh-wee. . . .

Another example of how family violence impacts the life of children and is associated with future criminal behavior was presented during a lengthy interview with Icepick. One of the characters featured in earlier portions of this study, Icepick is a thirty-seven-year-old who, by his own admission, has spent time in prison for crimes including attempted murder, murder, aggravated battery, armed robbery, and narcotics possession. Icepick refers to his childhood as "terrified," and he describes the pervasive physical abuse among family members and the manner in which the violence traveled with them to every new address.

Researcher: "Basically, just tell me your life story."

Icepick: I suffer from . . . major depression. It started out down . . . down south. You know, from abuse from my stepfather. And he brung us to the city. Man . . . I ain't, I ain't like it here, but you know he treated us real bad, so I took it to the streets. I been out here for numerous years like I say, going back and forwards to jail. And my mother, she basically, she basically just, just said grow up on ya own. But I've been around; I've been around the West Side. Really I growed up on the West Side. You know, but . . . I came to the South Side to live. I stayed on [an address in the beat] and uh . . . me and my cousin, we uh . . . caught a murder around here and uh . . . but first of all . . . I went to, I went to [a juvenile home] when I was fourteen.

Researcher: What was your childhood like?

Icepick: Childhood, terrorized! . . . My mama left and she had move wit my stepdad, terrorized! They use to just . . . I never did see him drink too much but you know, he was hell, he was hell. I saw him as wanting to be a controller, a woman 'buser [abuser], know what I'm saying? He always used to just beat my mama for no apparent reason.

He just come in the house, wake us up three in the morning and make us watch them while they fight. She don't be doing no fightin', she just cryin', and we hearing all this and shaking like a mug, they couldn't stop me from shaking.

Researcher: How old were you?

Icepick: Five.

Researcher: What was your relationship like with your mother?

Icepick: And me and my mother, we like talk every now and then but I'll snap. I'll snap and you know I'll get to telling her all different types of things, but it hurt me when I think about it. But I just want to know why I have the attitude, like I have. You know what I'm saying? How can I be talking to you one minute and then . . . it seem like, I just go into another person? Getting mad, upset, angry. You know, like I want to beat you up?

Researcher: Have you sought help for that?

Icepick: I been talking to this psychiatrist, but they telling me, you know, it's something that's in yo' past that you bitter about, that yo' mama allow to happen to you, and that's why I was thinking about my stepfather. You know he used to do us real bad.

Researcher: Tell me more about your stepfather and family life.

Icepick: My stepfather, I hated him. It make my blood boil up when I think about him. But, you know, it just things out here you gat to forget. They say it ain't no real Satan out here [and people change]. But the man was a trip, man. I told my mother, "What you was in love with?" I don't know, because the man, he did not believe in putting on no deodorant. He be funkier than a goat! . . . Yea, he be funkier than a goat. I said to her, "How could you lay upside that man and he like that? I see you in there in water everyday and you gat him." I said, oh no.

The man used to embarrass us, used to take us down Jew Town, you know. But I ain't look at it too much as embarrassing, but he could a gatten my sister a drum stick. He gat her trying to play drums with a bread spoon, and one drum stick. . . . You know those big long-handle bread spoons they gat? Down Jew Town. Hustling! I'm playing the bass. . . . He talking about "Move your hand up there" [teaching him how to play the bass guitar, playing a blues tune].

I was coming up there then, I was thirteen. I told my mama I'm tired of him. When I turn fourteen, if you don't get rid of him, I'm killing him! For real! That was on and everything, I was gone kill him. That man, that man, that man shot my mother in the hand.

Icepick explained that from an early age, his stepfather and mother began neglecting him and his sisters by leaving them alone at home for extended periods of time. Relatives became aware of the situation and allowed the children to live with them. He claims that his parents eventually decided to keep them after his stepfather learned that his mother could obtain money for them from the welfare system. The stepfather wanted that money. Icepick explained how he felt when he learned that he was about to be reunited with his mother and stepfather in what he considered a very disruptive home:

Icepick: He wanted to go out there and leave us. But when he found out that the [city] was giving you a lot of money for kids, my mama had six kids, they could be giving her a ugly check and food stamps. She used to come get us now and then. He heard, she can get some money off of us for him. So when I saw their car come and I see their faces, I was running. I did not want to go with them. I'm crying, "No, I don't wanna go with you all." . . . I ain't want to go with them. . . . That was when we were . . . with my aunty. . . .

No, you came and gat me not because you love, you came and gat me because you wanted to get some money off me to give to this little short man. . . . And that's why he wanted us. His kinfolks done told her, "Oh where your kids at, girl you can get on aid with them, go down there, and get you woo woo 'mount of money." Her and he come looking for us.

But anyway, my mom and them pull up, I started getting sick. Because that man had me so nervous and so upset all the time, I had developed ulcers at an early age. . . . That shows you how scared I was, shaking, because I know every time I see him is bad news. Is something always fittin' to go on, he fittin' to start something. And he gat kids just like him. My other brothers and sisters just like, just like him, they act just like him. I told them they all crazy.

Researcher: What was wrong with him? Why was he like that?

Icepick: Who?

Researcher: Your stepfather.

Icepick: My stepfather, he was just like that, he was a control freak. He wanted to control things and you know, wanna beat up on his woman. He used to whoop my mother all the time.

Researcher: Why did he want to control her? Did she make more money than he did, and he felt insecure about it?

Icepick: No, he kept her in the house all the time. She used to sing, had a beautiful voice. She used to back up for [a popular artist] and all this, she could have had her a little career. She let him take her from everything, just to get abuse for eighteen years, eighteen years he abused her.

Researcher: So did this make you angry, too?

Icepick: I figured that, you know, I am not saying that she is a woman and she ain't strong or nothing, being a woman. Because every time that you and me get into something, you want me to beat ma kids too, yea, like whoop us. But he ain't want his child whoop. In the summer, almost everyday, everyday he come home he let up all the windows in the house, open all the doors. I use to say, me and my sisters and them, "What you opening up all the windows for, what, if you can't get out the door you gone jump out the window?"

Researcher: What else did your stepfather do?

Icepick: That man was crazy, man, he shot her in the hand, broked all her fingers. She ranned again, and left us . . . this time [at a different address]. Him and her went and left us at another house. . . . Yes, she went with him. She went wit him and told them way at the hospital that she got shot by some gangbangers. They patched her up, him and her went ahead, again.

Now, he come on back, she come on back, we moved. Him and her fighting all the time again. . . . Well, she threw an ashtray trying to hit him. We had a mirror in our home wit the closet door, he opened the door and it busted, busted the mirror. He took a piece of the mirror and picked it up, and threw it down through there at her. She turned sideways, and it cut all in there [cheek]. She gat a scar up till this day. It cut up from here all the way 'round here. It was hanging out, blood just running. You could see her teeth.

Researcher: And you saw that?

Icepick: Yea, I say, "Oh man, he done killt her again!" They take her to the hospital, she got stitched up, she right back wit him, right back wit him.

Icepick explained that the violence moved with them again to another address:

Icepick: Okay, we moved from that spot, moved to another spot. This time, I'm with ma uncles. I'm feeling more secure; I ain't gone get beat up because I'm wit ma uncle now. I'm with ma uncle and my uncle gone protect me, my uncle don't play them games. So ma uncle gat me sitting up late at night watching matinee wit him. It was *Creature Feature* on.

Man, this man lay up there man, come in the house arguing. He slapped her at first, pow! It sounded like a gun shot out. 'Cause I had had a kernel stuck in ma nose, ma uncle was trying to get it out. He blew on the other side and it jumped out. . . . It was from the corn, popcorn, 'cause I was throwing it up in the air and catching it with ma mouth, and laughing. . . .

But anyway, I seen them in the kitchen, but I am starting to eat the popcorn, but I started shaking now. 'Cause I see him, shaking, like man, I'm finna get a whooping, for nothing, he just wanted her to beat on us.

Damn, so they in there arguing, I hear them saying something as he slap her again. She said, "You better go, [calling his name], you better go." Next thing I know, she wrapped her hand in his T-shirt and I just seen her doing like this [twisting her hands] and his T-shirt just turned red, red, red.

Researcher: Your mother and your stepdad?

Icepick: Yea. He talking 'bout, "I told you baby I love you, I love you." She stab that man eighteen times [laughing], and every time she stab him he say, "I love you, I told you that." I said, "Is he dead yet?" They talking 'bout no, the knife closed up on her finger. They said if she would a stabbed one more time, he would a died.

Man they lay him up there. He didn't die but they had to sell. We did have two couches, nice furniture in the house. They had to sell everything, refrigerator, stove, fridge, everything.

Researcher: Why?

Icepick: To bond ma mama out.

Researcher: Then what happened, did they get back together?

Icepick: Yes. We moved to Central Park, out west, in a house. He arguing with her. Now she got her feet stuck under the bed like this, and you know she kinda heavy-set, and he threw her backward, and twist her whole ankle around. Now right today she limp, she already walk on her tiptoes. I say, my, my, my!

Researcher: Is he still around?

Icepick: He the one I am saying down south carrying an air bag and all that around. He dying slowly now. All the hell he done raised. The man was crazy. One minute he a preacher, next minute he a plumber, the next day he a artist, next day, electrician again.

Icepick indicated that violence was the method many of his family members used to respond to disagreements and conflicts. As he grew into adulthood, he became both the perpetrator and the victim in many crimes, including battery. He explained how he became a victim of battery by his sister.

Researcher: You said that you have committed many crimes and stay in trouble. But how have your other siblings turned out?

Icepick: Naw, ain't none of my sisters never been to the penitentiary, but my other sista, she go to jail a lot.

Researcher: For what?

Icepick: Aggravated assault, indecent exposure, soliciting; she get drunk, she have that split personality. We just barely see her; she stay in the streets.

Researcher: You started telling me that one of your most recent injuries was from your sister. What happened?

Icepick: She turned the lights off on my mother and them, my nieces and everything was around. So . . . I told her don't do it and turn them back on. So I'm playing with the kids 'cause they know I carry a ice pick. I put the ice pick up. I'm playing with the kids, she come hit me on the side. She had a lil' knife 'bout this long; slid between my ribs and punctured my lungs. You know, I just got out the hospital four weeks ago. They had a tube in there keeping my lungs inflated.

Researcher: Did you do something else to aggravate her? How did you respond?

Icepick: Un huh, 'cause I told her don't be turning no lights out on my mama, 'cause she had went down in the basement and hit the power on all of us, everybody screaming. The kids hollering, my mother saying, "[Icepick], go down there and check that out, see who is that." I go out there, I see my sista runnin' up out the basement laughing. I say, "Get back up here and turn these lights on. Why you gon turn the lights off? You know you could've just said man, want ya'll hold it down or something, or you not feelin' good or something."

175

See, 'cause my mama lived wit her 'cause my mama don't get no type of money, no type of income. See, because back in '87 my mother was selling drugs; she was sellin' drugs in Indiana, rollin' hard. Police come in and caught her wit two ounces of cocaine; she use to cook it up so huh, she said when they came in one police said she didn't have it and the other say she did. But anyway, they won't give her no type of income 'cause they say she gotta go back to Indiana, straighten out that warrant. That's what's blocking her money, so she livin' wit my sista and my sista raise hell wit her almost every day and every night.

Yeah, you know, like I told you, she trying to feed this stud blow habit and her rock habit and she gotta give'em half of her rock, and I told her just don't be turning out the lights on my mama. I felt somethin' say boom, it's a lil' sting, I'm steady playing wit my lil' niece and she say, "Uncle [Icepick], you bleedin'." I say, "No I'm not."

I raise up my shirt and blood was skeetin' out like water; I had to press it back down. I say man and I flip my sista and I told her what you wanna stab me for. I say okay, you wanna play it like that? I went up on the counter and got that ice pick, she broke up out the door, I ran behind her but when I start runnin' I started getting dizzy. [When I got to the hospital] . . . immediately they had to give me some blood. . . .

But, I know . . . you know I'm steady saying, why is it that I'm having all this problem with my family? And I, you know, I want to be around them but then again I don't. You know, it just, it just be hurting at times, man. I have to walk around this, knowing all this pain . . . but I look at other people's family. Why . . . why they get along together and mines can't?

Family disruption exposed Icepick to violence, and sometimes made him a direct victim of battery. Family members also introduced Icepick to theft and hustling. He explains how he perceives his criminal career to have begun.

Researcher: At what age do you think you committed your first crime?
Icepick: Man, what age I committed my first crime; you talking 'bout wit the police or what I hadn't got caught for, or what?
Researcher: Any one, the one that stands out to you as your first robbery.
Icepick: When I first came to Chicago and I started hanging with my cousin. . . . He have no legs and no arms now. He was a good acrobat too, he could flip from. . . . He had a mental problem too. He started raping women, raping women, breaking into houses.

He used to have us out there stealing for him. He used to have a stick. Because he was older and bigger than us. We used to be out there on 63rd and Halsted, all them stores was up there. We used to go up in there and steal for him. He get the money, give us a dollar. He getting all the big money, we getting a dollar. He gat us stealing outta cabs, teaching us how to hit cabs with the cigarette boxes and all that. The cigar boxes, right.

So I was about . . . ten years then. That is first when I started doing crime. I saw that, man, it was getting good, and I can get all this money, give it to him, man. I can get ma own money, stand up against him. But I was so little, I was so little, I think I only weighed eighty-six pounds.

Icepick claims that his cousin, Legs, used assault and battery to coerce him and other younger relatives to commit thefts and robbery. Eventually, Icepick decided to break off and steal on his own. To him, this was also a way to stay out of an abusive household.

Researcher: So you said he got you started, your cousin, right?

Icepick: Yea, he got me started, his name is [Legs].

Researcher: Could you say no?

Icepick: If you say no, he would beat you to a puddle, and we was all scared of him. One day we just said forget it, man, we are not gonna be scared of you anymore.

Researcher: So once you started on your own, what made you continue?

Icepick: The money, and it was easy. And I could stay away from the house, stay away from the house. 'Cause see, when we turned twelve, we started cursing in the house and stuff. Ma mother told us, you all grown, start buying your own washing powder, your own bleach, and providing for yourself. Okay, cool, so we took it to the streets. I started going to the store stealing, man, I'm bringing all types of food back to the crib. All types of clothes. . . .

'Cause she was real fat, I get her coat and put it on, split the lining with a razor, and load it all the way up. And go to the store and buy one bubblegum, and out with 'bout $40 worth of merchandise. You know, come back, all my sweets and everything. "Icepick, who put all that food in here?" "I did." "Where you get it from?" "The lady down the street gave it to me for helping her take out the garbage."

I'm saying you let him tell you anything. This man [Icepick's stepfather] used to take her check every month. He would switch up in a different car. I don't know how much money she was getting on aid, plus the stamps, ma mother. I don't know how much money she was getting, but he took all of it and left us there starving, starving.

She ain't gat nothing but some Jiffy mix, some cornbread mix, and some Land O' Lakes butter. And we got that, we robbed a train and got that. And he come there, like he doing something, drop off some neck bones, a case of neck bones.

Researcher: How common is your kind of life experience among the guys you know who have committed crimes? How many of them had this kind of childhood, this kind of turmoil?

Icepick: I would say about 65 percent of them had a rough childhood, because it seems like that was [mostly] the type of peoples that I was running up on. You know, that they have been abused. So that's why they would section us off to see what kind of program that we need to be in, to try to help us out. But most of the guys I used to hand with was older guys. I ain't too much hang with the young guys in the penitentiary or in the streets. But I run into a couple of old fools, my mother said them the worse kinds you could meet.

Information from beat meetings, block club meetings, and the researcher's direct observation indicates that many domestic batteries involve stepfathers or other male figures such as uncles and cousins who cohabit in households where they are not the natural father to some or all of the children.[5] Within those disrupted families, as was the case with Icepick's, stepfathers often display less affection and concern toward their stepchildren than toward their natural offspring. Some stepfathers have admitted to this behavior. Others deny it and argue that the children and mother are often the ones who misinterpret their actions as favorable to their natural children. One mother of seven children explained what she considered a disparity in the affection her lovers showed toward their natural children compared to their stepchildren:

Respondent: I have seven children. There are four fathers. . . . The first one, he was murdered by some drug dealers because he was doing some dirt too. We had only one child together. . . . I got married to the father of my second set of children. We were married for four years and had two children. He's now in prison serving a life sentence. He was a good daddy except that he [the first child] did not get along too well with him. He said my husband was always picking on him. . . .

I got divorced from my husband in prison. I lived with [the father of the twins] for ten years. We had the twins and one girl. He was an asshole. A real jerk. But it was not his fault. It was the liquor and drugs he was involved in. We fought many times in the presence of the children. I had him going back and forth to jail for abuse. The children hated him.

5. It is important to note that there are several households in which stepfathers and other male figures treat children and women in the household with considerable respect and protect rather than abuse them.

He said the only ones he cared for in here was his children and he would have left me a long time if it was not for them. . . . My older son wanted to kill him. He was fifteen years old. He used to whoop him all the time and for the things he never laid hands on his children for.

Researcher: This is six children. Who fathered the seventh child?

Respondent: She is with my current husband. My second husband. He takes good care of all the children and treats me with respect. We are sort of old to have a baby, but we only got together three years ago and he wanted one of his own. The police met him one day and thanked him for getting with me because they said that they was too tired of coming over here to lock up [the father of the twins and the girl]. They have not been over here for the last three years. . . . They came here about eight to ten times a year for many years, because the neighbors and the children would call on him.

A stepfather believed that stepfathers are not always the cause of domestic violence. He explained that stepchildren and stepmothers are equally to blame:

Respondent: People say this sort of shit all the time—that stepfathers be abusing they children. But what they do not say is that the children be starting and perpetrating a lot of the shit. Don't trust them little rascals, thinking that they be innocent all the time. They can instigate some shit between you and your woman, and with they half-sisters and brothers. Me and ma baby mama be living together for ten years, you know, on and off. We been knowing each other from childhood. We grew up together from round here.

Her daughter from another stud, excuse the term, she is a lil'. . . . She tells her mother all sorts of lies about me and other women and cause havoc between us because she does not like me. She says I treat her lil' brother and sister better than I be treating her. That gets me angry and sometimes I leave the house. I slapped her one of the times she called the police. I spent the night in jail. It has happened a couple more times. Two times last year. Stepchildren be starting a lot of shit, and then the stepdaddy gets the blame because he s'posed to know better because he the adult. This is bullshit!

Researcher: You said that stepmothers are equally to blame; what do you mean?

Respondent: Oh, I have one baby by this other woman who died from a drug overdose. But I think somebody killed her. I think it was intentional because of something to do wit me. So I took my daughter from her grandmother so I could care for her because I felt bad about what happened to her mother; she looks just like her mother and I loved her mother.

So my daughter [name] lives with us 'round here, too. My girl starts shit with her, too. They like two women in the house. One does not want to let off for the other one. They like two strangers. She will not accept my daughter as her daughter because she said she is too rude. My daughter will not accept her as a mother because she said, "You ain't ma mama."

But as a stepmother, my woman don't act right sometimes. She picks on my daughter, too. She hardly asks her about school and my daughter get to thinking she likes her own children better. But as the adult, my woman should act better than that. You see, that's the shit I'm talking about. A double standard. My woman slapped my daughter many times. The police was never called on her, and she is seen by her sister as a disciplinarian for slapping her. But when I do it to her daughter, it is child abuse, the police gets called, and I go to jail. What's wrong with this picture?

It is important to note that as the official police statistics indicate, only a few blocks record high rates of battery. Most households in the research site do not display the sort of turmoil that has been described in this chapter. Most of the turmoil appears to be generated by a small number of families whose members engage in multiple offenses over extended periods of time. Such families are often neighbors to "intact" families that, although their income levels are quite similar, exhibit behaviors that are quite different. A neighborhood expert explained the variety of families that reside on her block:

Most of the families on our block, the blocks around us, and even the entire beat, I would say, are decent people. It is just a handful that cause most of the trouble most of the time. For example, on this block, my neighbors on the east side here are trouble. Their children turned out to be the same, and their grandparents were almost no better. But the other three families on this side of the street are really great people. The family on the second floor is in worse financial condition than the family over on that side, but they do not have much of the problems. They are God-fearing people that want better for themselves. They have done good for themselves and taught their children well, even though they are poor.

A police officer said that it would be a mistake to believe that although there are a considerable number of domestic and other batteries in this beat, most families are that way:

Now don't misunderstand me. The same small group of people commits most of the batteries in this beat. The families that stay out of problems one time seem to stay out of it most of the times. There are some areas that you never get called to. Once there is a call on one of these blocks, you can almost be certain about which families are involved, depending on the nature of the crime. A lot of it is predictable if you know the beat well. But again, do not make the mistake to believe that most families in this beat are troublemakers, even though most of them are poor. That would be a mistake.

Most domestic batteries are associated with quests to establish domination and control over others or revenge from spontaneous and long-standing unresolved conflicts that escalated, especially when drug and alcohol use was involved. These factors are also frequently associated with acquaintance battery, as along with other issues such borrowing money or extending credit for illegal drugs. High occurrences of battery are more likely in locations where disruptive families reside. Disruptive families are more likely to reside on blocks where the rent is the cheapest. Cheap rent is more commonly found in buildings that are not well maintained. However, even in these areas, most of the residents are decent families who do not engage in disruptive behaviors such as domestic violence. Residents are often reluctant to intervene in instances of domestic violence, as they perceive it to concern private matters among family members.

A Close Look at Acquaintance Battery

Acquaintance battery refers to physical injuries inflicted on a victim by another person with whom the victim is familiar, but who is not a domestic partner or a member of the household. Such batteries often occur in public places such as bars, streets, empty lots, alleyways, and dwelling units where at least one of the actors may reside. One beat police officer explains his experience with acquaintance batteries.

You may get called to a domestic, and it is clear what that is: some guy beating up on his woman is the case most of these times. I already told you about what happens there. But there are many batteries among people that just hang together. People they have some acquaintance with. They are not strangers; they are not living together. Now most of these batteries happen either in or close to a lounge, a liquor store, grocery store, or fast-food joint where people hang out.

Some of the drug guys beat up on each other when they are sitting around amusing themselves. If they have someone else selling the drugs for them, they sit around shooting dice or something like that. Then a fight breaks out among them for something stupid like one of them cheat, or laugh at the other one when he loses some money, call him a punk or something like that.

Some batteries also are among people who want some revenge for something stupid. They hang out with each other so much that they are bound to be irritated with them at some point because they say the same thing over and over again, and do the same thing: drink and talk. Eventually somebody gets hit because they did not settle some beef they had from some time ago. Sometimes from a long time ago. Some of them fight over money that they lend out and have not been paid back. But it is not a lot of batteries around here that are among people that are strangers to each other. They are mostly either domestics or people they know at least a little well. Often times, people they grew up with.

One sixty-eight-year-old resident said that there are some blocks in the beat that she has known to be notorious for acquaintance batteries since she was a child:

There used to be a bar on [a particular cross street] that we used to call the bloody bucket. Because almost every weekend, there would be a lot of blood on the street from fights that happened in the bars there. Mainly one bar. People would go there after work each day, but on the weekends they had more action. Gangs and regular people, too, used to get into fights there all the time, and the fights would end up on the streets. I saw a few of them from our window because we would be wakin' up from the sound of bottles breaking and people screaming or talking loudly during the fights. It was only neighborhood people that frequented the bars, except for a few regulars that did live further south. My father used to hang out there, so I heard when he told my mother and my aunt about what happened there. But this was a place where fights happened frequently because of the bars that were there, and that one bar we called the bloody bucket. I forget what its real name was.

One neighborhood expert explained that she thought two particular blocks were battery hotspots because acquaintances spend considerable time in the area "begging and hustling."

With [two particular blocks], there are many batteries there because of the people that are hanging out there begging and hustling. See, both of these blocks have grocery stores, liquor stores, and fast-food joints. People hang out there to beg because there are other people going in and out. They ask you to help them and you may spare them some change. Or they may just ask you to spare some change without asking you if you need help with the groceries to your car. There are a lot of people in this without work and no real recreation. They just hang around waiting for something to happen. They hang out in areas that are good for them in the sense that they will get some scraps here and there. This is a meeting place for them, and they are regulars. These are people that either grew up together or spent a lot of their lives as friends, since they have been down and out together. But sometimes they get into fights over little things.

I saw a guy punch another one in the head because he was trying to hustle a person he was hustling first. Sometimes they sit there and argue. Then they fight. But again, they hang out there for a reason, those two blocks, because of the businesses that are there. Then fighting breaks out among people that know each other because of something little and dumb. I see it all the time.

Another resident claimed that there are many fights close to grocery stores and liquor stores not only because people loiter there and fight over petty issues, but because people also sometimes go there to pick a fight:

There are some people that have some problems with others. If they want to find the person to get revenge, they go to where the person hangs out. Those persons hang out in places where they hustle, sell drugs, or whatever. So, for example, I saw two fights out on this block last week because one guy who hangs out here had cussed this other guy's woman. He slapped her, too. Now this happened some other place, but the woman that he slapped and her boyfriend came to the front of [a particular liquor store] to get him because this is where he be hanging out. They stabbed him and left. If you do not know what happened, you would think that this happened because of something that began here. But it did not begin here. This is just a place that they could get revenge because they know he will eventually show up here.

Another resident associates many batteries with informal loans and outstanding debts among the unemployed:

Many of the fights happening involve people fighting over money that was borrowed and not returned. Somebody might come to you and ask to borrow some dollars and say they will pay you when they check comes in. Then when they get they check, they buy alcohol, drugs, and other stuff without repaying you. And you want the money because you lent it to them. This happened to my cousin when he borrowed money and did not pay back in time. You might get beat up because of an argument that broke out. But not all people act that way. Mostly those who are on aid and do this shit all the time act that way. Working people who borrow money from people do not do this. None that I know of.

A police officer also associated batteries with the borrowing of money and failure to repay at the beginning of the month: "And most of them [batteries] occur during the first of the month. Because checks come in. Most of our robberies come in at the first of the month. Except that some people may get stuck up. They buy some dope on credit, the dopeman wants his money, he will take it, they will make it a robbery.

It is a robbery, technically. So they will call in and say that they got robbed."

Perhaps for these reasons, some neighborhood experts believe that most batteries are concentrated in cheap rental units and businesses such as bars, grocery stores, and check-cashing locations. When various neighborhood experts were asked to explain why they perceived certain locations as battery hotspots, many responded in much the same way as this senior citizen:

I think there are a lot more batteries on this block because the Ritz Motel and the Courtway building down the street are on this block. These are both places where the rent is cheap and they attract a certain crowd of people that find trouble with each other. There is a lounge in the basement of the Ritz, and people get into it with each other after a few drinks. I have seen a few fights there myself. Now, on [name of block] that is another issue. I know of fights out there mainly because of the hanging around outside of the grocery store and the check casher.

One former bar owner explained how his business became a hotspot for batteries:

I had to eventually shut the place down because of all the fighting that went on in there. It seems like it did not matter what I did: hire security, even shot at some people myself. I know it was wrong but it was tiresome. This is just what some people do. The building down the street is . . . a rooming house. Some of the people that live there have severe alcohol and drug problems. Some are mental. Something ain't too right with them up there. They seem like they always angry, always getting into something with somebody else. But they are your customers. It was always something or another. Sometimes really petty stuff.

Sometimes, batteries occur among acquaintances when someone is trusted to receive and manage money that belongs to others who, for some reason, often because of incarceration or drug and alcohol abuse problems. cannot receive it directly. Such persons are sometimes referred to as payees. Problems often result from such arrangements. For instance, a former prison inmate claimed that he was recently arrested for battery because he choked his former mother-in-law for spending his money, which was sent to her while he was in jail:

Respondent: Now she getting my checks, right; I get $430 a month for my living. I tell her would you get my checks until I get out, save up the money for me. I had counted it all up; it was $6,500. You know, I say I can use that money; I can get me a crib, you know, I can get a lil' car; I can pay for my lil' drivers ed. Man, that lady laid up there and kept all the money.

I agreed I went to jail for that year 'cause that the time I turnt myself in. I went to jail, man, every day that's all I'm thinking about, that money every day I'm down there. I . . . can do a year. I'm waiting on this year to run pass, man. Okay, they release me, man, I come. I get off the el down here. I come running down through here. . . . Man, I get there, she told me she ain't got a dime; ain't even got car fare for me, talkin' 'bout she gotta scrape up some change; and my whole body went to shaking. I grabbed her and start choking her.

Researcher: You grabbed her and started choking her, then what happened?

Respondent: Yeah, all that time I'm down here, you know I trusted you. Now, me and her daughter was going together. Now her daughter told me, "Mama took yo' money, she paid my rent and [my brother's] rent." Now this her brother, my ex-woman and her brother. Now they staying in the projects, her brother have to pay $115 a month; she pay $88. . . . See, that's what I don't be liking about the projects. They let you stay up in there and run up a tab, yeah, she then lay up in there ain't paid no rent and her rent is $2,000.

Researcher: From one hundred and something?

Respondent: No. From $88 a month to $2,000. She didn't know her brother . . . had to pay almost a hundred and a quarter every month; okay, they let his rent to $1,900.

Researcher: There should have been about $2,600 left; what happened to it?

Respondent: She say she bought the kids something. No, she wasn't thinking 'bout me; that's why she can't look at me to this day.

A self-proclaimed street prostitute, Anitar, explained how she and her boyfriend beat a neighbor in 1999 for spending money they had entrusted to her while the prostitute was enrolled in a drug rehabilitation program.

Researcher: How did you get this long cut on your arm?

Anitar: It happened when a fight broke out between me and my payee.

Researcher: What is a payee, and what happened?

Anitar: A payee is a person that gets your money on your behalf when you cannot get it for yourself. I was trying to get help for my heroin and crack habit, and I trusted her to hold the money until I got my act together after treatment. She would give me a little at a time when I requested it. But it was like being a child again. I agree that I pissed her off sometimes when I came for money too late, and she may not have any at home at that time.

Researcher: So how did she cut you?

Anitar: She did not cut me herself. I fell on a broken glass center table when we got to fighting. What happened, it was really my boyfriend [name] who got mad because he wanted the money for his drugs. I had checked myself in for four months. She was keeping the money until I went through the program. It was my aid. I went to her for the money with [boyfriend] and she started giving the run-around. Then her husband told us to get the hell out his house. [Boyfriend] got angry and pulled a gun on [the lady] and her husband. The man threw a chair at him and it hit him in the head. The gun fell. I picked it up and I fell on the table while it was in my hand.

Researcher: Did anybody get shot?

Anitar: No. When I got cut from falling on the glass center table, we all calmed down because I had to go to the hospital.

Researcher: How often does this sort of thing happen? I mean, people getting into fights because of situations similar to yours?

Anitar: Often enough, but not too often. Always somebody borrowing something and not returning it. You trust some people and they disappoint you. Sometimes a fight might break out.

These statements suggest that batteries occur in some locations, such as street corners where business establishments like liquor stores, grocery stores, and check cashing places are situated, because they bring together several people with pre-existing unresolved conflicts. Such areas frequently rank high for social disorder, as many people loiter and panhandle in such locations. Of course, others who congregate in such areas are those awaiting private or public transportation, but it is difficult to distinguish them from the others. Such locations show a high incidence of battery not because of high levels of physical or social disorder, or low levels of collective efficacy. Instead, people congregate in those areas because of the *ecological advantages* they offer—close proximity to business establishments that bring people together. Several low-rent units that house disruptive families are also located on or around these commercial and mixed-use blocks.

Batteries Associated with Other Crimes

In addition to domestic and acquaintance batteries, some batteries occur in the process of committing other crimes, and not necessarily as a result of strained domestic or acquaintance relationships. One police officer explained this category of batteries.

Researcher: You said earlier that some batteries are committed while perpetrators are in the quest of committing other crimes. Tell me more about that.

Police officer: Sometimes fights break out, or better put, people sometimes get battered for reasons that are not about the batteries as the end goal. I mean, the intention is to commit another crime. Or it may be as a result of committing another crime. I am not sure that it is a completely separate kind of battery but there is something different, at least for us as police officers. There is a different motive involved.

For example, battery is involved in robbery, but the end goal is not to batter the person, but to steal money. Battery gets involved in rape, but the goal may be about sexual domination. Battery comes in a homicide because often this is the vehicle through which people are killed, unless the person is poisoned or something. This is what I am talking about, and this is the way that many of us understand it.

One car thief and robber explained how batteries are "side effects" of his primary crimes:

Since I was a lil' shortie I began stealing cars and robbing wit ma older brother. We be wanting to get the car quick, or get the money quick. Ain't nobody want to beat up on nobody if you can avoid it, because is just too much stuff gets tangled up wit it. We want to get paid and move.

Every now and then you gat somebady who want to resist your game. You want no witnesses if you can. You want no more trouble than you already have. So you have to do something 'bout them when they resist. Some of them be tripping. So you use the gun or the knife to prevent them from resisting, to keep it cool. . . . So they may get beaten up . . . as a side effect, or something. Because that is not what you really out there to do.

A former drug dealer offered another example where battery was a "side effect" of another crime: drug dealing.

Researcher: Why is there so much violence involved in drug dealing?

Respondent: The violence is more rare than people make it out to be. Drug dealers would prefer not to have much attention to theyself because that ain't good for business. You want your customer to come in, buy, and go. You do not want too much police coming up in you business. But remember this is an illegal business and some guys not be wanting to be straight.

If you gat some debts not yet paid, you cannot go to the police and make a complaint about it. You gat to take it in your own hands. That is why gang members stick together; they run a business. Ain't no one guy doing everything.

187

Somebody selling, cashing, running, being the lookout. But you need security and enforcement. So when one of your workers or customers cheats you, they get roughed up. But generally, you want to keep down the violence, because you do not want police up in your business too much.

Battery is sometimes associated with public drunkenness, illegal drug abuse, assault, and murder. Icepick explained how public drunkenness, drug abuse, and assault led to battery and later, murder:

I'm on [a particular street]. I am just walking down the street, because I used to have real long hair, thinking I'm a pretty boy minding my own business. Girl get to talking to me, I get to talking to her. So she said later on come around my house, so later on I went around her house, but I was real drunk. Because it was my birthday, I was celebrating. I was going to buy her something too.

And I holla up at the balcony like that . . . trying to talk to this young gal. But he gone come and say I call his woman a bitch. So, he said, "Wait right there." So I'm thinking, "Yea, he can come down and talk to me," but he come down, and I'm looking at him, "Yea, I gat him."

Okay, now I turn around look again, I see a stud, man, he looked like Lou Ferrigno. Man, he had muscles on top of muscles, chests, legs. I was wearing a 26 in the waist. I was real small. And that man come out there and say, "You call my woman a bitch?" I say no, I say ask her. . . . The same girl on the balcony, not the girl that got done talking to me that told me to come around there. That's her sister, she kinda fat. So I'm starting to walk. Now my girlfriend over here cross the street cheating on me in the car, but she see it and she tell me, "Come on [Icepick]; they fitting to jump on you." I said no they ain't.

I get around the corner. Now my house right around the corner. They said, "Hold up homie, we just want to talk to you." I told her, "Wait, see, I told you they would come apologize." So when they get to the corner they said, "Look, you gat to fight one of us." I'm looking at the big guy, looking at the little guy. . . .

The little guy trying to swing, and I started maxing him out but I forgot about the big guy. And when I turned around, both of them hit me on both sides of my jaw. And they said I went to walking and fell straight on my face. So when I woke up, my mouth was locked like this. I told my girlfriend to go around there and tell them to come and apologize. If they don't, I'm 'a kill'em, simple as that.

Bam. She went around there. They told her to tell me that if I come around there again, they will kick my ass some more. I said okay. I had a .25 automatic and a Chinese Butterfly, that knife, the Chinese Butterfly, that knife with the wings and the knife comes out in the middle.

So I went around there and they let me in. I did not sit on the couch. I sit on the back of they couch, put my feet on they couch, told they mama, "I ain't trying to hear nothing you talking about, lady; where they at, I know they in there." They were keeping them in the bedroom and they would not come out, so I left.

See, then I was messing with a bunch of PCP. I loved that PCP, so I just went to the West Side to get PCP and I was smoking it. But I am still thinking about that, 'cause my mouth still ain't opening up too much. But he come around here talking about "Yea, there he is, I knocked him out."

Icepick said that he stalked the men who punched him for twelve days and eventually killed one of them:

Now we see the girl again, the same girl that I was talking to, we see her because I gat a friend with me now. So he [wanted to talk to them] and I said no, that's [the girl's name]; I don't want to talk to her now. I said to her, "Last time you got me jumped on. I come around your house you got me jumped on." She said, "I told him he should not have did that" and this and that. I say okay, cool.

But I been stalking this man for twelve days. Stalking, watching his every move. I have been looking for him; I have been stalking him. So now I am smoking that PCP. He go out to get some Chinese food, up on [a particular block]; I walk on the other side of him, watching him.

He get the food, heading back home. I break to the head of him. And I come sit inside the hallway, and I'm drinking. "What'd I tell you, didn't I tell you?" . . . I get up right, he hit me, he hit real hard. So when he knock me down, he tried to square up over me.

I went to my pocket, got the Chinese butterfly, I said bye. Pop!! Hit him in the neck. Hit that artery. Bled to death. I'm sitting there with him, pouring that drink in his mouth. For real, pouring the drink in his mouth . . . the big guy, he had just gotten out of the penitentiary, too.

As the quotations in this chapter have indicated, batteries occur for various reasons among persons in domestic relationships, acquaintances, or persons in the process of committing other crimes. There is a considerable amount of overlap among the factors involved in these various situations in which batteries are prominent. Alcohol and drug abuse, the inability to resolve spontaneous and longstanding conflicts, and the desire to dominate others are common factors involved in batteries.

Summary and Conclusion

In Appendix A, analyses of the statistical data left a few important questions to be addressed by the qualitative data. These questions can be briefly restated as follows. First, why is there such a weak association between physical disorder and batteries? Second, since I concluded that the significant association between social disorder and batteries was because the absence of social disorder was strongly matched with lower incidence of battery, but not because high social disorder was a necessary condition for high incidence of battery, what then is the missing link between social disorder and batteries? Third, what is the missing link between collective efficacy and batteries? The association between collective efficacy and batteries was explained chiefly by the observation that when collective efficacy is high, most blocks are likely to have a low incidence of battery; however, low collective efficacy is not a sufficient condition to produce high incidence of battery.

Ethnographic data indicated that there are three main types of battery: domestic battery, acquaintance battery, and batteries that result in conjunction with other crimes. Most domestic batteries are related to the desire of perpetrators to establish domination and control over others, or they are forms of revenge that occur in the context of spontaneous or longstanding unresolved conflicts. All of these factors are associated with acquaintance batteries, but in addition, delays in payment of outstanding debts and illegal drugs are commonly involved. Sometimes batteries are part of the process of perpetrating other crimes. As the qualitative data indicated, drug entrepreneurship, robberies, assaults, and murder often involve batteries at one stage or another. The use and abuse of illegal drugs and alcohol are also commonly associated with batteries.

Interviews with residents and police officers suggest that domestic and acquaintance batteries are the most common types that occur in Beat 213. The presence of disruptive families on a block has considerable impact on observed levels of both domestic and acquaintance battery. As the narratives from Icepick and various neighborhood experts, other residents, and police officers suggest, for various reasons, batteries occur frequently in disruptive families. Also, when disruptive families relocate, their combative habits continue. Therefore, the presence of disruptive families is an important condition for high levels of domestic batteries.

Disruptive families also contribute considerably to acquaintance batteries. Since their method of domestic conflict negotiation frequently involves physical violence, they exercise the same behavior in relationships with acquaintances. Simply put, disruptive families frequently socialize and produce troublemakers who often batter both their loved ones and their associates.

Table 7.1. Correlations between 2000 Population and Selected Variables.

Variables	Coefficient	p-value	N
2000 populations and 1999 batteries	.32**	.01	58
2000 populations and 2000 batteries	.47**	.00	58
2000 populations and physical disorder	−.34**	.01	58
2000 populations and social disorder	.12	.37	58
2000 populations and collective efficacy	−.30*	.04	47

The Weak Association between Physical Disorder and Batteries

The weak association between physical disorder and batteries is explained by field observation indicating that while many of the blocks that were battery hotspots also ranked high on physical disorder, most high physical disorder blocks did not have high incidence of battery. Most of the blocks that ranked high on batteries also tended to have larger populations. Blocks with larger populations tended to have lower physical disorder. This claim is made based on ethnographic field notes that indicate that most of the buildings that were high on physical disorder are indeed abandoned, and abandoned buildings have no residential population. Furthermore, blocks that are higher on physical disorder tend to have more commercial or mixed-use properties than strictly residential units. There are no residential populations on commercial properties, and only a few persons reside in mixed-use structures. Moreover, as stated earlier in this chapter, most batteries in the beat take place within domestic domains. Since most domestic batteries occur within houses or residential properties, it is expected that, other conditions being equal, there will be more battery incidents on blocks with higher residential populations.

Analyses of statistical data are consistent with the qualitative observation that blocks with higher reported rates of battery tend to have higher populations, and blocks that are higher on physical disorder are lower in population size. Table 7.1 indicates that the Pearson bivariate coefficients between 2000 block populations and batteries were .32** for 1999 and .47** for 2000. The coefficient between 2000 population and physical disorder is negative and strongly significant, as denoted by the two asterisks (−.34**).

Table 7.1 implies that since most batteries tend to be domestic, and high physical disorder blocks have smaller populations, there are fewer people there to become perpetrators or victims of battery. Of course, this is affected by the type of persons who reside in such locations. Although some disruptive family members reside on high physical disorder blocks, they also occupy units on blocks that are low on physical disorder. Ethnographic data suggest that in Beat 213, disruptive families tend to live on blocks that are more densely populated. Thus, the relationship between population size and batteries is complicated by the presence of disruptive families.

Domestic batteries are not generated based on the external condition of buildings in which families reside. Instead, they are often directly related to what happens behind closed doors. As the qualitative data suggest, the most dominant factor associated with batteries is the presence of disruptive families. Although many disruptive families often occupy low-rent properties, not all of them do. Furthermore, low-rent properties are not necessarily high on physical disorder. In fact, many known disruptive families utilize Section Eight[6] subsidized dwelling units that have been constructed over the last four years. Moreover, as is discussed in chapter 5, many residential structures that are high on physical disorder are occupied by residents who are actively involved in crime prevention efforts in their neighborhoods and who maintain relatively stable family lifestyles. Therefore, more important than analyzing the external condition of a neighborhood structure is understanding what is happening within it.

The Missing Link between High Social Disorder
and High Incidence of Battery

Why is it that when social disorder is high, a similar proportion of blocks are battery hotspots as well as coldspots? This research finds that two important factors bridge the link between high social disorder and high incidence of battery: (1) the sort of participants involved in particular social disorder episodes, and (2) the different levels of ecological challenge faced by neighborhood blocks.

Ethnographic data suggest that knowledge about who is involved in loitering, panhandling, scavenging, and public drinking is important to understanding the association between social disorder and batteries. On several occasions, idlers by the wayside are guardians of public order (aside from the disorder they are creating by their very presence). Some of the examples were outlined in chapter 5, when it was explained that

---

6. Section Eight is a federal government income subsidy for low-income persons.

persons such as Bike and Bird, who are public drinkers and loiterers, are frequently actively involved in mediating conflicts among their associates and acting as guardians to schoolchildren.

It is not simply whether people are loitering, begging, scavenging, or drinking in public that is important, but *where* those activities are occurring. Blocks with high social disorder and proximity to liquor stores, bars, and check-cashing locations are more likely to be associated with acquaintance batteries than blocks without those characteristics. As the ethnographic data indicated, on some occasions, in the quest for revenge, persons seek each other out in locations where they "hang out." Moreover, vicinities with high social disorder that are occupied by or are located very close to disruptive families are more likely to be associated with high incidence of battery. This is part of the ecological challenge.

The Missing Link between Low Collective
Efficacy and High Incidence of Battery

The tasks here are to explain why low levels of collective efficacy are insufficient to produce high incidence of battery and to clarify what appears to be a bi-directional relationship between high collective efficacy and low incidence of battery. This study suggests that the ecological challenge disruptive families and their associates place on the blocks where they reside and on those around them is the missing link between low collective efficacy and high incidence of battery. What is important is not simply whether collective efficacy levels are low, but where the low collective efficacy blocks are situated. If low collective efficacy blocks are situated in areas dominated by disruptive families, battery encounters will be higher. However, low collective efficacy on blocks that are not dominated by disruptive families will be matched with low incidence of batteries. Over time, collective action can encourage disruptive family members to moderate their domestic behavior, but the lack of such action is not a primary cause of those crimes. They are instead rooted in unresolved interpersonal conflicts and private quests aimed at establishing domination over others.

Earlier sections of this chapter suggest that when disruptive families are dominant on a block, other residents tend to be more reluctant to intervene in their conflicts because of perceived high costs associated with retaliation. Instances were presented in which, because of fear of retaliation associated with violence among cohabitants, perceived levels of trust, solidarity, and the willingness of residents to intervene were reduced over time. There were also several instances when intervention resulted in escalation of conflict. Therefore, the issue is not whether people intervene, but what form of intervention they employ and whom they are called upon to intervene against. Since many disruptive families frequently change residences, it is not easy to trace their violent and abusive behaviors to low levels of collective efficacy in earlier stages of their lives. If disruptive families are absent or only a minor presence on a block, low levels of collective efficacy will not be sufficient to produce high incidence of batteries. However, once such families are present, depending on the particular form it takes, collective action against crime can help resolve personal conflicts before they escalate into batteries.

EIGHT

What This All Means

Summary, Conclusions, and Implications

Summary and Conclusions

This book began by questioning how well, when taken directly into the world of hardened offenders, broken windows and collective efficacy theories would explain why some city blocks experience considerably more crime[1] than others. The research found some support for both broken windows and collective efficacy theories. However, it also found data indicating that, by themselves, the conditions proposed by both theories are insufficient to explain high levels of drug dealing, robbery, and battery on neighborhood street blocks. Consequently, I have introduced the concept of *ecological disadvantage* and have used it to extend both theories.

In response to critiques of broken windows theory, Bratton and Kelling (2006) stress that the theory is often misrepresented by scholars who insist that it assumes a *direct* link between neighborhood disorder and serious crime. To the contrary, they posit that the relationship is *indirect*. Disorder causes fear of crime, and leads to weakened social controls, "creating the conditions in which crimes can flourish" (Bratton and Kelling 2006, 2). However, the focus of this book has been on how disorder influences neighborhood crime not from the law-abiding citizen's perspective,

---

1. The crimes of narcotics violations (drug dealing), robbery, and battery that were reported to the Chicago Police Department as having occurred in Beat 213 during 1999 and 2000 were analyzed.

but rather from the offenders' point of view. A close reading of the logic of broken windows theory presented in chapter 2 indicated that the link between neighborhood disorder and crime is more direct from the perspective of offenders than from that of law-abiding residents. From the offenders' perspective, neighborhood disorder is more directly linked to crime because it signals to offenders that people do not care about their neighborhoods, and that therefore there are little or no costs for committing crime there (Wilson and Kelling 1982). This book has focused more specifically on that claim. Neighborhood disorder exists in both physical and social forms. Physical disorder refers to unpleasant neighborhood characteristics created by abandoned buildings, boarded-up windows, broken windows, overgrown lawns, and trash. Social disorder is the unpleasant and potentially intimidating interactions among people in public space—such as loitering, panhandling, and public drinking. As disorder increases, criminal activities will also increase, and a series of events such as fear of crime and the exodus of law-abiding citizens will ensue, leading to further problems and criminal invasion (ibid.).

Collective efficacy theorists, by contrast, argue that neighborhood disorder and crime are linked because both come from the same source: the concentration of disadvantage and weakened collective efficacy. The concentration of disadvantage refers to poverty and the paucity of resources that often accompanies it—such as unemployment, underemployment, financial dependency, lack of investment potential, low home ownership, high residential turnover, density, and mixed land use (Sampson and Raudenbush 2001, 2). However, while the structural constraints of concentrated disadvantage are working to produce both crime and disorder, human intervention, characterized by collective efficacy, is a force working to inhibit them (ibid). Collective efficacy theorists contend, therefore, that collective efficacy also mediates the impact that concentrated disadvantage has on both crime and disorder. Collective efficacy is defined as mutual trust and solidarity among neighbors along with their willingness to intervene on behalf of social control (Sampson, Raudenbush, and Earls 1997; Sampson and Raudenbush 1999).

The research utilized multiple sources of data that include crime statistics, a survey of neighborhood experts, systematic social observation, field research, and interviews with offenders. Data gathering was conducted from 1997 through 2002 in Grand Boulevard (Beat 213), a subsection of Wentworth Police District, which has historically had one of the highest rates of violent and predatory crime in Chicago, Illinois. The crimes of narcotics violations, robbery, and battery reported to the police in 1999 and 2000 were analyzed and cross-validated with results from the neighborhood experts' survey and my field observations to identify the blocks that were hotspots for the various crimes. These three types of crime were selected because as examples of entrepreneurial, predatory, and grievance crimes, they provide an opportunity to examine closely how different types of crimes function in terms of the claims of broken windows and collective efficacy theories. Only 1999 and 2000 crimes were selected because at the time of the study, they were the only years for which detailed block-level crime data were available from the Chicago Police Department.

Quantitative analyses indicated that in both 1999 and 2000, there were weak (insignificant) positive associations between physical disorder and all three types of crime. For each year (except for 1999 batteries and collective efficacy) there were statistically significant relationships between social disorder, collective efficacy, and all three types of crime (see Table A.5). Moreover, it was observed that while low social disorder was primarily matched with low crime, high social disorder was not predominantly matched with high crime (see Tables A.12–A.17). This led to the conclusion that low social disorder may be among the important conditions for low crime, but that high social disorder was not sufficient to produce high crime.

Also, high collective efficacy blocks were predominantly matched with low crime, but low collective efficacy blocks were observed to be almost equally crime hotspots and coldspots (see Tables A.18–A.23). These puzzling results of the analysis of the statistical data were further supported by field observations. GIS maps were then used to display the spatial positioning of crime hotspots in reference to the different levels of physical disorder, social disorder, and collective efficacy. The maps allowed for a better understanding of where the crime hotspots were spatially distributed in the research site.

Figure 8.1 shows that the crime hotspots were mainly at or near the northwestern and southeastern corners, at the intersections of Pershing Road and King Drive, and Cottage Grove and 43rd Street, respectively. These are the busiest intersections in Grand Boulevard, with the most frequent public bus transportation, and they are the sites of a majority of the business outlets that include grocery stores, liquor stores, check-cashing outlets, and take-out restaurants. Interviews with drug dealers and robbers indicate that such blocks are attractive mainly because the businesses within them bring different people together—people who can be clandestine clients of drug dealers, or easy targets for robbers. The chapter on batteries showed that such busy intersections also bring together people with longstanding and/or unresolved conflicts, people

Neighborhood Disorder, Collective Efficacy, and Street Crimes, per Face Block, 1999-2000

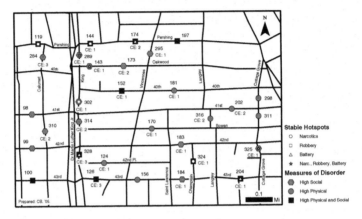

Figure 8.1. Neighborhood disorder, collective efficacy, and street crimes, per face block (1999-2000).

who sometimes spontaneously fight with and injure each other. These locations are also nearby the residence of disruptive families and their acquaintances, people who frequently, in public and private spaces, resolve outstanding conflicts by recourse to physical violence. Figure 8.1 also demonstrates how various crime hotspots were spatially distributed in reference to different levels of physical disorder, social disorder, and collective efficacy (CE).[2]

The observations that (1) neighborhood spaces are unevenly zoned, used, and developed, and (2) offenders habitually commit crimes in locations that offer them particular spatial advantages have led to the introduction of the term *ecological disadvantage,* which I use to extend both broken windows and collective efficacy theories. The logic of *ecological disadvantage* is that the particular space where a location of interest is situated independently contributes to criminal opportunities, and this must be considered before analyzing potential impacts of additional factors such as neighborhood disorder and collective efficacy.

Indeed, ecological disadvantage impacts the interpretations and uses of neighborhood disorder and conditions the demands and returns of collective efficacy. For instance, as can be observed in Figure 8.1, several

2. In Figure 8.1, CE: 1 = low collective efficacy, CE: 2 = midrange collective efficacy, and CE: 3 = high collective efficacy.

blocks located in the interior of Grand Boulevard are high on neighborhood disorder but are low on narcotic violations and robberies. This is mainly because they are not situated along the busy mixed-use and commercial intersections where drug dealers and robbers primarily go to service clients or to find prey. Disorder in busy mixed-use street intersections and business areas is interpreted by offenders as a public issue—failure of the city's government and local businesses to develop the area—whereas disorder in remote private residential spaces is interpreted as evidence of personal struggles associated with inadequate income. In neither case is disorder interpreted by offenders to mean that residents do not care about their neighborhood.

Collective efficacy is also conditioned by ecological disadvantage because collective action is not undertaken without a challenge. Ecological disadvantage provides challenges that activate the need for collective action. For instance, persons residing near busy intersections or mixed-use areas (like blocks 143, 144, 174, 204, and 126) that are of interest to offenders are challenged to organize themselves to act collectively against crime. By contrast, residents of blocks in remote and exclusively residential sections of the area (like blocks 152, 181, and 170) are challenged less because crime entrepreneurs such as drug dealers and robbers do not consider their block geographically advantageous for business.[3] Therefore, they may enjoy a life of low crime even under conditions of low collective efficacy.

Physical Disorder and Narcotic Violations

Interviews with drug dealers, their clients, law-abiding residents, and police officers indicated that physical disorder is not of primary importance for street drug dealing, for several reasons. First, contrary to the belief of broken windows theorists, street drug dealers do not interpret physical disorder as an invitation to conduct business in the location because people do not care about their neighborhood. Instead, drug dealers view high levels of physical disorder as a sign that the city's government does not consider that section of town as a priority, and allows deterioration to take place—often as an early stage of gentrification. Drug dealers consider high drug demand, high supply of bulk drugs, high availability of unemployed youths, and high exchange opportunities as most important for their business to flourish.

---

3. Keeping in mind that sometimes drug dealers capitalize on sales wherever they are at the moment, and robbers capitalize on spontaneous opportunities.

Street drug dealers provided different interpretations of physical disorder on the macro and micro neighborhood levels. They consider a large dilapidated section of the city—such as a 20- to 60-block radius—to be a depressed area because of governmental neglect and other factors associated with poverty and unemployment. Such areas are expected to contain a considerable number of residents and visitors who self-medicate with illegal drugs in order to deal with the pressures of everyday life. Such areas are expected by drug dealers to contain a high availability of young persons who are willing to peddle street drugs as a source of income. However, when street drug dealers select micro neighborhood locations such as street corners to sell drugs, they pay little attention to physical disorder. Instead, they select locations based on the easy availability of exchange opportunities: secure transactions, deniability, and the presence of enablers.[4]

Second, to drug dealers and their customers, place matters most. However, what matters most about place is not its appearance, but where is it situated and what sorts of activities occur within it. Therefore, to motivated narcotics offenders, knowledge about how the space functions is much more important than its appearance. This knowledge includes an understanding of the place's reputation in reference to particular criminal opportunities. As some of them indicated in chapter 5, drug dealers often stumble upon places and gradually "build up the spot" until it becomes popular with their customers. After drugs are successfully sold in that place for an extended period of time, the reputation of the place as a lucrative drug location becomes crystallized. Once that reputation is crystallized, drug dealers are more likely to retaliate against efforts to remove them from that location. Before the reputation is crystallized, drug dealers are more likely to flee in the face of collective action against their activities. When certain locations gain a reputation as "problem narcotic areas," they often become "dumping grounds" to which residents from neighboring locations attempt to push the drug problems that occur on their blocks. Furthermore, problems of neighborhood decline, including rising physical disorder, sometimes occur as drug dealing flourishes on a neighborhood block. Therefore, when physical disorder and street drug dealing are present in the same micro neighborhood location such as a street corner, their coexistence is not based on the expectations of broken windows theory—that dealers have interpreted disorder to mean that no one cares about the neighborhood and that therefore there are little or no costs to their actions.

4. See chapter 5 for a detailed discussion of these factors.

Third, there is a very weak association between physical disorder and narcotic violations partly because most of the blocks that rank highest on physical disorder contain abandoned properties in remote locations that are of no interest to drug dealers. As was explained in chapter 5, some abandoned properties are of interest to drug dealers, but not simply because of the way the place looks—rather, the important consideration is where it is situated and what other activities occur in and around it.

Physical Disorder and Robberies

Reasons for the very weak association between physical disorder and robberies are quite similar to those that explain the association between narcotics violations and physical disorder. Ethnographic data indicate that robbers do not select targets based on levels of physical disorder. Instead, target selection is based on spontaneous access, predictable access, and predictable escape. Chapter 6 indicated that in this research site, robbers most frequently monitor strategic locations and spontaneously select their target when they "see the money." The places that robbers primarily monitor for suitable targets are selected based on what activities occur there. As statements from robbers indicate, they mostly monitor locations that are near transit stops, check-cashing establishments, grocery stores, hair salons, fast-food restaurants, and other businesses where most persons are likely to have cash in their possession. Victims are then spontaneously selected when they act in ways the robbers consider to be vulnerable and when easy escape seems quite possible. As one active robber articulated, and this was supported by narratives from other robbers, "I want it, I see it, I take it" is the mode of street robbers in this area.

Physical Disorder and Batteries

As was discussed in chapter 7, the very weak association between physical disorder and batteries is explained mainly by the finding that most batteries result from domestic conflicts among disruptive family members who reside mainly on more densely populated blocks in the beat. The blocks that ranked highest on physical disorder were dominated by abandoned properties, many of which, therefore, had no residents to be victims or perpetrators of domestic batteries. Furthermore, most nondomestic batteries are less likely to occur in such abandoned areas of high physical disorder unless they host business establishments such as fast-food restaurants, grocery stores, hair salons, laundromats, and certain types of liquor outlets. These business establishments are located in buildings characterized by varying levels of physical disorder, and they bring together many idlers and persons with longstanding and/or unresolved conflicts who sometimes batter each other at those locations.

Social Disorder and Narcotics Violations

While physical disorder was not found to have significant associations with narcotics violations, robberies, and batteries, the reverse was found for the association between those crimes and social disorder. However, when these significant associations were closely examined both statistically and qualitatively, it was determined that the relationships were quite complex. For each of these three crimes, the significant association was mostly due to the observation that those crimes do not flourish in the absence of social disorder; but high social disorder was insufficient to produce high crime rates.

The overall explanation for this puzzle is that social disorder matters generally, but the particular aspects of social disorder that matter most are (1) the location where the social disorder is present, and (2) the identity of the key actors involved in the social disorder episodes. If social disorder is in a location that is attractive to drug dealers because of the ecological advantages the place offers and its established reputation as a lucrative location for narcotics sales, some drug dealers will use that social disorder to help disguise their activities by "blending in" with the crowd. However, depending on who the key actors are in the social disorder episodes, drug dealers who attempt to blend in may be chased away or otherwise made to feel unwelcome among that group. However, even if social disorder is high in a particular location and participants in the social disorder episodes are welcoming, drug dealers will not be interested in operating their business among that crowd if the location is not a geographically convenient one. This mainly explains why spaces that are high on social disorder are almost equally likely to be high or low on narcotics violations—because drug dealers are more interested in where a place is located than in the presence or absence of social disorder.

Narcotics violations did not flourish on blocks characterized by low social disorder mainly because most areas of low social disorder are not situated in the strategic locations many drug dealers consider to be convenient. Furthermore, as stated earlier, social disorder is sometimes important for street drug dealing, but it must be in a strategic location and executed by a group of actors who are sympathetic to drug dealing or to the socioeconomic plight of particular drug dealers. In several instances, drug dealing itself brings about street-corner congregations that are considered loitering. Dealers sometimes congregate on street corners awaiting clients. In other instances, clients are known to await the arrival of their dealers. Therefore, sometimes social disorder is not a precursor to drug dealing, but rather, drug dealing in progress.

Drug dealers and their clients also utilize particular forms of social disorder in strategic locations to conduct business; and except when drugs are quietly and swiftly sold behind closed doors, drug sales are frequently accompanied by social disorder. Junkies frequently "hang out" and "hustle" in locations near drug supplies so that they can access drug dealers as soon as they obtain money to purchase substances for their next fix. Drug dealing, therefore, is sometimes an enabling condition for social disorder.

The data suggest that there is often a reciprocal relationship between social disorder and narcotics violations. Certain forms of social disorder can be useful conditions for drug dealing; on other occasions, drug dealing leads to social disorder because certain clients loiter, beg, and hustle while they await their next fix. This partly explains why, in public spaces, few narcotic violations are observed in locations characterized by low social disorder.

Social Disorder and Robberies

The positive and significant association between social disorder and robberies is also complex. For instance, in 1999 only one of the 25 blocks that ranked low on social disorder was a robbery hotspot. In 2002, none of those 25 blocks were robbery hotspots (see Figures 4.13 and 4.14). However, for both years, among the 23 blocks that ranked high on social disorder, more were coldspots than were hotspots. There are very few robberies in locations of low social disorder because the robberies that occur most frequently in that area are conducted at or near business establishments such as grocery stores, fast-food restaurants, check cashers, and liquor stores. Such locations are not low on social disorder. High social disorder is insufficient for high robberies because, as with narcotics violations, what matters most to the offender is not the level of social disorder, but where the acts of social disorder are located and who the actors are that are involved in the episodes. Robbers are often selective about who they target because they need some assurance that the victims will have money in their possession. Therefore, even though social disorder is high in a particular location, if the people there are known or believed to have little or no cash, they will be of little use to the motivated robber. Thus, they are less likely to become targets. Furthermore, not all locations that are high on social disorder are necessarily suitable spots for robberies because, as explained in the earlier chapters, some of the participants in social disorder episodes are themselves guardians against crimes such as robbery, theft, and child molestation. Thus, robbers do not select their targets on the basis of high levels of social disorder. However, as stated in the robbery chapter, when victims are selected, they are frequently in strategic neighborhood locations where they are distracted, with money in their possession. Such areas of distraction are frequently at or near business establishments. In this research site, most blocks on which business establishments are situated are observed to be at least midrange on levels of social disorder.

Social Disorder and Batteries

The positive and significant association between social disorder and batteries is chiefly explained by the finding that blocks that rank low on social disorder are mostly battery coldspots (68 percent in 1999 and 52 percent in 2000); however, blocks that rank high on social disorder are as likely to rank high as to rank low on batteries.[5] In chapter 7, ethnographic data indicated that batteries were most common on blocks dominated by the presence of disruptive family members who frequently engaged in domestic and other conflicts. In this research site, very few known members of disruptive families reside on the blocks observed to be low on social disorder. Blocks observed to be low on social disorder are often predominantly occupied by single-family homes or the area's more expensive condominiums and apartments. Most known members of disruptive families are either unemployed or underemployed. Therefore, disruptive family members, who are known to be from lower-income backgrounds, cannot afford access to those more expensive properties that characterize most of the blocks that are lower on social disorder. Known members of disruptive families typically occupy low-rent properties, many of which are on or close to blocks with business establishments. Blocks with business establishments usually rank higher in social disorder than other blocks. Furthermore, being frequently unemployed, many members of disruptive families often engage in acts of social disorder at or near their place of residence. Either way, very few

5. See Tables A.17 and A.18.

members of disruptive families that frequently commit batteries reside on blocks that are low on social disorder. This mostly explains why there are very few known batteries on blocks that are low on social disorder. The rule appears to be, fewer disruptive family members results in fewer batteries.

Why are blocks that rank high in social disorder as likely to be battery hotspots as coldspots? Ethnographic data indicate that most members of disruptive families in the area are clustered in lower-rent buildings (on blocks that are often closer to business establishments) that are also high in social disorder. However, nondisruptive family members also occupy many blocks that are high in social disorder. Even if a block is high in social disorder, it is likely to have a low incidence of battery if members of nondisruptive families predominantly occupy it. In other words, blocks that are high in social disorder and are also dominated by members of disruptive families have a higher incidence of batteries, while blocks that are high in social disorder but are home to predominantly non-disruptive family members are observed to be low on batteries. Therefore, the salient factor in the relationship of high social disorder and high batteries is the presence of disruptive family members.

Collective Efficacy and Street Drug Dealing

The findings also indicated that there were significant negative associations between collective efficacy and all three selected crimes (narcotics violations, robberies, and batteries). However, as was the case with social disorder, the relationships between collective efficacy and those three crimes were found to be quite complex.

The significant associations between collective efficacy and these crimes were explained mainly by the finding that very few crime hotspots were observed under conditions of high collective efficacy. For instance, for each year, among the sixteen high collective efficacy blocks, no more than three blocks (19 percent)[6] emerged as crime hotspots. However, low collective efficacy was insufficient to result in high levels of narcotics violations, robberies, or batteries. For instance, with the exception of robberies and batteries in 2000, among the seventeen blocks that ranked low on collective efficacy, more were crime coldspots than hotspots.[7]

Ethnographic data indicated that low levels of drug dealing are observed under conditions of high collective efficacy mainly because of

6. 1999 batteries and collective efficacy—see Table A.22.
7. See Tables A.18–A.23.

a reciprocal effect—low drug dealing encourages high levels of collective efficacy, and high collective efficacy diminishes neighborhood drug dealing. In chapter 5, there were several instances when collective action by residents resulted in a decline in narcotics sales on a particular street block. However, as was explained earlier in this book, drug dealers become attracted to locations not primarily because of levels of neighborhood disorder or collective efficacy, but based on the ecological advantages that are available to them. Thus, under conditions of low narcotics violations, residents are more likely to report a greater willingness to intervene. This is because their willingness to intervene is seldom placed under challenge, and they perceive the cost of intervention to be quite low. Therefore, they are more likely to perceive higher levels of trust, solidarity, and others' willingness to intervene when something wrong is in progress on their block.

On several occasions, persons (especially newcomers) who reside on blocks with very low crime indicated to me that they trusted their neighbors very much, felt as if they were the same type of people, and thought that their neighbors would be very willing to intervene should something "wrong" unfold on their block. However, I was often astonished to discover that many of those residents did not know their neighbors very well. They were sometimes unable to tell the names and number of adults and children in the neighboring households, the occupation of their neighbors, and how actively they had seen those neighbors intervene against "something wrong" in the last year. These instances led me to question whether people can really develop high trust of persons they do not know well, and whether they can genuinely feel that persons they do not know well are "like themselves." Furthermore, how can residents who have not seen their neighbors actively intervene against "something wrong" be confident that those neighbors will do so if something wrong actually occurs in the future?

I have concluded that the high levels of trust and solidarity such residents expressed toward their neighbors were not due to the fact that they knew them well; rather, residents assumed certain things about their neighbors because they live together on a quiet block. Newcomers to quiet blocks often believe that the low crime rate is because residents actively "do something" about crime-related problems. They are often surprised to learn later that there are no block clubs, and that residents often do not know each other very well or spend much time in the neighborhood. Their sense of trust, solidarity, and shared expectations for action is frequently based not on what they know about their neighbors, but on their observation that very few crimes occur on their block.

Residents sometimes deduce that since it appears that certain crimes are low or almost nonexistent on their block, their neighbors must be trustworthy; these neighbors are most likely people with whom residents can bond; and that they are most likely willing to intervene to help the neighborhood maintain its quiet status.

For example, in several instances, after observing that very few or no crimes were reported from particular blocks, I proceeded to question residents about their knowledge of crimes and why they believed so few crimes occurred there. While some residents pointed to concrete examples of collective guardianship that indicated their trust for and personal knowledge of each other, as well as their intervention against troublemakers in the past, others argued, "we are just lucky," "I guess they have not gotten to us yet," "I guess they are busy someplace else," and "I really don't know."

To the researcher, these statements and other observations mean that motivated offenders do not challenge each block on the beat equally. Therefore, many blocks are low on crime for reasons other than the active participation of residents. When crime is low on a block, many residents are likely to feel a sense of security that leads them to assume high levels of trust, solidarity, and the willingness of their neighbors to intervene on behalf of the common good, even without concrete knowledge. In many instances, residents actually point to low crime on their block as one reason that they trust their neighbors, perceive their neighbors as like themselves, and think their neighbors are willing to intervene to keep the block safe. Therefore, there is a reciprocal relationship between high collective efficacy and low rates of such crimes as narcotics violations.

The data also indicate that for both 1999 and 2000, blocks on which collective efficacy was low were more likely to be drug-dealing coldspots than hotspots.[8] This means that many blocks that are low on collective efficacy are missing a characteristic needed to result in high rates of narcotics violations. As was indicated in chapter 5, this characteristic is ecological disadvantage: where the block is located, what is in and around it, and the reputation it has gained over time. Depending on where a block is situated in reference to the broader neighborhood, and depending on the type of commercial activities conducted within it, the same level of collective efficacy might yield significantly different returns in terms of reduction of narcotics violations. Blocks that drug dealers consider to be lucrative for business will see less results for the same level of collective

8. See Tables A.18 and A.19.

efficacy than will blocks that are of little interest to drug dealers and their clients. This means that ecological disadvantage conditions the demands for collective efficacy and its likely returns.

Furthermore, under certain neighborhood conditions, collective efficacy is used as a private good in the form of aiding and abetting the sale of narcotics, rather than as a public good such as suppressing those sales. This observation highlights the need to determine under what conditions collective efficacy will be used to produce a private as opposed to a public good. The broader socioeconomic conditions under which the place and its actors function must be given serious consideration. Under strained conditions of concentrated disadvantage, and being positioned in certain kinship and friendship networks with chronic motivated offenders, residents are more likely to use collective action, a form of social capital, as a resource toward certain private benefits[9] than as a public good such as neighborhood safety—a dynamic suggested by several examples in chapter 5.

Collective Efficacy and Robberies

The association between collective efficacy and robberies is also an interesting one. Out of the sixteen high collective efficacy blocks, only two (13 percent) were battery hotspots in 1999, and none were hotspots in 2000. As with the relationship between high collective efficacy and drug dealing, there is a reciprocal association between robberies and high collective efficacy. High collective efficacy conditions lower the incidence of robberies because watchful neighbors and other capable guardians sometimes serve as effective constraints against neighborhood robberies. Robbers have admitted that watchful eyes have a deterrent effect on the timing of their activities. When neighbors trust each other, they estimate lower costs of retaliation in the belief that others will support them if the perpetrators retaliate. When neighbors know each other well and believe that others are like themselves,[10] they are more likely to estimate low costs associated with their actions against crime and are more likely to intervene. Thus, unless they expect payoffs

9. Such as profiting financially from drug deals, or "purchasing" personal security and other social favors from motivated offenders by turning a blind eye to their actions even though they are perceived to be "bad" for the neighborhood in general. Residents may also reap private benefits by not being perceived as the "rat." There can be other perceived private benefits as well.

10. Depending on who they perceive themselves to be. When they believe that others are like themselves, they are more likely to feel confident that they can anticipate how others will act under given circumstances.

to be very high, robbers often avoid operating in locations where they perceive that there is high trust[11] among neighbors who are willing to intervene to prevent robberies, to interrupt robberies that are in progress, or to provide incriminating evidence after witnessing robberies.

However, low collective efficacy is an insufficient condition to produce robbery hotspots. This is because place matters most to robbers. Certain low collective efficacy locations are not of interest to robbers because they are not frequented by vulnerable persons with cash in their possession. Robbers, typically preferring the path of least resistance, select their victims based mainly on spontaneous opportunities. When suitable victims are encountered in strategic neighborhood locations and payoffs appear to be high, robbers pay little attention to what scholars perceive to be levels of collective efficacy. "I want it, I see it, I take it" is the most common logic used by robbers who find prey within the research site. Therefore, to most robbers, low levels of collective efficacy mean nothing unless they are matched with spontaneous opportunities in strategic neighborhood locations.

Collective Efficacy and Batteries

Among the sixteen high collective efficacy blocks, respectively, only three were considered battery hotspots in 1999, and only one in 2000. However, among the seventeen low collective efficacy blocks, eight were battery coldspots in 1999 and only one in 2000; six were battery hotspots in both 1999 and 2000.[12] Few batteries were observed under conditions of high collective efficacy. Moreover, in 2000, most batteries were observed under conditions of low collective efficacy. This suggests that low collective efficacy is also insufficient for high levels of battery. Discussions in chapter 7 indicated that the presence of disruptive family members is the key variable in the relationship between low collective efficacy and high incidence of battery.

Chapter 5 also indicated that trust, solidarity, and the willingness of residents to intervene sometimes serve as a useful motivation for cooperation and a measure to prevent conflicts from escalating to the point where they result in violent physical exchanges. On some occasions, trust, solidarity, and the willingness of residents to intervene serve to prevent physical conflicts from continuing over time.

11. Observations suggest that high trust is high assurance of protection imbedded in social relations. When neighborhood actors speak about trust, they often refer to levels of assurance that, in their presence or absence, others will not cause them harm.
12. See Tables A.22 and A.23.

However, as was illustrated in chapter 7, certain forms of intervention in interpersonal conflicts can make matters worse, even over time. Members of disruptive families, and sometime others, frequently intervene by taking sides and throwing punches themselves. This often results in a series of retaliatory combative episodes that sometimes lead to severe injury or even death. Therefore, the important issue is not simply whether neighbors are willing to intervene, but what forms of intervention they are willing and able to employ. This is important because some forms of intervention actually make matters worse, while others may reduce batteries over time. Domestic disputes that occur behind closed doors are often beyond the scope of intervention by neighbors. Residents often consider domestic violence to be a private matter. Collective action to reduce domestic violence may be more effective when it takes the form of awareness and prevention than when it surfaces as intervention during heated moments.

Theoretical Implications

Several theoretical implications can be derived from this study. First, the study advances knowledge about crime and place by challenging conventional wisdom that tends to discuss large high-crime neighborhoods as if all of their sub-neighborhood units are about equally dangerous. This study reveals that like the broader city, high crime areas show considerable variation in concentrations of crime across micro-locations. Therefore, socioeconomic and race variables are inadequate to explain variations in concentration of crime over place and time. There is a need to look at this phenomenon over multiple cities and sub-areas to further examine this observation.

Second, this study further supports the need to look at neighborhoods, and at particular places within them, as units of analysis in their own rights. A place is a commodified space—a location of specific consumption value to various neighborhood actors. However, the value of place is not arbitrary; rather, it is dependent on its context, on what is going on in and around it, and on the reputation it has gained over time. Like legitimate business entrepreneurs, when considering opportunities for lucrative business transactions, crime entrepreneurs such as drug dealers, prostitutes,[13] and robbers pay close attention to the ecological

13. Although not discussed at length in this book.

advantages places offer them. Simply by virtue of their close proximity to transit stops and certain business establishments, some places offer crime entrepreneurs spatial opportunities for easy access to customers or victims, quick escape from police, and an ability to deny that they are present in the area solely for illegal activities. To robbers, place matters greatly because different spaces do not equally attract and socialize suitable targets. Members of disruptive families who frequently engage in domestic and acquaintance violence often find housing in less desirable sections of the neighborhood where the rent is lower.

The reputation a place has gained over time is also an important component of its ecological advantage or disadvantage, because this assigns the place a certain profile and value in reference to other spaces around it. On most occasions, the place acquires a particular reputation because of repeated actions that occur there over time. Again, certain actions are more likely to occur in places because of their location than because of what they look like. Therefore, the ecology of place has an independent effect on providing opportunities for certain crimes to flourish.

Third, the independent effect of place has considerable impact on the relationships between broken windows and collective efficacy variables and crimes. As the preceding discussions indicated, there are other significant factors besides simply what a place looks like, how much disorderly conduct is visible within it, and the sense of community among its residents. Location matters considerably; knowledge of the key actors in social disorder is important too. It is also crucial to determine the purpose to which collective efficacy is directed. That is to say, one must seek to comprehend what communities are organized for, how, and in what ways the very location within which they are imbedded influences the demand for particular forms of collective action. Therefore, future research concerned with physical disorder, social disorder, and collective efficacy should pay specific attention to the independent effects of the ecological advantages and disadvantages of place.

Fourth, future research on collective efficacy needs to pay close attention to the reciprocal relationship between high collective efficacy and low crime rates. It is evident that some neighborhoods experience low levels of crime partly because of collective action toward intervention. Those acts of intervention are frequently made possible by substantial trust and subjective solidarity among neighbors. Yet, under conditions of low crime, neighbors are quite likely to report high estimates of trust and solidarity among themselves, and of the willingness of others to intervene. An important question is whether the perceived willingness to intervene will actually translate into active intervention when the neighborhood is faced with a crime challenge. How will we know that?[14] Or is the willingness to intervene alone a deterrent to motivated offenders? If so, how do motivated offenders come to know what residents are willing to do or what they are actually *able* to do? Often, motivated offenders become aware of what other residents are willing to do because there has been a history of confrontations between them. Quite often, such confrontations are the genesis of collective efficacy because they expose neighbors to opportunities for knowing who they can trust in certain ways, who has values similar to theirs, and who is willing to intervene in particular ways on behalf of a safer neighborhood for all.

In most situations, residents do not build a strong sense of community unless they have been faced with a common external enemy. They are often ambivalent about whether they and their neighbors trust each other, how well they know and identify with each other, and what they are willing to do on behalf of the common good until they are faced with crime or other threatening problems. These challenges force them to look within, and to discover, evaluate, and develop their capacities for action. Therefore, if some micro neighborhoods are seldom placed under direct challenge, often because of where they are located, how can perceptions of collective efficacy in these areas be clearly ascertained? Future research needs to consider this question.

Toward Improving Collective Efficacy Measures:
Questioning the Reliability of Global Trust

These findings raise some important questions about the real-world implications for variables used to measure collective efficacy. It was observed that a global measure of trust may be problematic because there are different types of trust that sometimes function in contradictory ways in relation to crime. For example, in this study, trust was divided into trust with property and trust with information. Trust with property questioned the extent to which residents trusted their neighbors to look after their residence while they were away and to return borrowed items. Trust with information related to the extent to which neighbors trusted each other with information about themselves that could be used to

14. These questions arose frequently during the author's communications with Robert J. Sampson while the research was in progress and we were both at the University of Chicago's Department of Sociology.

harm them (i.e., personal secrets). Trust with property had a significant negative association with all three crimes; this was not the case, however, for trust with information. Therefore, future studies should find ways to inquire about and measure the relationships between specific types of trust and various crimes.

Toward Improving Collective Efficacy Measures: Questioning
the Willingness to Intervene as a Predictor for Action

The findings of this study also question whether the willingness to intervene is a reliable predictor of what residents will actually do if faced with a challenge that compromises neighborhood safety. Many residents who reported low willingness to intervene were frequently observed engaging in direct acts of intervention aimed at increasing safety in their neighborhood. This was rather puzzling until field notes revealed many statements made by those residents indicating that they intervene reluctantly. Because of high expectations about the costs of retaliation, many residents are not willing to intervene on behalf of neighborhood safety. However, faced with the daily challenges posed by crime problems in the neighborhood, the same residents were observed engaging in several spontaneous acts of active intervention. On other occasions, residents who expressed strong willingness to intervene did not engage in active intervention because of the network ties they shared with perpetrators. These perpetrators were often their children, parents, siblings, or other close relatives, or friends with whom they felt they could not afford suffering the break in affective affiliation that would entail from a direct intervention. Having high willingness to intervene, but not having what is perceived as the opportunity or leverage to do so, such residents become empathetic or afraid and allow their troublemaking associates to continue their wrongful actions with impunity.

Lack of confidence in the criminal justice system is one key reason residents gave for reluctance to engage in collective action against criminal activities. They expressed concerns about engaging in acts of intervention that would lead to young persons, such as drug dealers, going to prison. Although they do not want drug dealing in their neighborhoods, they are concerned that many young persons who are incarcerated return to their neighborhoods in worse psychological and social condition than before they went to prison. Often, the people neighbors are called upon to intervene against are their close relatives or friends who have returned home after serving time in prison. Incarceration has major impacts on local capacities for social control; since inmates are seldom rehabilitated, residents wonder if it is productive to engage in acts of intervention that may cause others to serve time in prison. They develop *bonds of sympathy* with many local offenders. Meanwhile, offenders interpret this lack of intervention to mean that residents either approve of their behavior or fear them, so they continue with their illegal activities. This observation suggests that future research on collective efficacy should consider the impact of mass incarceration on local social control, and should find ways to resolve this tension by formulating measures that can more directly determine what residents will actually do if faced with the complex challenges that often threaten neighborhood tranquility and capacities for collective action.

One possibility is to gather information about how residents have actually responded in the past and to use this information as a predictor of what they may do in the future, in similar circumstances. Considerable emphasis needs to be placed on determining the conditions under which residents would be willing to compromise affective personal ties or other perceived personal benefits in order to produce a safer neighborhood. The paradox in this regard is that many residents feel that their involvement in neighborhood safety efforts comes at great personal cost, which will increase others' safety but jeopardize their own. Therefore, residents will be more willing to intervene when the situation in which they are called upon to act does not jeopardize their affective ties and other perceived private benefits or further compromise their personal safety. This implies that the willingness to act is not a sufficient condition for action. Other conditions determine the extent to which such willingness will actually translate into action.

Residents need the opportunity to act in ways that are not perceived to have high personal or group costs. The perceived level of personal cost is often contingent on the affective and other ties the actors have with those they are called to intervene against. In this area of concentrated disadvantage, many residents use personal ties to obtain help, supplies, and favors, and to meet other wants and needs. They are constantly faced with compromising individual or small-group personal interests for the common good. Stripped from those intense networks of dependency, they may have more leverage and opportunities to act and follow up on behalf of the common good. It is important for future research to determine how residents construct perceptions of the common good and how it can be attained. Furthermore, under what conditions will the common good be perceived as a concurrent personal good of about the same magnitude? Involvement in neighborhood block clubs often presents situations where private and public goods are realized concurrently. For instance, residents engage in developing local flower gardens and clean-up campaigns that yield personal benefits in the form of stabilized real estate values and sense of neighborhood attachment as well as the public good of creating a clean and pleasing environment for all to enjoy. Collective action against crime also concurrently yields private and public goods when many block club members are seriously involved in the effort. The private benefit is often attained when certain offenders are chased away from the block, and the public good is the safer neighborhood that results when residents on adjacent blocks do the same. However, if the intervention is not well coordinated by groups, offenders will retaliate against those who were most actively involved in the intervention. Larger coordinated group interventions, such as those often undertaken by neighborhood block clubs, seem to reduce the personal costs incurred by individual residents.

Toward Improving Collective Efficacy Measures:
Subjective versus Objective Solidarity

The measure of solidarity among neighbors also requires some attention. This study made a distinction between objective and subjective solidarity, and found that there are notable differences in their association with crime. Subjective solidarity referred to the extent to which residents believed that others on their blocks were "like them." By contrast, objective solidarity referred to the length of time persons resided on the block. The measure of subjective solidarity showed a stronger association with all three types of crime. As explained in chapters 5 through 7, there were also substantive differences in the ways these forms of solidarity related to trust among neighbors and their willingness to intervene. Some residents reported that the longer they lived among some neighbors, the better they got to know them, but the less they trusted them. In addition, under certain conditions, some residents showed considerable reluctance to intervene against others with whom they felt subjective solidarity, and instead found ways to excuse their wrongful behavior and sometimes even aid and abet their criminal activities. Under what conditions do stronger bonds develop among neighbors over time, and under what conditions don't they? When bonds do develop, what determines whether they will be used to produce lower crime neighborhoods as a public good? It is important for future research on collective efficacy to test these questions.

Methodological Implications

This study serves as an example of how multiple data gathering techniques can be harmoniously used to study neighborhood issues. The quantitative, ethnographic, survey, mapping, and Systematic Social Observation (SSO) data all served as cross-validations of each other. An important question in the mind of all field researchers should be, "how will I know if I am wrong?" The use of multiple methods to gather diverse sources of data is one way of guarding against collecting data that cannot be cross-validated for accuracy. Official statistics were cross-referenced against neighborhood experts' survey and ethnographic data to determine whether they provided a reliable portrait of the spatial distribution of crime hotspots. Dialogues were then conducted among the quantitative, ethnographic, map, and SSO data to scrutinize and explain the relationships among social disorder, physical disorder, and collective efficacy variables. This book also advances the technique of SSO by creating a movie from the data that was then used during field interviews with offenders. The SSO movie was also used to provide a video ethnographic account of Beat 213. These procedures have several implications for the future of neighborhood context research.

Policy and Programmatic Implications

One major finding of this book in reference to policy implications is that even within a high crime area only a few micro locations such as street blocks may be crime hotspots—habitual crime locales.[15] This is partly because urban and other spaces are not evenly zoned and developed, providing different structures of criminal opportunities to different offenders who capitalize on spatial (dis)advantages. For instance, among the 58 blocks analyzed, only 10 (1 percent) were hotspots for at least one of the three types of crime in both 1999 and 2000. Among these 10 blocks, only 3 were stable hotspots for all three types of crime; the other 7 blocks were stable hotspots for only one type of crime. Stated otherwise, among the 58 blocks in the beat, only 3 (5 percent)[16] were stable hotspots for all three types of crime analyzed by this study. Detailed explanations were provided as to why these blocks and not others were higher crime locales.

15. Keeping in mind that the equation used to tabulate crime hotspots will also influence the raw number of crimes that will be required for a location to be considered a hotspot, and how many hotspots there will be.

16. Blocks 143, 289, and 325.

Most of the blocks in high-crime areas are likely to have low crime rates, and the few blocks that have high crime rates are likely to remain that way over time. Therefore, one policy implication is that even in high crime areas, it is important to avoid employing one overall crime reduction strategy for all micro neighborhood units such as blocks. It would be more useful to categorize and understand blocks in terms of hotspots, warmspots, and coldspots, paying close attention to the factors that make them similarly vulnerable, and to devise strategies accordingly. In other words, variation in concentrations of crime over place and time will demand diverse strategies to address neighborhood crime problems effectively. This means that although a general neighborhood anticrime strategy may be developed, in order to be effective it must consider multiple strategies to be used across different micro neighborhood units. Since each micro neighborhood will not be faced with the same crime challenges, strategies should be employed that are specifically sensitive to the challenges of certain types of blocks. This does not necessarily mean that each block requires its own special program. After all, only a few places will be major problems; others will be either midrange or low problem areas for particular types of crime.

The few high crime areas need special attention to determine if they all require the same or similar sorts of intervention. Many blocks are midrange in crime, and they are vulnerable to becoming *the next hotspots* if efforts are not made to transform them into coldspots. Warmspots (and some coldspots) sometimes offer the same ecological advantages as hotspots. However, as ironic as this may seem, there are not enough active motivated offenders to capitalize on every ecological and other opportunity that exists. For narcotics violations, for example, there are considerably more potentially lucrative spots than are being utilized at any given time. Active drug dealers easily identify locations perceived to be on hold as the "next spot" in the event that the older lucrative location becomes no longer available. These potential "next spots" will likely require different strategies than the current hotspots.

Coldspots should not be forgotten, because they too can later emerge as hotspots. When older hotspots decline, motivated offenders may capitalize on some of the ecological advantages offered by certain coldspots, thereby transforming them into hotspots. Efforts must be made, then, to preserve whatever is responsible for the persistence of low-crime micro neighborhoods. The study indicates that it is unlikely that a block will be a hotspot one year and a coldspot the next, and vice versa. However, this only means that the probability was small based on recent and current conditions in the research site. Over a one-year period, a few blocks have displayed drastic low to high shifts in their criminogenic profile. Therefore, although coldspots are more likely to remain stable than to change into hotspots, this cannot be taken for granted.

Policy and programmatic efforts should also be sensitive to the additional challenges imposed by the ecological position of the place itself. Some blocks will yield lower returns for the same level and type of intervention if they are situated in locations of greater interest to motivated offenders who will retaliate more fiercely. Crime problems in other locations will require less effort for higher returns if those locations are, because of certain ecological disadvantages,[17] not of great interest to certain motivated offenders. Offenders will simply move to another, more welcoming and potentially lucrative location, or retire when forced or encouraged to do so. Ecological disadvantage has considerable consequences for the relevance of physical disorder and social disorder. It also affects the demand[18] for, the returns[19] of, and the costs[20] of collective efficacy. Policy and programmatic efforts need to take these findings into consideration.

Effects of Broad Socioeconomic Constraints on Neighborhoods

While it is important to consider factors associated with criminal opportunities, policy and programmatic efforts need to consider equally forces such as concentrated disadvantage which influence criminal motivation. Concentrated disadvantage influences criminal motivation by creating a milieu of extremely limited resources and networks that further compromise social values and priorities. These factors cause many residents and businesspersons alike to remain in conflict over transforming limited resources into private goods, for strictly personal gains, instead of working together toward public goods such as safer and healthier neighborhoods.

Criminal opportunities are worth nothing if motivated offenders do not take advantage of them. Criminal opportunities outnumber motivated offenders; offenders can only take advantage of a limited number

17. Note that this term is relative because, for instance, an ecological "disadvantage" to the motivated offender will be considered an ecological "advantage" to the neighborhood reformer.

18. How many and what type of collective efforts are needed to eliminate or significantly reduce the crime problem in question.

19. How much headway will actually be made by activating certain forms of collective action against crime.

20. How frequently actors in collective action episodes will encounter resistance from motivated offenders, and the severity of retaliatory threats motivated offenders will make against neighborhood reformers.

of opportunities. The opportunities certain motivated offenders capitalize on are often within reasonable proximity to where they live or in preferred targeted locations that exist further away. Concentrated disadvantage often brings motivated offenders and criminal opportunities together, or converts what would otherwise have been a community good, such as a small business area, into a criminal opportunity.

The concentration of socioeconomic constraints such as unemployment, underemployment, and underdevelopment affect the manner in which micro neighborhood issues are perceived, prioritized, and approached. Socioeconomic constraints intensely experienced in micro neighborhoods influence the particular ways neighborhood actors[21] construct notions of what are actually *crime problems*. Neighborhood actors often refer to broad socioeconomic conditions when they express perceptions of which *crime issues* are worthy of attention as major *problems*[22] in the neighborhood. For example, although many residents express a great desire for low crime neighborhoods, they also understand that, as one neighborhood expert put it, "every man has the right to eat."[23] Therefore, neighborhood actors often spontaneously ponder whether or not, and how, they should respond to suspected or known criminal activities. This is especially the case with nonviolent entrepreneurial crimes such as narcotics violations, prostitution, and illegal vending. Often, in addition to perceiving the actions being observed as completely wrong because they look bad and are illegal, neighborhood actors seek more information. They often make concerted efforts to identify what is really "the problem with the problem."[24] These discussions are frequent in community policing beat meetings, where residents have said, for instance, "prostitution is not the problem; it is where and how they do it,"[25] "it is not the drug dealing I am concerned about, it is the violence," "I do not want to send them to jail; I just want help for them because I understand that they are trying to make a living," "the problem is that we have to let them know that they cannot be so bold with what they are doing," and "they need to take this someplace else."[26] Concentrated

---

21. Local residents and business persons alike.

22. A problem is often perceived as an issue that is persistent, that is of significant concern, and that cannot be eliminated or significantly reduced through human or other forms of intervention.

23. Many neighborhood actors, even some police officers, have made similar statements.

24. This is a direct quote that expresses an idea encountered several times during field interviews with police officers, neighborhood reformers, and motivated offenders.

25. Such as on the hoods of cars, on church steps, in alleyways, in cars on vacant lots, in parking lots, and on private driveways.

26. These are all direct quotes from police beat meetings.

disadvantage affects how neighborhood actors perceive and are likely to respond to potential crime problems.

Under conditions of concentrated disadvantage, residents often feel helpless to reduce the motivation of their neighbors to become involved in violent and predatory crimes. This is because residents frequently associate motivations to commit violent and predatory crimes with the frustrations that accompany concentrated disadvantage or other forms of socioeconomic strain. Faced with these conditions, and concurrently desiring as much peace of mind as they can muster, many neighborhood residents do not place much emphasis on actively seeking ways to completely eliminate neighborhood crime problems. They are convinced that as long as those broad socioeconomic conditions exist, the motivation for violent and predatory crimes will persist. Once such disenfranchised persons are motivated to commit crimes, they will find places to do so. The question remains, in what particular neighborhood places will motivated offenders find the best opportunities to commit crimes? As this study has indicated, criminal opportunities in a specific place vary based on the type of crime in question. Therefore, all places will not be equally attractive to, or reflective of, the actions of all types of motivated offenders.

Moreover, many residents in highly disadvantaged neighborhoods realize that although they do not have the power and resources to uproot motivations for involvement in violent and predatory criminal activities by removing these broad socioeconomic constraints, they are not completely helpless. They can have an impact on where crimes occur most frequently by reducing opportunities in some locations.

Many neighborhood residents perceive that the biggest threat of neighborhood crime is the threat of becoming a random victim. Therefore, faced with conditions of concentrated disadvantage, they attempt to control certain crimes by influencing where they occur most frequently—organizing themselves to cluster or push certain crimes into strategic neighborhood locations such as adjacent street blocks with passive residents.[27] In this way, they attempt to "de-randomize" crime, hoping that it will also be reduced in the process. Meanwhile, motivated offenders, especially crime entrepreneurs, go about selecting places based on the ecological and social advantages they offer. So when crimes become clustered,[28] motivated offenders feed off the perceived

---

27. This is what I refer to as consecutive displacement.

28. This is often accomplished with the assistance of well-intentioned neighborhood reformers.

advantages offered by that place and keep their activities there until they are forced to move elsewhere or to find other ways to occupy their time. These micro-level processes are repeated on intermediate neighborhood levels of organization and are further observed as macro neighborhood–level crime rates.

When neighborhoods maintain high levels of crime over an extended period, they gain a certain criminal reputation that makes eliminating or significantly reducing crime in that place even more difficult. Such persistent high crime places frequently become dumping grounds onto which police and residents of more efficacious neighborhoods push questionable behavior.[29] In such places, where crime reputations have become crystallized, considerably more time and effort is necessary to significantly reduce or eliminate certain types of crime.

For these reasons, intervention at early stages of criminal involvement is important. Early intervention prevents crime problems from escalating to levels where the place gains a reputation that reduces the effects of subsequent modest efforts. Early intervention also limits the investments some motivated offenders, such as drug dealers, have made in the area. When drug dealers have spent a considerable amount of time attempting to make a location such as a street corner more lucrative, they are more likely to engage in fight than in flight. When motivated offenders fight back, this reduces the active participation of residents toward producing neighborhood safety as a common good.

Early intervention can also reduce offense motivation. As the ethnographic data in this study indicate, criminal involvement often begins at an early age, when persons are very adaptable to whatever habits are introduced to them. Once those good or bad habits are imbued, they often continue through the life course. As the statements made by motivated offenders have indicated, criminal habits are very hard to break, especially when they were nourished from an early age. Many motivated offenders learn criminal behavior from close friends and relatives. For this reason, children who are socialized in certain types of disruptive families need to be exposed to alternative forms of socialization. Over time, early intervention will likely diminish both structures of opportunity in place and offense motivation among people.

So we return to the question raised at the beginning of this book—within the same broadly defined high crime area, when placed under ethnographic scrutiny, how well do broken windows and collective

---

29. Another form of consecutive displacement; in this instance it is organized more on the macro neighborhood level.

efficacy theories explain the formation of higher crime locales on smaller neighborhood levels such as street blocks? It is clear from the data that offenders do not unequivocally interpret disorder to mean that no one cares[30] about the neighborhood and that they can commit crimes there at little or no cost. However, while neighborhood disorder is not an invitation to offenders to commit crimes with impunity, it does have harmful effects on neighborhoods. Perhaps the most detrimental impact of neighborhood disorder is that it chases away potentially good and productive residents and business persons. Potential homeowners avoid making purchases in areas where property values seem to be at great risk of declining. During interviews, neighborhood disorder was often interpreted as an indication of such decline. Neighborhood disorder also causes some residents and outsiders to believe that since the area is in rapid decline, little can be done to rescue it, and that one should therefore extract as much as possible from the area before nothing is left. By the same token, other residents and outsiders interpret disorder as a call to action—those who care must work harder to turn conditions around.

Collective efficacy, or collective action for problem solving, has been observed to possess the potential for reducing both neighborhood disorder and crime. However, this study has pointed to several complex issues worthy of attention. One of these issues is the realization that based on where they are located, neighborhoods face different ecological disadvantages that activate the need for certain forms of collective action in response to problems. Moreover, because of those ecological disadvantages, neighborhoods do not realize the same return for the same level of collective action. Therefore, efforts aimed at reducing neighborhood crime to increase quality of life should not only seek to reduce disorder, increase trust, increase solidarity, and increase the willingness of residents to intervene on behalf of social control; they should also pay attention to factors such as lopsided planning and development, collaborative surveillance among business establishments, and diminishing the constraints of concentrated disadvantage that fuel criminal motivation. Collective action for problem solving should not only be reactive to existing neighborhood problems, but also be proactive to avoid other problems in the future. I have increasingly wondered why residents expend so much energy on responding to crime problems and pay so little attention to organizing themselves to address other quality of life issues

30. Offenders often interpret disorder to mean that the city's government does not care about the area, but residents still care about their neighborhood.

such as increased employment, strengthening business communities, actively promoting moral and normative development, and advocating effective conflict management skills. In addition to improving capacities for social control, these actions will likely reduce incidence of certain crimes as well as criminal motivation.

This leaves the question of what specific policies and programs are recommended, based on the findings, to reduce neighborhood crime. I do not propose to offer any magic bullets, nor do I expect any single program to solve the majority of crime problems. I also expect that effective policies and programs can emerge from the readers' own understanding of the findings I have presented, combined with their interests and expertise. The findings in this book indicate that although multiple crimes may regularly occur on the same neighborhood blocks, they do so for different reasons. Therefore, no single strategy[31] is likely to result in significant reductions of all these crimes at once. The fact that multiple types of crime occur consistently on the same neighborhood blocks draws our attention to the need to consider the forces of ecological disadvantage.

It would not be appropriate to suggest that residential neighborhoods should not contain any business outlets such as grocery stores, check cashing outlets, and fast-food restaurants (i.e., to eliminate mixed-use neighborhoods). Such businesses are established for the public good but sometimes also serve as lucrative places for crime entrepreneurs and predators—mainly because they bring potential victims and perpetrators together. Zoning and land use laws may be effective in determining where such businesses can best be located, and it may be possible to design them in ways that make shared surveillance relatively easy. This does not mean that strip malls are the only solution, or that cameras should be indiscriminately installed. It is quite possible that the "mom and pop" stores that are essential to many neighborhoods can be less vulnerable to incidents of violent and predatory crime if business owners, customers, local police, and others devise strategies in response to the particular challenges at hand.

Although strategies may be similar, some variations will be needed to address crime problems effectively. Such strategies should include soliciting the input of stakeholders from all major categories: residents, customers, business owners, local and other governmental representatives, law-enforcement representatives, employment agencies, drug treatment

---

31. Except for demolishing an entire area, as was done to the Robert Taylor Homes and State Way Gardens on State Street in Chicago.

and rehabilitation agencies, schools, churches, block clubs and other neighborhood organizations, and offenders who are reformed or are serious about becoming reformed.[32] All crime reduction strategies should include two major components: one focused on reducing criminal opportunity (through shared surveillance among the business community, residential community, visitors, customers, and responsible law enforcement); and another focused on reducing criminal motivation (through increased socioeconomic opportunities[33] and/or moral development).[34] If criminal motivation is not reduced, offenders will continue to employ creative measures to capitalize on criminal opportunities. Drug dependency, thrill-seeking, severe economic strain, limited coping and conflict management skills, and lack of moral development are often at the root of criminal motivation. Criminal opportunities with little motivation produce little crime; therefore, it is important for crime reduction strategies to seek to reduce criminal motivation, and not simply assume that motivation will decrease if opportunities are diminished. These can be attained under the current organizational structure of community policing, but alternative approaches can also be utilized.

Plans for economic development of neighborhood space should also simultaneously consider the development of neighborhood people. If efforts are not made to develop people and reduce criminal motivation, business establishments intended to benefit the public will continue to serve as incubators for their criminal victimization. Crimes occur when motivated offenders find suitable opportunities in suitable locations. Suitable opportunities and locations do not produce crime if they are not engaged by motivated offenders. Most of the crimes analyzed in this study were committed by offenders who reside in close proximity to the crime locales. Therefore, if the social, economic, and moral dimensions of people who reside near business establishments are developed, neighborhood establishments will less likely become sites for criminal activities. Persons who reside near those establishments can participate in community policing or other similar efforts aimed at making their neighborhood less conducive to criminal activities and violence perpetrated by neighbors and visitors alike. All of this responsibility should

32. Thinking of reformed offenders or those who are serious about being reformed as stakeholders may seem a peculiar position. However, I have found that when such persons are included in discussions of crime prevention strategies, they add a real-world perspective stocked with insights that many law-abiding citizens overlook.

33. This is except in instances when crime is motivated more by greed than by need.

34. This is especially instances when crime is motivated more by geed than by need, and when there is clear disrespect for human life and positive social values.

not fall solely on the shoulders of residents and other informal agents; law enforcement agents also need to be actively involved in street patrols, site visits, and other forms of responsible and proactive policing.

Violent crimes were found to be closely related to the presence of disruptive families who attempt to resolve conflicts with violence. Neighborhood conflict management programs may be effective at reducing incidence of interpersonal violence. The most promising policies and programs would consider social, economic, and moral development of neighborhood persons together with improvement of the façades of public spaces. In this way, trust, solidarity, and the willingness of residents and others to intervene may be more closely aligned with producing public as opposed to private goods.

It should be clear by now that the problem of crime in urban neighborhoods is produced by a confluence of factors, and that policy and programmatic attempts to address the problem must emphasize early intervention from multiple angles, including social, economic, and moral development and uplifting neighborhood space together with neighborhood people. The multifaceted character of the problem and possible solutions is exemplified by Icepick, a former murderer, pimp, armed robber, and drug dealer who was one of the most cooperative collaborators in this study:

No more coming outside, no more sitting on your porch. We done took over. All they say is, "There is a pack of sellers out here, you know, I don't know what they fitting to do in a minute, so I only want to be out there seldom." So I go in, but now I go in, and the police come up and bust'em. Now they think I went in and called the police. So they come and see me, and give me a warning: "You better quit calling them police." "I haven't done anything." But they keep saying watch out for her because she keep calling the police. So what if, they start moving, they start moving. You have some that try to stand hard, and as I said, if they stay out and build up, and put in time, that's what they say, it's a business; nothing personal, just business. They been here for a while. It is just business. They think this is all they know.

If I stand out there and I devote all my time and energy into this, I deserve this. For real, that's how they be thinking. I deserve this, this is mines, and I'm not moving for nobody. Yea, I'm not moving my business for nobody. My money is coming in here, you know, this is bread and butter for my family.

But you know what I'm gonna do for my family when I get the money? I'm gone move them out this neighborhood. I'm gonna move them out in the suburbs where this here ain't going on there. And I'm 'a come back over through here and rake everything. I'll keep peoples looking down and whatnot. But for my family, I get tired of being over here. I gats some people now, selling my drugs, I can go in the suburbs, where it's clean and everything ain't none of this. It may be going on but you won't hear about it too much. My kids can come out and play.

I'm just like a parasite; I need a host to live on. So this is where my bread and butter comes from. I am getting fed through it. You know, I tell you, this is the way it gone be unless they get some jobs up in here and help us strengthen families. How you gone try to take what I gat to feed my family when you took away the little jobs that I once had? What did you expect? Then you call me a monster, when you are the one that done made me so from the time I was little! How can you be scared of something you done made?

Appendix A

METHODOLOGICAL APPENDIX

Introduction

Statistical findings regarding the relationships between neighborhood disorder (physical disorder, social disorder), collective efficacy, and the three crimes of narcotics violations, robbery, and battery for the years 1999 and 2000 are presented and discussed in this appendix.[1] These analyses begin with bivariate correlations that depict strengths of associations between the independent variables of physical disorder, social disorder, and collective efficacy, and the dependent variables of narcotics violations, robbery, and batteries for the years 1999 and 2000. These correlations show the direction (negative or positive) and strength of these relationships; the strength measures serve as points of departure to determine whether those relationships are significant enough to be worthy of further investigation.[2] While they should not be interpreted as causation, these correlations serve as springboards to further inquiries intended to increase our understanding of causal relationships. The data in this study are not appropriate for advanced statistical analyses such as hierarchical linear modeling to determine causality, mainly because this study is focused on a small area of 58 blocks, and so does not offer sufficient multilevel

---

1. See footnotes in chapter 1 for an understanding of how physical disorder, social disorder, and collective efficacy were measured.
2. Except in the case where insignificant relationships could still warrant further investigation to determine whether suppressor variables exist.

units and variations. Causal arguments are left as a task of chapters 5, 6, and 7, which provide thick ethnographic descriptions to explain how offenders select particular locations to commit crimes.

After reviewing bivariate coefficients to determine the direction and strengths of the relationships, cross-tabulations tables are used to dissect the data—to determine what proportion of street blocks observed within various measures of physical disorder, social disorder, and collective efficacy are matched with various levels of crime. To this end, for each year and for each of the three crimes, blocks that were more than a standard deviation above the mean of that type of crime for that year, were labeled hotspots, while those observed as less than a standard deviation below the mean were labeled coldspots; all others were labeled warmspots. The same criteria were used to categorize blocks as high, midrange, and low on physical disorder, social disorder, and collective efficacy. These quantitative findings set the stage for chapters 5, 6, and 7, which present qualitative findings that question, support, contradict, and explain them.

The official crime statistics provide an indication of where various 1999 and 2000 crime hotspots[3] were situated in Beat 213. However, since it was evident from the ethnography that, for many reasons, some criminal incidents are not reflected in official police statistics, independent sources of data were mined to provide information about unreported crimes. To this end, police crime statistics are cross-validated with results from a survey of neighborhood experts[4] who were asked, among other things, to identify based on their knowledge and experience blocks they considered to have high incidence of various crimes. The neighborhood expert survey also generated responses used to assign collective efficacy measures for each block. This information was further cross-validated with my field notes, which included sketches of where I observed crimes in progress or knew about where they occurred through local communication networks. Many similarities were apparent among the statistical, neighborhood experts', and ethnographic accounts of crime hotspots.

3. A block was designated as a hotspot if the crime reported to the police to have occurred there during a given period of time was 1/2 standard deviation above the mean of the total counts of that crime reported in the beat for the same time period. The analysis also included the designation of "cold spots" which is a standard deviation measure below the mean. The 1/2 standard deviation measure was used instead of a 1 standard deviation measure because the latter was often larger than the mean, resulting in a negative number of crimes for the designation of coldspot. That problem was eliminated with a 1 standard deviation measure.

4. Each block was represented by the knowledge of six neighborhood experts: two police officers, two reformers (persons active in neighborhood change), and two motivated offenders (persons known to have offended in the past; some of these informants have served time in prison or jail for drug dealing, armed robbery, theft, homicide, prostitution, burglary, battery, or aggravated assaults) or persons not actively involved in neighborhood reform.

Table A.1. Descriptive Statistics for 1999 and 2000 Crimes.

	N	Minimum	Maximum	Sum	Mean	Std. Deviation
1999 Narcotics	58	0	8	35	.60	1.297
1999 Robberies	58	0	11	59	1.02	2.073
1999 Batteries	58	0	14	59	1.02	2.132
2000 Narcotics	58	0	8	42	.72	1.554
2000 Robberies	58	0	18	74	1.28	2.694
2000 Batteries	58	0	38	267	4.60	7.076
Valid N (list wise)	58					

After official crime statistics are cross-validated, Geographic Information Systems (GIS) maps are presented to depict the spatial distributions. I then present cross-tabulations and Pearson bivariate coefficients to assess the theoretical claims of broken windows and collective efficacy theories aimed at explaining variation in the concentrations of crime over place and time. This quantitative approach is immediately followed by a qualitative approach that explains social processes.

A Close Look at the Hotspots

Table A.1 shows that in 1999, 35 narcotics violations, 59 robberies, and 59 batteries were reported to the Chicago Police Department as having occurred within Beat 213. In 2000, 42 narcotics violations, 74 robberies, and 267 batteries were reported for the same area.

Based on the definition of crime hotspots used in this study,[5] it was determined that 9 blocks were narcotics hotspots in both 1999 and 2000 (Table A.2). Blocks that were robbery hotspots numbered 9 in 1999; that number declined to 5 in 2000 (Table A.3). In 1999, 15 blocks were battery hotspots; in 2000 the number was 9 (Table A.4).

Blocks that were hotspots in both 1999 and 2000 were labeled stable hotspots. Note from Tables A.2–A.4 that there were five stable drug

---

5. Half a standard deviation above the mean = hotspot, half a standard deviation below the mean = coldspot. Also see note 1. To identify hotspots and coldspots, a relative cutoff point such as a standard deviation measure from the mean was used instead of an absolute cutoff such as highest 25 percent because the intention was to understand hotspots and coldspots as locations that are higher and lower in crime, relative to the patterns of distribution among all of the blocks in the beat.

Table A.2. Cross-validating Accounts of Narcotic Violations Hotspots.

Black Code	1999 Official Statistics	2000 Official Statistics	Stable Hotspots	Beat Police	Reformers	Motivated Offenders
143	Yes	Yes	Yes	No	Yes	Yes
144	No	Yes	No	No	Yes	Yes
152	No	No	No	Yes	Yes	Yes
174	Yes	No	No	No	No	No
181	No	No	No	Yes	Yes	Yes
204	No	No	No	Yes	Yes	Yes
223	No	No	No	No	No	No
289	Yes	Yes	Yes	Yes	Yes	Yes
297	Yes	No	No	No	No	No
298	Yes	No	No	No	No	No
302	Yes	Yes	Yes	Yes	Yes	Yes
314	No	Yes	No	No	No	No
323	No	Yes	No	No	No	No
324	Yes	Yes	Yes	Yes	Yes	Yes
325	Yes	Yes	Yes	Yes	Yes	Yes
328	No	Yes	No	No	No	No
335	Yes	No	No	No	No	No
Totals	9	9	5	7	9	9

Table A.3. Cross-validating Accounts of Robbery Hotspots.

Black Code	1999 Official Statistics	2000 Official Statistics	Stable Hotspots	Beat Police	Reformers	Motivated Offenders
119	Yes	Yes	Yes	Yes	Yes	Yes
143	Yes	Yes	Yes	Yes	Yes	Yes
144	Yes	Yes	Yes	Yes	Yes	Yes
173	Yes	No	No	No	No	No
181	No	No	No	No	No	Yes
204	No	No	No	Yes	Yes	Yes
289	Yes	Yes	Yes	Yes	Yes	Yes
302	Yes	No	No	No	No	No
321	Yes	No	No	No	No	No
324	No	No	No	Yes	No	Yes
325	Yes	Yes	Yes	Yes	Yes	Yes
328	Yes	No	No	No	No	No
Totals	9	5	5	7	6	8

Table A.4. Cross-validating Accounts of Battery Hotspots.

Black Code	1999 Official Statistics	2000 Official Statistics	Stable Hotspots	Beat Police	Reformers	Motivated Offenders
119	Yes	No	No	No	No	Yes
143	Yes	Yes	Yes	Yes	Yes	Yes
144	No	Yes	No	Yes	No	Yes
152	Yes	No	No	No	No	Yes
156	Yes	No	No	No	No	No
174	Yes	Yes	Yes	Yes	Yes	Yes
181	No	No	No	No	No	Yes
195	Yes	No	No	No	No	No
204	Yes	Yes	Yes	Yes	Yes	Yes
289	Yes	Yes	Yes	Yes	Yes	Yes
298	Yes	No	No	No	No	No
302	Yes	No	No	No	No	No
311	Yes	No	No	No	No	No
319	Yes	No	No	No	No	No
321	Yes	No	No	No	No	No
324	No	Yes	No	Yes	Yes	Yes
325	Yes	Yes	Yes	Yes	Yes	Yes
328	Yes	Yes	Yes	Yes	Yes	Yes
333	No	Yes	No	Yes	Yes	Yes
Totals	15	9	6	9	8	12

dealing hotspots, five stable robbery hotspots, and six stable battery hotspots. Note further that while four new drug dealing hotspots emerged in 2000, no new robbery hotspots emerged. This finding is supported by ethnographic data that suggest that drug dealers appear to occupy about the same number of blocks at any given time, but that the locations usedand the volume of business conducted within them changes frequently. By contrast, the robbers in this area return to the same locations quite frequently. Figures A.1–A.3 illustrate the spatial distribution of those hotspots. It is clear that the various hotspots are strategically clustered[6] in the northwestern and southeastern corners of the beat.

Ethnographic data presented in the narcotics and robbery chapters (chapters 5 and 6) further highlight these observations. For instance, residents and police officers report several instances when drug dealers appear to function out of "seasonal locations." They conduct business in several locations at one time but at different levels of intensity,

6. Existing very close to each other.

Spatial Distribution of Narcotic Violations
per Face Block, 1999–2000

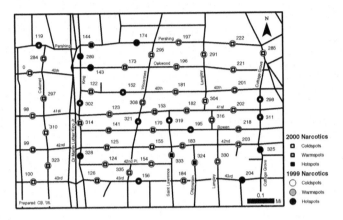

Figure A.1. Narcotics violations, per block (1999-2000).

Spatial Distribution of Robberies
per Face Block, 1999–2000

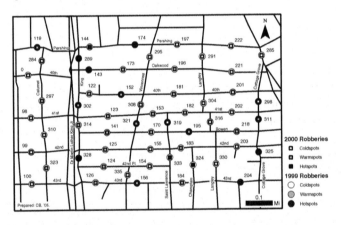

Figure A.2. Robberies, per block (1999-2000).

depending on the presence of opposing factors such as police enforcement, neighborhood complaints and intervention, gang turf fights, changes in the type of street drug that is "hot" on the market, and other exogenous factors. It is common knowledge in these communities that markets for different street drugs are located in different sections of the

Spatial Distribution of Batteries
per Face Block, 1999–2000

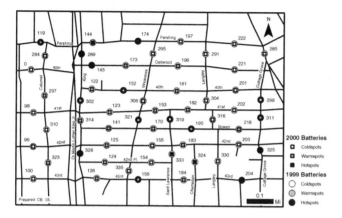

Figure A.3. Batteries, per block (1999-2000).

beat. One who is very knowledgeable about the streets can almost determine which drug is "hot" at the time simply by observing the blocks that have the highest level of "drug traffic" at a particular point in time and among a certain clientele. The stable drug-dealing hotspots (blocks 143, 289, 302, 324, and 325) have been identified as the most notorious and lucrative drug-dealing spots in the beat. This explains why all categories of neighborhood experts and the statistical analysis have identified these blocks as hotspots for street drug dealing.[7]

Ethnographic data explain some of the reasons particular blocks labeled as hotspots in 1999 were not identified as such in 2000, and why no new robbery hotspots emerged in 2000. For example, on Block 321, residents organized to close a small liquor and grocery store they perceived as a locus of questionable behaviors that often led to crime and violence. At their November 1997 beat meeting, residents and local businesspersons intensified discussions among themselves and complained to the police, aldermen, and other city officials about undesirable activities that had been ongoing on Block 321. That location remained on their list as a priority problem until October 2000, when the store was finally closed. The strategy they developed was that the residents would keep a watchful eye out for undesirable activities, and police officers would investigate the code compliance of the building and also issue citations where

7. See Tables A.2–A.4.

necessary. The store was found to be in violation of liquor laws, and in September 2000, the business license was suspended pending a hearing before a city commissioner. During subsequent beat meetings, residents reported an acceptable decrease in the loitering they saw as a precursor to violent and predatory crimes on that block. Concerned residents and local police used similar collaborative strategies on various other neighborhood blocks to affect perceived precursors to crime.

During beat meetings, the reduction in robberies on Block 302 was credited to efforts made by citizens involved in community policing who took action to alert senior citizens about neighborhood robberies. All of the robbery victims on that block in 1999 were senior citizens on their way to or from a nearby bus stop. In 2000, community policing meetings were sometimes held near that location, and special emphasis was placed on alerting seniors about their safety. During subsequent meetings, although seniors seemed to have exhibited increased fear of crime, they expressed better knowledge about how to avoid becoming a crime victim in public space. Several of them gave detailed narratives of the actions they took to change routine activities that may have placed them in danger of victimization.

All of the stable robbery hotspots (blocks 119, 143, 144, 289, and 325) are situated along the major thoroughfares of the beat, where local businesses are most heavily concentrated. Because of the ecological advantages they offer, such places are of great interest to motivated robbers and drug dealers. Those locations are of particular interest to robbers because businesses within them, such as the liquor stores, grocery stores, check-cashing outlets, and fast-food restaurants, are frequented by suitable targets— persons who are both distracted and likely to have money in their possession.

Cross-validating Official Data with Neighborhood Experts' Accounts of Hotspots

Tables A.2–A.4 compare official police statistical accounts of crime hotspots with neighborhood experts' perceptions of the same. These tables indicate that for all three crimes, although there were some differences concerning which blocks were identified as hotspots by whom, all of the blocks tabulated as stable hotspots by use of the official crime statistics were also identified as hotspots by all informants. It was clear that the official police crime statistics did not capture every crime that occurred on a block. Offenders and residents knew of isolated incidents of crime that occurred on certain blocks but were not reported to the police. However, since there was so much agreement among the offenders, residents, and beat police officers about the blocks that seemed to host the most crimes for both years (the stable hotspots), and that those agreements completely matched the hotspots identified by analyzing the official crime statistics, I am confident that the official crime statistics provide a reasonable estimate of the blocks that were crime hotspots in Beat 213 in 1999 and 2000. The next step was to examine correlations between indicators of neighborhood disorder and collective efficacy.

Correlations between Neighborhood Disorder, Collective Efficacy, and Crime

Eighteen correlations were examined between physical disorder, social disorder, collective efficacy, and the crimes of narcotics violations, robbery, and battery. Those figures are presented in Table A.5.

Physical Disorder and Crimes

Table A.5 indicates that in both 1999 and 2000, physical disorder was found to be positively associated with all three crimes. However, those relationships were not statistically significant. Tables A.6–A.11 explain these associations further by outlining cross-tabulations that show how various crime hotspots and coldspots were matched with various levels of physical disorder, social disorder, and collective efficacy. On the basis of Tables A.6 and A.7, it can be observed that for each year, 14 (78 percent) of the 18 blocks that ranked low on physical disorder were also drug-dealing coldspots. This finding supports broken windows theory, which suggests that low physical disorder will be matched with low crimes.

Broken windows theory also predicts that high physical disorder will be predominantly matched with high levels of drug dealing. However, this is not the case. For each year, only 3 (17 percent) of the 18 blocks that ranked high on physical disorder were drug-dealing hotspots, while 11 (61 percent) and 15 (83 percent) were drug-dealing coldspots, in 1999 and 2000 respectively. This finding contradicts broken windows theory, which would expect a large proportion of the blocks that were high on physical disorder to be drug dealing hotspots.

The same patterns hold true for robberies. Moreover, it is interesting to observe from Tables A.10 and A.11 that for each year, 8 (44 percent)

Table A.5. Bivariate Correlations for Physical Disorder, Social Disorder, Collective Efficacy, and 1999 and 2000 Crimes.

Variables	Coefficients	p-values	N
Crime and Physical Disorder			
1999 Narcotic Violations and Physical Disorder	.21	.11	58
1999 Robberies and Physical Disorder	.09	.50	58
1999 Batteries and Physical Disorder	.25	.06	58
2000 Narcotic Violations and Physical Disorder	.12	.38	58
2000 Robberies and Physical Disorder	.09	.49	58
2000 Batteries and Physical Disorder	.24	.07	58
Crime and Social Disorder			
1999 Narcotic Violations and Social Disorder	.33*	.01	58
1999 Robberies and Social Disorder	.32*	.01	58
1999 Batteries and Social Disorder	.31*	.02	58
2000 Narcotic Violations and Social Disorder	.36**	.01	58
2000 Robberies and Social Disorder	.36**	.01	58
2000 Batteries and Social Disorder	.44**	.001	58
Crimes and Collective Efficacy			
1999 Narcotic Violations and Collective Efficacy	−.43**	.002	47
1999 Robberies and Collective Efficacy	−.33**	.02	47
1999 Batteries and Collective Efficacy	−.23	.11	47
2000 Narcotic Violations and Collective Efficacy	−.58**	.000	47
2000 Robberies and Collective Efficacy	−.55**	.000	47
2000 Batteries and Collective Efficacy	−.54**	.000	47
Other Related Associations			
1999 and 2000 Narcotic Violations	.74**	.000	58
1999 and 2000 Robberies	.69**	.000	58
1999 and 2000 Batteries	.72**	.000	58
Physical Disorder and Social Disorder	.34**	.01	58
Physical Disorder and Collective Efficacy	−.11	.48	47
Social Disorder and Collective Efficacy	−.53**	.000	47

of the 18 blocks that ranked low on physical disorder were battery cold-spots; however, among the 18 blocks that ranked high on physical disorder, 5 (28 percent) were battery hotspots and 5 were battery coldspots.

These cross-tabulation figures suggest that although low physical disorder may have an important relationship with low levels of street drug dealing, robberies, and batteries, high physical disorder is insufficient to produce high levels of those crimes. Since high physical disorder does not appear to be strongly related to high levels of those three crimes, it is reasonable to question whether a low level of physical dis-

Table A.6. Physical Disorder *1999 Narcotic Cross-tabulation.

			1999 Narcotic			
			Coldspot	Warmspot	Hotspot	Total
Physical Disorder	High	Count	11	4	3	18
		% within Physical Disorder	61.1%	22.2%	16.7%	100.0%
	Mid	Count	15	3	4	22
		% within Physical Disorder	68.2%	13.6%	18.2%	100.0%
	Low	Count	14	2	2	18
		% within Physical Disorder	77.8%	11.1%	11.1%	100.0%
Total		Count	40	9	9	58
		% within Physical Disorder	69.0%	15.5%	15.5%	100.0%

Table A.7. Physical Disorder *2000 Narcotic Cross-tabulation.

			2000 Narcotic			
			Coldspot	Warmspot	Hotspot	Total
Physical Disorder	High	Count	15	0	3	18
		% within Physical Disorder	83.3%	.0%	16.7%	100.0%
	Mid	Count	11	7	4	22
		% within Physical Disorder	50.0%	31.8%	18.2%	100.0%
	Low	Count	14	2	2	18
		% within Physical Disorder	77.8%	11.1%	11.1%	100.0%
Total		Count	40	9	9	58
		% within Physical Disorder	69.0%	15.5%	15.5%	100.0%

order causes low crime. Is it possible for low crime to be caused by some other factor that, simultaneously or in turn, also produces low physical disorder?

It is important to note that there is likely a reciprocal relationship between low physical disorder and low crimes, a relationship that needs

Table A.8. Physical Disorder *1999 Robbery Cross-tabulation.

| | | | 1999 Robbery | | | |
			Coldspot	Warmspot	Hotspot	Total
Physical Disorder	High	Count	8	7	3	18
		% within Physical Disorder	44.4%	38.9%	16.7%	100.0%
	Mid	Count	13	6	3	22
		% within Physical Disorder	59.1%	27.3%	13.6%	100.0%
	Low	Count	11	4	3	18
		% within Physical Disorder	61.1%	22.2%	16.7%	100.0%
Total		Count	32	17	9	58
		% within Physical Disorder	55.2%	29.3%	15.5%	100.0%

Table A.9. Physical Disorder *2000 Robbery Cross-tabulation.

| | | | 2000 Robbery | | | |
			Coldspot	Warmspot	Hotspot	Total
Physical Disorder	High	Count	8	8	2	18
		% within Physical Disorder	44.4%	44.4%	11.1%	100.0%
	Mid	Count	11	8	3	22
		% within Physical Disorder	50.0%	36.4%	13.6%	100.0%
	Low	Count	8	10	0	18
		% within Physical Disorder	44.4%	55.6%	.0%	100.0%
Total		Count	27	26	5	58
		% within Physical Disorder	46.6%	44.8%	8.6%	100.0%

clarification. For instance, are low levels of narcotics violations really a result of low physical disorder, or is low physical disorder largely a result of the absence (or near absence) of street drug dealing? If the association is indeed reciprocal, what social conditions determine how each causal direction is formed? Moreover, what is it about the manner in which

Table A.10. Physical Disorder *1999 Battery Cross-tabulation.

| | | | 1999 Battery | | | |
			Coldspot	Warmspot	Hotspot	Total
Physical Disorder	High	Count	8	2	8	18
		% within Physical Disorder	44.4%	11.1%	44.4%	100.0%
	Mid	Count	13	4	5	22
		% within Physical Disorder	59.1%	18.2%	22.7%	100.0%
	Low	Count	14	2	2	18
		% within Physical Disorder	77.8%	11.1%	11.1%	100.0%
Total		Count	35	8	15	58
		% within Physical Disorder	60.3%	13.8%	25.9%	100.0%

Table A.11. Physical Disorder *2000 Battery Cross-tabulation.

| | | | 2000 Battery | | | |
			Coldspot	Warmspot	Hotspot	Total
Physical Disorder	High	Count	5	8	5	18
		% within Physical Disorder	27.8%	44.4%	27.8%	100.0%
	Mid	Count	11	7	4	22
		% within Physical Disorder	50.0%	31.8%	18.2%	100.0%
	Low	Count	8	10	0	18
		% within Physical Disorder	44.4%	55.6%	.0%	100.0%
Total		Count	24	25	9	58
		% within Physical Disorder	41.4%	43.1%	15.5%	100.0%

street drug dealing, robberies, and batteries occur that makes high physical disorder an insufficient condition to produce such crime hotspots? Answers to these and other relevant questions are suggested in the ethnographic data through which offenders explain in detail how and where they commit crimes.

Table A.12. Social Disorder *1999 Narcotic Cross-tabulation.

			1999 Narcotic			
			Coldspot	Warmspot	Hotspot	Total
Social Disorder	High	Count	13	4	6	23
		% within Social Disorder	*56.5%*	17.4%	*26.1%*	100.0%
	Mid	Count	8	1	1	10
		% within Social Disorder	80.0%	10.0%	10.0%	100.0%
	Low	Count	19	4	2	25
		% within Social Disorder	*76.0%*	*16.0%*	*8.0%*	100.0%
Total		Count	40	9	9	58
		% within Social Disorder	69.0%	15.5%	15.5%	100.0%

Social Disorder and Crimes

For both 1999 and 2000, social disorder was found to have positive and statistically significant associations with all three types of crime (Table A.5). Cross-tabulations between social disorder and the various crimes further explain these relationships (Tables A.12–A.17). These tables show that in both 1999 and 2000, an overwhelming majority of the 25 blocks that were low on social disorder were drug-dealing coldspots (19 or 76 percent and 20 or 80 percent, respectively). Also, 64 percent (1999) and 60 percent (2000) of the blocks that were low on social disorder were robbery coldspots, and 68 percent (1999) and 52 percent (2000) were battery coldspots (Tables A.14–A.17). These findings are consistent with broken windows theory, which would predict that most blocks that are low on social disorder would be drug-dealing, robbery, and battery coldspots.

However, although low social disorder is somewhat strongly matched with low crime rates, high social disorder is not so well matched with high crime rates. Among the 23 blocks that showed high social disorder in 1999 and 2000, only 6 (26 percent) and 8 (35 percent) were narcotics hotspots, respectively (Tables A.12 and A.13). Similarly, only 35 percent and 22 percent, and 39 percent and 35 percent of high social disorder blocks were robbery and battery hotspots, respectively (Tables A.14–A.17). Therefore, these cross-tabulations indicate that the statistically significant associations between social disorder and all three types

Table A.13. Social Disorder *2000 Narcotic Cross-tabulation.

			Coldspot	Warmspot	Hotspot	Total
				2000 Narcotic		
Social Disorder	High	Count	11	4	8	23
		% within Social Disorder	47.8%	17.4%	34.8%	100.0%
	Mid	Count	9	1	0	10
		% within Social Disorder	90.0%	10.0%	.0%	100.0%
	Low	Count	20	4	1	25
		% within Social Disorder	80.0%	16.0%	4.0%	100.0%
Total		Count	40	9	9	58
		% within Social Disorder	69.0%	15.5%	15.5%	100.0%

Table A.14. Social Disorder *1999 Robbery Cross-tabulation.

			Coldspot	Warmspot	Hotspot	Total
				1999 Robbery		
Social Disorder	High	Count	9	6	8	23
		% within Social Disorder	39.1%	26.1%	34.8%	100.0%
	Mid	Count	7	3	0	10
		% within Social Disorder	70.0%	30.0%	.0%	100.0%
	Low	Count	16	8	1	25
		% within Social Disorder	64.0%	32.0%	4.0%	100.0%
Total		Count	32	17	9	58
		% within Social Disorder	55.2%	29.3%	15.5%	100.0%

of crime are explained by the observation that low social disorder is more strongly linked to low crime rates than high social disorder is linked to high crime rates. In other words, the significant relationship between social disorder and the crimes of street drug dealing, robbery, and battery may tell us more about what does not happen in the absence of low social

Table A.15. Social Disorder *2000 Robbery Cross-tabulation.

			2000 Robbery			
			Coldspot	Warmspot	Hotspot	Total
Social Disorder	High	Count	8	10	5	23
		% within Social Disorder	*34.8%*	43.5%	*21.7%*	100.0%
	Mid	Count	4	6	0	10
		% within Social Disorder	40.0%	60.0%	.0%	100.0%
	Low	Count	15	10	0	25
		% within Social Disorder	*60.0%*	40.0%	.0%	100.0%
Total		Count	27	26	5	58
		% within Social Disorder	46.6%	44.8%	8.6%	100.0%

Table A.16. Social Disorder *1999 Battery Cross-tabulation.

			1999 Battery			
			Coldspot	Warmspot	Hotspot	Total
Social Disorder	High	Count	11	3	9	23
		% within Social Disorder	*47.8%*	13.0%	*39.1%*	100.0%
	Mid	Count	7	1	2	10
		% within Social Disorder	70.0%	10.0%	20.0%	100.0%
	Low	Count	17	4	4	25
		% within Social Disorder	*68.0%*	16.0%	*16.0%*	100.0%
Total		Count	35	8	15	58
		% within Social Disorder	60.3%	13.8%	25.9%	100.0%

disorder (crimes do not flourish) than about what high social disorder actually causes. By and large, in the absence of social disorder, street drug dealing, robberies, and batteries are considerably less likely to flourish. However, the presence of high social disorder is not a sufficient condition to produce high levels of street drug dealing, robberies, and batteries. For

Table A.17. Social Disorder *2000 Battery Cross-tabulation.

			2000 Battery			
			Coldspot	Warmspot	Hotspot	Total
Social Disorder	High	Count	7	8	8	23
		% within Social Disorder	30.4%	34.8%	34.8%	100.0%
	Mid	Count	4	6	0	10
		% within Social Disorder	40.0%	60.0%	.0%	100.0%
	Low	Count	13	11	1	25
		% within Social Disorder	52.0%	44.0%	4.0%	100.0%
Total		Count	24	25	9	58
		% within Social Disorder	41.4%	43.1%	15.5%	100.0%

instance, in 1999, among the 23 blocks that ranked high in social disorder, a majority (13, or 57 percent) were drug-dealing coldspots. This suggests that many blocks that rank high for social disorder are still lacking certain characteristics that are needed to produce high crime rates. What are those missing ingredients? Moreover, why doesn't street drug dealing flourish under conditions of low social disorder? These data raise some important questions that require attention.

Collective Efficacy and Crimes

The central claim of collective efficacy theory is that when multilevel inter-neighborhood comparisons are conducted, higher levels of trust, solidarity, and willingness among residents to intervene on behalf of neighborhood safety as a common good (shared expectations for action) will have stronger negative associations with neighborhood crime (Sampson, Raudenbush, and Earls 1997, 918). In this study, collective efficacy is measured as the combination of trust and solidarity among neighbors, along with their willingness to intervene when "something perceived to be wrong" is in progress on their block. These responses were obtained from a survey of neighborhood experts. One advantage of using neighborhood experts rather than randomly selected residents is that they are much more knowledgeable about day-to-day neighborhood processes than most residents, who know little about what happens there because

Table A.18. Collective Efficacy *1999 Narcotic Cross-tabulation.

| | | | 1999 Narcotic | | | |
			Coldspot	Warmspot	Hotspot	Total
Collective Efficacy	High	Count	12	3	1	16
		% within Collective Efficacy	75.0%	18.8%	6.3%	100.0%
	Mid	Count	10	2	2	14
		% within Collective Efficacy	71.4%	14.3%	14.3%	100.0%
	Low	Count	10	2	5	17
		% within Collective Efficacy	58.8%	11.8%	29.4%	100.0%
Total		Count	32	7	8	47
		% within Collective Efficacy	68.1%	14.9%	17.0%	100.0%

they are not actively involved. During the three years of ethnographic research that preceded the neighborhood experts' survey, I observed that many residents were not very aware of the actions of their neighbors because they either had not lived there for very long or had mainly kept to themselves. One drawback of using results from a neighborhood experts' survey is that it may not appear to represent the voice of many in the community. However, this may be balanced by the fact that activities on each block were represented by the responses of reformers, police officers, and offenders.

Pearson bivariate coefficients between collective efficacy and the three crimes in question were significantly negative for both years, except for 1999 batteries (Table A.5). The strongest relationship in 1999 was with street drug dealing $-.43**$ ($p = .002$) and with robberies $-.55$ ($p = .000$) in 2000. There were also stronger relationships between collective efficacy and all three crimes in 1999 compared to 2000. Since collective efficacy was not independently measured for each year, the change is not reflective of variations in levels of collective efficacy between 1999 and 2000. Instead, it suggests that in 2000 crime declines were greater on blocks with higher levels of collective efficacy.

Cross-tabulations (Tables A.18–A.23) further outline the relationships between the various crimes and collective efficacy. For both years, an overwhelming majority of the 16 blocks that ranked high for collective efficacy were narcotics coldspots (12, or 75 percent in 1999; and 13, or

Table A.19. Collective Efficacy *2000 Narcotic Cross-tabulation.

			2000 Narcotic			
			Coldspot	Warmspot	Hotspot	Total
Collective Efficacy	High	Count	13	2	1	16
		% within Collective Efficacy	81.3%	12.5%	6.3%	100.0%
	Mid	Count	8	4	2	14
		% within Collective Efficacy	57.1%	28.6%	14.3%	100.0%
	Low	Count	9	2	6	17
		% within Collective Efficacy	52.9%	11.8%	35.3%	100.0%
Total		Count	30	8	9	47
		% within Collective Efficacy	63.8%	17.0%	19.1%	100.0%

Table A.20. Collective Efficacy *1999 Robbery Cross-tabulation.

			1999 Robbery			
			Coldspot	Warmspot	Hotspot	Total
Collective Efficacy	High	Count	10	4	2	16
		% within Collective Efficacy	62.5%	25.0%	12.5%	100.0%
	Mid	Count	9	4	1	14
		% within Collective Efficacy	64.3%	28.6%	7.1%	100.0%
	Low	Count	6	6	5	17
		% within Collective Efficacy	35.3%	35.3%	29.4%	100.0%
Total		Count	25	14	8	47
		% within Collective Efficacy	53.2%	29.8%	17.0%	100.0%

81 percent in 2000). Although the percentages were smaller, similar patterns were observed for robberies and batteries, except for 2000, when only 50 percent of the blocks that were high on collective efficacy were battery coldspots. These statistics suggest that high collective efficacy may be an important condition for low crimes. However, there is likely

Table A.21. Collective Efficacy *2000 Robbery Cross-tabulation.

| | | | 2000 Robbery | | | |
			Coldspot	Warmspot	Hotspot	Total
Collective Efficacy	High	Count	10	6	0	16
		% within Collective Efficacy	*62.5%*	37.5%	*.0%*	100.0%
	Mid	Count	7	7	0	14
		% within Collective Efficacy	50.0%	50.0%	.0%	100.0%
	Low	Count	3	10	4	17
		% within Collective Efficacy	*17.6%*	58.8%	*23.5%*	100.0%
Total		Count	20	23	4	47
		% within Collective Efficacy	42.6%	48.9%	8.5%	100.0%

Table A.22. Collective Efficacy *1999 Battery Cross-tabulation.

| | | | 1999 Battery | | | |
			Coldspot	Warmspot	Hotspot	Total
Collective Efficacy	High	Count	11	2	3	16
		% within Collective Efficacy	*68.8%*	12.5%	*18.8%*	100.0%
	Mid	Count	10	2	2	14
		% within Collective Efficacy	71.4%	14.3%	14.3%	100.0%
	Low	Count	8	3	6	17
		% within Collective Efficacy	*47.1%*	17.6%	*35.3%*	100.0%
Total		Count	29	7	11	47
		% within Collective Efficacy	61.7%	14.9%	23.4%	100.0%

a reciprocal relationship between the two variables. Low neighborhood narcotic violations, robberies, and batteries can also lead to high collective efficacy.

The relationship between collective efficacy and crime is quite complex. Collective efficacy theorist would also expect that among the

Table A.23. Collective Efficacy *2000 Battery Cross-tabulation.

			2000 Battery			
			Coldspot	Warmspot	Hotspot	Total
Collective Efficacy	High	Count	8	7	1	16
		% within Collective Efficacy	50.0%	43.8%	6.3%	100.0%
	Mid	Count	7	5	2	14
		% within Collective Efficacy	50.0%	35.7%	14.3%	100.0%
	Low	Count	1	10	6	17
		% within Collective Efficacy	5.9%	58.8%	35.3%	100.0%
Total		Count	16	22	9	47
		% within Collective Efficacy	34.0%	46.8%	19.1%	100.0%

blocks observed as low on collective efficacy, a majority would be crime hotspots. However, cross-tabulations show that in 1999 and 2000, among the 17 blocks that were low on collective efficacy only 5 (29 percent) and 6 (35 percent) were narcotics hotspots, respectively. Similar patterns are observed with robberies and batteries. In 1999 and 2000, only 5 (29 percent) and 4 (24 percent) of the 17 low-collective-efficacy blocks were robbery hotspots, respectively. Furthermore, for each year, 6 (35 percent) of the low-collective-efficacy blocks were battery hotspots. Therefore, while high collective efficacy was a strong match with low level of street drug dealing, robberies, and batteries, low collective efficacy was an insufficient condition to produce high levels of those crimes. Why is that the case? What is the missing criterion between low collective efficacy and high crimes?

Ethnographic data reveal several instances when neighborhood collective action resulted in displacement or elimination of criminal activities. During beat meetings, residents, business owners, political representatives, and others frequently organize to identify and prioritize perceived neighborhood problems. Reducing narcotics violations, robberies, and batteries frequently topped residents' prioritized lists. The year 2000 was a particularly strong year for neighborhood organizing in Beat 213 because of several issues on the table at the time. For the previous two years, neighborhood actors were busy organizing to create the sort of neighborhoods they believed would mark the new millennium. This often meant lower crime, stronger citizen involvement, holding elected officials more accountable, and addressing issues of affordable housing.

Homeowners also showed greater concern about property values than they had in the previous two years. Many of these concerns centered on the future of the neighborhoods as public housing units were being demolished daily. In a rather haphazard fashion, public housing residents were being placed in rooming houses, motels, and other locations in the beat. Although the possible placement of public housing tenants in smaller nearby housing units was a concern, residents seemed to be more worried about what would replace the many empty lots throughout the Bronzeville area. Many of the new homeowners who began entering the area in 1998, 1999, and 2000 attended beat meetings faithfully for at least the first six months of residence. Such interest gave the more seasoned residents some reason to believe they were supported in their quest to create a neighborhood that looked and felt safer, so that they could keep the new homeowners and attract desirable others, especially young middle-class African Americans, to the Grand Boulevard and Bronzeville area. These vibrant years of collective action seem to have contributed to the shift in crimes that occurred away from high collective efficacy areas in 2000.

Summary and Conclusion

Overall, the statistical findings outlined in this appendix both support and challenge broken windows and collective efficacy theories. Counter to the expectation of broken windows theory, physical disorder was not found to be significantly related to any of the three types of crimes (narcotics violations, robbery, and battery) for either 1999 or 2000. In general support of broken windows theory, for both years, social disorder was found to be significantly related to all three types of crime. However, when this relationship was examined more closely, it became apparent that, consistent with the expectations of broken windows theory, low social disorder was predominantly matched with low crime. In contradiction of broken windows theory, high social disorder blocks were not predominantly crime hotspots. Instead, they appeared to be just as likely to be coldspots. This led to the conclusion that high social disorder is insufficient for high crime, and highlights the need for further inquiries into these puzzles.

With the exception of 1999 batteries, all three types of crime were found to be significantly and negatively related to levels of collective efficacy. Consistent with the expectations of collective efficacy theorists, high collective efficacy was predominantly matched with low crime. However, in contradiction to collective efficacy theory, low collective efficacy blocks were just as likely to be crime coldspots as to be hotspots. This suggests that low collective efficacy is insufficient to produce high crime rates. These findings set the stage for introducing the qualitative data that were gathered with the explicit purpose of deciphering meaning-making and causal relationships.

Finally, discussion of the quantitative data in this appendix and elsewhere in this book may give the impression that the ethnographic data were gathered with the intention of explaining the puzzles posed by the quantitative data. However, that is not the case. Indeed, collection of ethnographic data began in 1997, while the statistical data used (from 1999 and 2000) were not available from the Chicago Police Department until July 2001. By that date, most of the field interviews, including the survey of neighborhood experts that provided an independent account of crime hotspots, were already completed and analyzed. In other words, before obtaining the statistical data outlined in this appendix, I already knew where the drug dealing, robbery, battery, and other crime hotspots were—based on the accounts of offenders, law-abiding residents, police officers, business persons, visitors to the area, and my own direct observations. Based on these non-quantitative data, I had already produced a hand-drawn sketch of various neighborhood crime hotspots. When the quantitative data were finally cleaned and analyzed in SPSS and GIS toward the end of 2001, I was astonished to discover how perfectly the ethnographic and survey accounts of crime hotspots were matched with the analyses of the official crime statistics on hotspots.

The quantitative data presented in this appendix should be understood as an independent source of verification for the qualitative data that form the core of this book. The independent sources of data can also be understood as verifications of each other; but it is important to know the sequence in which the data were gathered and analyzed. It is hoped that although the statistical data presented in this chapter are quite descriptive, they will serve as a foundation for more rigorous statistical analyses based on data from larger samples, which seek to test various new hypotheses derived from the qualitative data. Most notably, future statistical analyses should calculate scales of ecological disadvantage and explain associated interaction effects with broken windows and collective efficacy variables. The key question is, to what extent does the way space/place becomes imbedded within larger space/place, and the non-criminal events that occur within the space/place in question, influence the effects of broken windows, collective efficacy, and perhaps other variables on crime?

The qualitative data in this book have explained *how* this occurs, and the independently gathered quantitative data in this appendix support the conclusions derived from the qualitative data. However, because of the small sample sizes and the fact that this is a study of only one broad neighborhood, key findings from this book should be tested with larger sample sizes obtained across multiple research sites. The hypotheses, however, should be formulated based on the processes explained by the qualitative data.

Appendix B

Author and Citation	Research Methods	Research Focus	Major Findings	Supports BW Theory?
Corman, Hope and Naci Mocan. 2002.	-Quantitative- *Uses unemployment rates and real minimum wage to measure economic conditions. *Uses felony arrests, police force size, and NYC residents in prison to measure sanctions. *Uses misdemeanor arrest rates to measure broken windows policing.	Analyze impact of economic conditions and various deterrence measures on 5 different index crimes (murder, assault, robbery, burglary, motor vehicle theft). Investigate the validity of the broken windows hypothesis.	*Increased police presence accounted for 20% decline in motor vehicle theft but had no effect on other crimes. *Increase in murder arrests, prison population, and the real minimum wage explained 53% of drop in murders. *Felony arrests deter all 5 crimes analyzed. *Unemployment rate has impact on burglary and motor vehicle theft. *Real minimum wage as impact on murder and robbery.	YES- But only in reference to motor vehicle theft and robbery.
Crank, J.P., A. Giacomazzi, and C. Heck. 2003	-Quantitative- *Uses a random telephone survey of 806 county residents.	Assess citizens' attitudes toward crime and disorder to assist local law enforcement in the development of crime prevention strategies.	*Residents who observed drug/gang activity were more likely to believe that all types of criminal and disorderly activity were heightened. *Residents did not confuse what they saw on television with perceptions of crime in the areas where they lived. *Generally weak linkages between perceptions of crime and disorder problems, residents' fears of crime, and concerns over safety. *Consistently found that concerns over personal safety and fear of victimization affected the extent to which respondents left their houses for recreational or social reasons.	MIXED RESULTS

Author	Method	Purpose	Findings	Deterrence
Funk, P. and P. Kugler. 2003.	-Quantitative- *Uses Swiss quarterly time series data to measure increases in crime.	Investigate interrelationships between crimes of different severity levels.	*An increase in minor crimes dynamically triggers more severe crimes without the reverse being true. *Tougher enforcement when it comes to mild offenses reduces minor crimes and also significantly deters more severe offenses.	YES
Giacopassi, D. and D. R. Forde. 2000.	-Quantitative- *Uses state- and city-level homicide and traffic fatality data. *Uses correlational analysis and regression analyses to compute the relationship between homicide rates and traffic fatality rates.	Assess the relationship between homicide rates and traffic fatality rates. Traffic fatalities are assumed to be indices of incivility and aggression, indicating a disregard for social conventions, leading to more serious violations, such as homicide.	*Significant relationship between the traffic fatality rates and homicide rates hold true for both state- and city-level data.	YES
Golub, Andrew, et al. 2003.	-Quantitative- *Uses the Arrestee Drug Abuse Monitoring (ADAM) Policing Study, which asked NYC arrestees about their awareness of response to Quality of Life (QOL) policing. *The authors limited their analysis to 539 arrestees.	Look at whether Quality of Life (QOL) policing deters offenders from engaging in these types of disorderly behaviors.	*The majority of arrestees were aware of QOL policing initiatives. *About 1/2 of arrestees stopped or cut back on each QOL behavior. *About 2/3 of those reporting reductions listed police presence as their main reason. *Fewer than 10% indicated that they reduced their behavior because of direct criminal justice contact.	YES- Increased enforcement of QOL laws deterred arrestees from engaging in such disorderly behaviors.

(continued)

Author and Citation	Research Methods	Research Focus	Major Findings	Supports BW Theory?
Harcourt, Bernard E. 1998, 2001	-Quantitative- *Replicates Skogan's Disorder and Decline: Crime and the Spiral of Decay in American Neighborhoods (1987) study.	Examine the empirical evidence and the social influence explanation supporting New York City's experiment with order-maintenance policing.	*Certain types of crimes like rape, purse snatching, and pick-pocketing are not significantly related to disorder. *Other types of crimes like physical assault and burglary are not significantly related to disorder when neighborhood poverty, stability, and race are held constant. *Although robbery remains significantly related to disorder, a cluster of five Newark neighborhoods exert excessive influence on the statistical findings. When these neighborhoods are set aside, the relationship between robbery victimization and disorder disappears.	NO
Herbert, Steve. 2001.	-Qualitative- *Compares community policing and broken windows (order maintenance) policing and provides a history of recent policing and a review of the debates about police effectiveness.	Focus on police culture and organization, public attitudes about crime and criminal justice, and the activities of political elites while attempting to explain why community policing and broken windows policing are often conflated.	*The author concludes that, though there may be little reason to accept that broken windows policing is responsible for reducing crime, it does work, albeit in cultural and political terms because it fits comfortably with established patterns within police departments and American culture and politics.	YES

Citation	Methodology	Purpose	Findings	Supports?
Kelling, George L. and Catherine M. Coles. 1996	-Qualitative- *Uses case studies of Baltimore, Boston, New York, San Francisco, and Seattle.	Examine crime prevention and the applications of broken windows policing.	*The authors argue that police efforts to control disorderly behavior in public places have succeeded in reducing more serious crimes.	YES
Kelling, George L. and William J. Bratton. 1998.	-Qualitative- *Recounts how and why New York City decided to employ broken windows policing to combat crime.	Attempt to explain why police played an important role in crime reduction in New York City.	*The authors assert that the restoration of assertive policing in 1994 and 1995 interacted with community forces to achieve an unprecedented "tipping point" in violent and other forms of crime.	YES
Taylor, Ralph. 2001.	-Quantitative- *Uses surveys, police records, Census data, and assessments of disorder to produce a longitudinal profile of Baltimore neighborhoods.	Examines Broken Windows Theory by looking at Baltimore neighborhoods.	*Observed disorder predicted several violent crimes. *Home ownership rates and racial composition of neighborhoods were stronger predictors of changes in crime rates than were levels of disorder.	MIXED RESULTS- But raises serious questions about broken windows policing and theory.

Appendix C

RECENT TRENDS IN RESEARCH ON COLLECTIVE EFFICACY

Author and Citation	Research Methods	Research Focus	Major Findings	Supports CE Theory?
Atkinson, Rowland and John Flint. 2004.	-Mixed Methods- *Uses survey and interview techniques. *Looks at crime and disorder in adjacent neighborhoods of differing social composition.	Focus on community responses to crime and the relationship between formal and informal agents and mechanisms of social control.	*Residents of deprived neighborhoods had more friends and family in the area. *People tended to trust others to help them; however, this was significantly more true in affluent neighborhoods. *In all neighborhoods the police and "looking out for neighbors" were regarded as by far the most important mechanisms of social control. *Outside officials and agencies were twice as likely to be viewed as important in deprived neighborhoods.	YES
Browning, Christopher R. 2002.	-Quantitative- *Uses Census data , 1994–1995 Project on Human Development in Chicago Neighborhoods Community Survey, 1994–1995 Chicago homicide data, and the 1995–1997 Chicago Health and Social Life Survey	Apply social disorganization perspective on the neighborhood-level determinants of crime to partner violence.	*Both population and concentrated disadvantage are positively and significantly associated with intimate-partner homicide. *Concentrated disadvantage is associated with intimate-partner homicide, though this is mediated by collective efficacy. *The average effect of collective efficacy is negative and significantly associated with partner violence independent of individual and relationship features that increase the risk of violence.	YES

Carr, Patrick J. 2003.	-Qualitative- *Presents a five-year ethnographic study of informal social control in the "Beltway" neighborhood of Chicago.	Examine informal social control at the private, parochial, and public levels.	*Controls at the private and parochial level can be weaker and less important than previously assumed. *The parochial and the public arenas are inseparable from each other, not independent as others have argued.	YES- But, questions whether strong social ties are crucial to neighborhood control.
DeKeseredy, W. S., et al. 2003	Quantitative- *Uses data from the Quality of Neighborhood Life Survey of an urban area in Eastern Ontario, Canada.	Test and apply a model of collective efficacy to domestic violence and other crimes in Canadian public housing.	*Concerns about street crimes and informal means of social control designed to prevent such harms are not effective forms of alleviating intimate partner violence in public housing. *Collective efficacy was related to victimization. *Only 23.2% of residents reported that they got together in the homes of their neighbors. *For all questions about engaging in activities with neighbors, more than 50% of respondents indicated that they very rarely or never participated with neighbors in various activities. *78.5% of the respondents indicated that they do not belong to any social clubs or organizations.	YES

(continued)

Author and Citation	Research Methods	Research Focus	Major Findings	Supports CE Theory?
Duncan, Terry E., et al. 2003.	-Quantitative- *Uses data collected from 1,105 individuals from 392 families.	Examine relations among neighborhood-, family-, and individual-level variables, and perceptions of neighborhood collective efficacy.	*Significant variation was evident at the individual, family, and neighborhood levels. *Higher neighborhood violent crime was significantly related to lower levels of perceived collective efficacy. *Neighborhoods characterized by disorder have high levels of fear and mistrust, and weak community social ties. *Did NOT find a relation between neighborhood demographic indicators and perceived neighborhood collective efficacy. *Two-parent families had higher perceptions of collective efficacy than did single-parent families. *Perceptions of collective efficacy were higher among older respondents.	YES- Partial support.
Ford, Julie M., and Andrew A. Beveridge. 2004.	-Quantitative- Uses date from the community-based program Fighting Back, the 1990 Census, and Select Phone data from 1997.	Provide a more comprehensive view of the ecological profile of neighborhoods that have to cope with drug dealing in public places and to present a preliminary test of the potential dimensions of collective efficacy as it pertains to business location in such neighborhoods.	*Census tracts where visible drug sales are highest are more frequently located in poor, predominantly black neighborhoods with higher unemployment and dropout rates. *Neighborhoods with high levels of visible drug sales differ dramatically from their low visibility counterparts as a result of the absence of desirable businesses. *High visibility tracts have significantly fewer banks, supermarkets, clothing stores, bookstores, sporting goods stores, movie theaters, and gyms, when compared to low visibility tracts.	YES

(continued)

Citation	Method	Purpose	Findings	
Lowenkamp, Christopher T., Francis T. Cullen, and Travis C. Pratt. 2003.	-Quantitative- *Replicates Sampson and Groves's 1989 Test of Social Disorganization Theory.	Test social disorganization theory using the 1994 British Crime Survey.	*SES, ethnic heterogeneity, and urbanization all exert a statistically significant inverse effect on local friendship networks. *Ethnic heterogeneity, residential stability, and family disruption were all significantly related to organizational participation in the expected direction. *SES and urbanization was NOT a significant predictor of organizational participation. *Residential stability and family disruption had a significant relationship with total victimization.	YES
Morenoff, Jeffrey D., Robert J. Sampson, and Stephen W. Raudenbush. 2001.	-Quantitative- Uses Census data and survey data from 8,872 Chicago residents to predict homicide variations in 1996–1998 across 343 neighborhoods.	Look at resource inequality, social processes, and spatial interdependence to predict homicide rates in Chicago.	*Spatial proximity to homicide is strongly related to increased homicide rates. *Concentrated disadvantage and low collective efficacy also independently predict increased homicide.	YES
Pattillo, Mary E. 1998.	-Qualitative- Uses participant observation methods to collect data from a black middle-class neighborhood in Chicago.	Examine how residents of a black middle-class neighborhood manage high internal poverty rates and close proximity to high-crime areas.	*The residents of this neighborhood have formed strong primary and institutional ties based on high rates of home ownership and residential stability. These ties promote neighborhood-level familiarity, integrate disparate networks, and facilitate informal and formal social control. *However, these ties also thwart efforts to totally rid the neighborhood of gangs and drugs.	YES

Author and Citation	Research Methods	Research Focus	Major Findings	Supports CE Theory?
Sabol, William J., Claudia J. Coulton, and Jill E. Korbin. 2004.	-Qualitative- Reviews literature regarding community violence prevention when it comes to youth violence, child maltreatment, and domestic violence.	Examine the capacity of communities to prevent violence.	*Strong social ties alone within communities may not be sufficient to produce the capacity to prevent violence. *Neighborhoods with strong ties and dense networks may not be able to maintain informal social controls and safety if these neighborhoods are isolated from contacts with the broader society. *Though violence prevention programs rarely have an explicit goal of building community capacity to prevent violence, they can nevertheless be part of a community-building effort. *Community capacity consists of the social capital and formal and informal organizations that can be drawn on to reduce violence.	YES
Sampson, Robert J., and Stephen J. Raudenbush. 1999.	-Quantitative- *Uses Census data, police records, an independent survey, and videotaping and systematic social observation of Chicago streets.	Assess the sources and consequences of public disorder and test the theory of collective efficacy and structural constraints.	*Structural characteristics, especially concentrated poverty and mixed land use, were strongly associated with physical and social disorder. *Collective efficacy predicted lower observed disorder after controlling sociodemographic and land use characteristics and perceived disorder and prior rates of predatory crime. *Collective efficacy also maintained a significant relationship with violent crime after adjusting for simultaneous feedback effects. *Observed disorder did not match the theoretical expectations set up by the main thesis of "broken windows."	YES

Sampson, Robert J., Stephen W. Raudenbush, and Felton Earls. 1997	-Quantitative- *Uses a 1995 survey of 8,782 respondents of 343 Chicago neighborhoods to conduct a multilevel analysis.	Test the hypothesis that collective efficacy is linked to reduced violence.	*A measure of collective efficacy yields a high between-neighborhood reliability and is negatively associated with variations in violence, when individual-level characteristics, measurement error, and prior violence are controlled. *Associations of concentrated disadvantaged and residential instability with violence are largely mediated by collective efficacy. *High SES, home ownership, and age were associated with elevated levels of collective efficacy, whereas high mobility was negatively associated with collective efficacy. *Concentrated disadvantage and immigrant concentration were significantly negatively associated with collective efficacy, whereas residential stability was significantly positively associated with collective efficacy.	YES
Silver, Eric, and Lisa L. Miller. 2004	-Quantitative- *Examines multilevel data from the Project on Human Development in Chicago Neighborhoods and uses hierarchical regression.	Examine why youth in structurally disadvantaged neighborhoods experience lower levels of informal social control.	*Neighborhood attachment and satisfaction with police contributed significantly to neighborhood levels of informal social control. *Neighborhood attachment and satisfaction with police mediated a substantial portion of the association between informal social control and neighborhood levels of concentrated disadvantage and immigrant concentration.	YES

(continued)

Author and Citation	Research Methods	Research Focus	Major Findings	Supports CE Theory?
Triplett, Ruth A., Randy R. Gainey, and Ivan Y. Sun. 2003	-Qualitative- *Reviews existing empirical support for various paths in the model of institutional control and neighborhood crime.	Propose a model of neighborhood-based institutional control.	*No test of the overall model proposed here exists, but the various paths described in the model have received varying levels of support from past empirical research. *Families with social ties that provide re-sources, both social capital and social support, lay the groundwork for social control in the neighborhood. *Social ties, however, may sometimes drain resources. When resources are weak, ability to intervene is weakened. *When social networks include parties involved with criminal activities, the ability of the family to intervene is diminished at the same time that the ability to reward deviance increases.	YES
Warner, Barbara D., and Pamela Wilcox Rountree. 1997.	-Quantitative- *Uses Census data, Seattle Police Department annual reports, and a 1990 survey of 5,302 Seattle residents to examine burglary and assault.	Examine to what extent local social ties affect official rates of crime and whether they mediate the effects of exogenous variables on crime rates. Also, examine whether local social ties' effects on assault rates are conditioned by the racial composition of the community.	*Ethnic heterogeneity significantly lowers social ties and residential stability. *Local social ties decrease the assault rate significantly but have little mediating effect between community structure and crime rates. *Social ties have differing effects in different types of neighborhoods. Social ties significan-tly and negatively affect assault rates in predominantly white neighborhoods, while they have no significant effect in predominan-tly minority or racially mixed neighborhoods.	MIXED RESULTS

References

Andreas, A. T. 1975. *History of Chicago: From the Earliest Period to the Present Time.* New York: Arno Press.

Atkinson, Rowland, and John Flint. 2004. "Order Born of Chaos? The Capacity for Informal Social Control in Disempowered and 'Disorganised' Neighbourhoods." *Politics & Policy* 33: 333–50.

Barnes, Patricia G. 1998. "Safer Streets at What Cost?" *American Bar Association Journal* 84 (June): 24.

Bernstein, Richard. 1998. "A Thinker Attuned to Thinking: James Q. Wilson Has Insight, Like Those on Cutting Crime, that Tend to Prove Out." *New York Times,* August 22, B7.

Block, R., and C. Block. 1995. "Space, Place and Crime." In *Crime and Place,* ed. J. Eck and D. Weisburd, 145–84. Monsey, N.Y.: Criminal Justice Press.

Brantingham, P. J., and P. L. Brantingham. 1991. *Environmental Criminology,* 2d ed. Prospect Heights, Ill.: Waveland Press.

———. 1998. *Reducing Crime though Real Estate Development and Management.* Washington, DC: Urban Land Institute.

———. 1999. "A Theoretical Model of Crime Hot Spot Generation." *Studies on Crime and Crime Prevention* 8: 7–26.

Bratton, William J., and George L. Kelling. 2006. "There Are No Cracks in the Broken Windows: Ideological Academics Are Trying to Undermine a Perfectly Good Idea." *National Review Online,* February 28, 2006. www.nationalreview.com.

Browning, Christopher R. 2002. "The Span of Collective Efficacy: Extending Social Disorganization Theory to Partner Violence." *Journal of Marriage and Family* 64: 833–50.

Burawoy, Michael, et al. 1991. *Ethnography Unbound: Power and Resistance in the Modern Metropolis.* Berkeley: University of California Press.

Burgess, E. 1967 [1925]. "The Growth of the City: An Introduction to a Research Project." In *The City,* ed. Robert E. Park, Ernest Burgess, and Roderick D. McKenzie. Chicago: University of Chicago Press.

Bursik, Robert J. Jr. 1986. "Delinquency Rates as Sources of Ecological Change." In *The Social Ecology of Crime,* ed. J. M. Byrne and R. J. Sampson, 63–76. New York: Springer-Verlag.

———. 1999. "The Informal Control of Crime through Neighborhood Networks." *Sociological Focus* 32: 85–97.

Byrne, James M., and Robert J. Sampson, eds. 1986. "Key Issues in the Social Ecology of Crime." In *The Social Ecology of Crime,* ed. J. M. Byrne and R. J. Sampson, 1–22. New York: Springer-Verlag.

Carr, Patrick J. 2003. "The New Parochialism: The Implications of the Beltway Case for Arguments Concerning Informal Social Control." *American Journal of Sociology* 108: 1249–91.

Chicago Community Policing Evaluation Consortium. 1995. *Community Policing in Chicago, Year Two: An Interim Report.* Unpublished report available at the Illinois Criminal Justice Information Authority, Chicago.

Chicago Police Department. 1997. "Chicago Police Department 1996 Annual Report." Unpublished report available from the Chicago Police Department.

———. 2005. "The Chicago Police Department Annual Report 2004 Year in Review." Unpublished report available from the Chicago Police Department.

Conklin, John E. 2003. *Why Crime Rates Fell.* New York: Allyn and Bacon.

Corman, Hope, and Naci Mocan. 2002. "Carrots, Sticks and Broken Windows." National Bureau of Economic Research. Working Paper 9061. http://www.nber.org/papers/w9061.

Crank, John P., Andrew Giacomazzi, and Cary Heck. 2003. "Fear of Crime in a Nonurban Setting." *Journal of Criminal Justice* 31: 249–64.

Cromie, Robert. 1984. *A Short History of Chicago.* San Franciso: Lexikos.

Decker, Scott, and Carol Kohfeld. 1985. "Crimes, Crime Rates, Arrests, and Arrest Ratios: Implications for Deterrence Theory." *Criminology* 23: 437–50.

DeKeseredy, Walter S., et al. 2003. "Perceived Collective Efficacy and Women's Victimization in Public Housing." *Criminal Justice* 3: 5–28.

Duncan, Terry E., et al. 2003. "A Multilevel Contextual Model of Neighborhood Collective Efficacy." *American Journal of Community Psychology* 32: 245–52.

Eck, J. 2001. "Problem-Oriented Policing and Crime Event Concentration." In *The Process and Structure of Crime,* ed. R. Meier, L. Kennedy, and V. Sacco. Piscataway, N.J.: Transaction Press.

Eck, J., J. Gersh, and C. Taylor. 2000. "Finding Crime Hotspots through Repeat Address Mapping." In *Analyzing Crime Patterns: Frontiers of Practice,* ed. V. Goldsmith, P. Maguire, J. Mollenkopf, and T. Ross, 49–64. Thousand Oaks, Calif.: Sage Publications.

Felson, M. 1986. "Linking Criminal Choices, Routine Activities, Informal Control, and Criminal Outcomes." In *The Reasoning Criminal,* ed. D. Cronish and R. Clarke. New York: Springer–Verlag.

Ford, Julie M., and Andrew A. Beveridge. 2004. "'Bad' Neighborhoods, Fast

Food, 'Sleazy' Businesses, and Drug Dealers: Relations between the Location of Licit and Illicit Businesses in the Urban Environment." *Journal of Drug Issues* 34: 51–77.

Funk, Patricia, and Peter Kugler. 2003. "Dynamic Interactions between Crimes." *Economic Letters* 79: 291–99.

Geis, Karlyn J., and Catherine E. Ross. 1998. "A New Look at Urban Alienation: The Effect of Neighborhood Disorder on Perceived Powerlessness." *Social Psychology Quarterly* 61: 232–46.

Giacopassi, David, and David R. Forde. 2000. "Broken Windows, Crumpled Fenders, and Crime." *Journal of Criminal Justice* 28: 397–406.

Golub, Andrew, et al. 2003. "Quality-of-Life Policing: Do Offenders Get the Message?" *Policing: An International Journal of Police Strategies and Management* 26: 690–708.

Harcourt, Bernard E. 1998. "Reflecting on the Subject: A Critique of the Social Influence Conception of Deterrence, the Broken Windows Theory, and Order-Maintenance Policing New York Style." *Michigan Law Review* 97: 299–398.

———. 2001. *Illusions of Order: The False Promise of Broken Windows Policing.* Cambridge, Mass.: Harvard University Press.

Herbert, Steve. 2001. "Policing the Contemporary City: Fixing Broken Windows or Shoring up Neo-liberalism?" *Theoretical Criminology* 5: 445–67.

Jacob, Herbert, and Michael J. Rich. 1981. "The Effects of the Police in Crime: A Second Look." *Law and Society Review* 15: 109–22.

Janowitz, Morris. 1975. "Social Theory and Social Control." *American Journal of Sociology* 81, no. 1: 82–107.

Jeffery, C. R. 1971. *Crime Prevention through Environmental Design.* Beverly Hills, Calif.: Sage.

Jones, Robert. 1997. "The Puzzle Waiting for the New Chief." *Los Angeles Times,* August 10, 1997.

Kahan, Dan A. 1997. "Social Influence, Social Meaning, and Deterrence." *Virginia Law Review* 95: 2477–97.

Kelling, George L., and William J. Bratton. 1998. "Declining Crime Rates: Insiders' Views of the New York City Story." *Journal of Criminal Law and Criminology* 88: 1217–31.

Kelling, George L., and Catherine M. Coles. 1996. *Fixing Broken Windows: Restoring and Reducing Crime in Our Communities.* New York: Martin Kessler Books.

Kubrin, Charis E., and Ronald Weitzer. 2003. "New Directions in Social Disorganization Theory." *Journal of Research in Crime and Delinquency* 40: 374–402.

Langworthy, R., and E. Jefferis. 2000. "The Utility of Standard Deviation Ellipses for Evaluating Hot Spots." In *Analyzing Crime Patterns: Frontiers of Practice,* ed. V. Goldsmith, P. McGuire, J. Mollenkopf, and T. Ross, 87–104. Thousand Oaks,Calif.: Sage Publications.

Lersch, Kim Michelle. 2004. *Space, Time and Crime.* Durham, N.C.: Carolina Academic Press.

Lowenkamp, Christopher T., Francis T. Cullen, and Travis C. Pratt. 2003. "Replicating Sampson and Grove's Test of Social Disorganization Theory: Revisiting a Criminological Classic." *Journal of Research in Crime and Delinquency* 40:351–73.

Miethe, T., and McCorle, R. 2001. *Crime Profiles: The Anatomy of Dangerous Persons, Places, and Situations,* 2d ed. Los Angeles, Calif.: Roxbury.

Morenoff, Jeffrey D., Robert J. Sampson, and Stephen W. Raudenbush. 2001. "Neighborhood Inequality, Collective Efficacy, and the Spatial Dynamics of Urban Violence." *Criminology* 39: 517.

Nifong, Christina. 1997. "One Man's Theory Is Cutting Crime in Urban Streets." *Christian Science Monitor,* February 18, 1.

Nolan, James J. III, Norman Conti, and Jack McDevitt. 2004. "Situational Policing: Neighbourhood Development and Crime Control." *Policing & Society* 14: 99–117.

Pattillo, Mary E. 1998. "Sweet Mothers and Gangbangers: Crime in a Black Middle-Class Neighborhood." *Social Forces* 76: 747–74.

Perkins, D. D., and R. B. Taylor. 1996. "Ecological Assessments of Community Disorder. Their Relationship to Fear of Crime and Theoretical Implications." *American Journal of Community Psychology* 24: 63–107.

Roberts, Dorothy E. 1999. "Race, Vagueness, and the Social Meaning of Order-Maintenance Policing." *The Journal of Criminal Law & Criminology* 89: 775–836.

Rosen, Jeffery. 2000. "Excessive Force." *New Republic,* April 10, 24–27.

Sabol, William J., Claudia J. Coulton, and Jill E. Korbin. 2004. "Building Community Capacity for Violence Prevention." *Journal of Interpersonal Violence* 19: 322–40.

Sampson, Robert J. 1985. "Neighborhood and Crime: The Structural Determinants of Personal Victimization." *Journal of Research in Crime and Delinquency* 22: 7–40.

———. 1986. "The Effects of Urbanization and Neighborhood Characteristics on Criminal Victimization." In *Metropolitan Crime Patterns,* ed. Robert Figlio, Simon Hakim, and George Rengert, 3–26. Monsey, N.Y.: Criminal Justice Press.

———. 2003. "The Neighborhood Context of Well Being." *Perspectives in Biology and Medicine* 46: 53–73.

———. 2004a. "Networks and Neighbourhoods: The Implications of Connectivity for Thinking about Crime in the Modern City." In *Network Logic: Who Governs in an Interconnected World?* 157–66. London: Demos.

———. 2004b. "Neighborhood and Community: Collective Efficacy and Community Safety." *New Economy* 11: 106–13.

Sampson, Robert J., and Jacqueline Cohen. 1988. "Deterrence Effect of the Police in Crime: A Replication and Theoretical Extension." *Law and Society Review* 22: 166.

Sampson, Robert J., and W. B. Groves. 1989. "Community Structure and Crime:

Testing Social Disorganization Theory." *American Journal of Sociology* 94: 774–802.

Sampson, Robert J., and Jeffrey D. Morenoff. 2004. "Spatial (Dis)advantage and Homicide in Chicago Neighborhoods." In *Spatially Integrated Social Science,* ed. M. Goodchild and D. Janelle, 145–70. New York: Oxford University Press.

Sampson, Robert J., and Stephen W. Raudenbush. 1999. "Systematic Social Observation of Public Spaces: A New Look at Disorder in Urban Neighborhoods." *American Journal of Sociology* 105: 603–51.

———. 2001. "Disorder in Urban Neighborhoods—Does It Lead to Crime?" *Research Brief Washington, D.C.: U.S. Department of Justice, National Institute of Justice.*

Sampson, Robert J., Stephen W. Raudenbush, and Felton Earls. 1997. "Neighborhoods and Violent Crimes: A Multilevel Study of Collective Efficacy." *Science* 227: 918–24.

Shaw, Clifford, and Henry McKay. 1942. *Juvenile Delinquency and Urban Areas.* Chicago: University of Chicago Press.

Sherman, L. 1995. "Hot Spots of Crime and Criminal Careers of Places." In *Crime and Place,* ed. J. Eck and D. Weisburd, 35–52. Monsey, N.Y.: Willow Tree Press.

Sherman, L., and D. Weisburd. 1995. "General Deterrent Effects of Police Patrol in Crime 'Hot Spots': A Randomized, Controlled Trial." *Justice Quarterly* 2: 625–48.

Silver, Eric, and Lisa L. Miller. 2004. "Sources of Informal Social Control in Chicago Neighborhoods." *Criminology* 42: 551–83.

Skogan, Wesley G. 1987. "Disorder and Community Decline: Final Report to the National Institute of Justice." Unpublished report, Center for Urban Affairs and Policy Research, Northwestern University.

———. 1990. *Disorder and Community Decline: Final Report to the National Institute of Justice.* Center for Urban Affairs and Policy Research, Northwestern University.

Skogan, Wesley G., and Susan Hartnett. 1997. *Community Policing Chicago Style.* New York: Oxford University Press.

Skogan, Wesley G., et al. 1994. "Community Policing in Chicago, Year One: An Interim Report." Unpublished report available from the Illinois Criminal Justice Information Authority, Chicago.

St. Clair, Drake, and Horace R. Cayton. 1970. *Black Metropolis: A Study of Negro Life in a Northern City.* New York: Harcourt, Brace & World.

Taub, Richard P., D. Garth Taylor, and Jan D. Dunham. 1984. *Paths of Neighborhood Change.* Chicago: University of Chicago Press.

Taylor, Ralph. 2001. *Breaking Away from Broken Windows: Baltimore Neighbor-Hoods and the Nationwide Fight against Crime, Grime, Fear, and Decline.* Boulder, Colo.: Westview Press.

Taylor, R. B. 1996. "Neighborhood Responses to Disorder and Local Attachments: The Systemic Model of Attachment, Social Disorganization, and Neighborhood Use Value." *Sociological Forum* 11: 41–74.

Taylor, R. B., S. D. Gottfredson, and S. Brower. 1985. "Attachment to Place: Discriminant Validity and Impacts of Disorder and Diversity." *American Journal of Community Psychology* 13: 525–542.

Taylor, R., and A. Harrell. 1996. *Physical Environment and Crime*. Washington, D.C.: National Institute of Justice.

Taylor, R. B., and S. Shumaker. 1990. "Local Crime as a Natural Hazard: Implications for Understanding the Relationship between Disorder and Fear of Crime." *American Journal of Community Psychology* 18: 619–642.

Taylor, R. B., S. Shumaker, and S. D. Gottfredson. 1985. "Neighborhood-level Links between Physical Features and Local Sentiments: Deterioration, Fear of Crime, and Confidence." *Journal of Architectural Planning and Research* 2: 261–75.

Thrasher, Frederic. 1927. *The Gang: A Study of 1313 Gangs in Chicago*. Chicago: University of Chicago Press.

Triplett, Ruth A., Randy R. Gainy, and Ivan Y. Sun. 2003. "Institutional Strength, Social Control and Neighborhood Crime Rates." *Theoretical Criminology* 7: 439–67.

Warner, Barbara D., and Pamela Wilcox Rountree. 1997. "Local Social Ties in a Community and Crime Model: Questioning the Systematic Nature of Informal Social Control." *Social Problems* 44: 520–36.

Whittaker, David, Charles Phillips, Peter Haas, and Robert Worden. 1985. "Aggressive Policing and the Deterrence of Crime." *Law and Policy* 7: 395–416.

Wilson, James Q. 1968. *Varieties of Police Behavior*. Cambridge: Harvard University Press.

———. 1981. "The Effects of Police on Crime: A Response to Jacob and Rich." *Law and Society Review* 16: 163–69.

———. 1985. *Thinking about Crime*. New York: Vintage Books.

Wilson, James Q., and Barbara Boland. 1978. "The Effect of the Police on Crime." *Law and Society Review* 12: 367–90.

Wilson, James Q., and Richard J. Herrnstein. 1985. *Crime and Human Nature*. New York: Simon and Schuster.

Wilson, James Q., and George L. Kelling. 1982. "The Police and Neighborhood Safety: Broken Windows." *The Atlantic Monthly,* March 1982, 29–38.

Witkin, Gordon. 1998. "The Crime Bust." *U.S. News and World Report,* May 25, 28.

Wright, Richard. 1945. "Introduction." In Drake St. Clair and Horace R. Cayton, *Black Metropolis: A Study of Negro Life in a Northern City*. Chicago: University of Chicago Press.

———. 1964. *Black Boy: A Record of Childhood and Youth*. New York: Harper and Row.

Wikipedia. 2006. "History of Chicago." From Wikipedia, the free Encyclopedia. http://en.wikipedia.org/wiki/History_of_Chicago.

Index

Note: Page numbers in italics refer to illustrations or tables